SCIENCE ESSENTIALS

GRADES 5-6

AMERICAN EDUCATION PUBLISHING™
Columbus, Ohio

Copyright © 2005 School Specialty Publishing. Published by American Education Publishing™, an imprint of School Specialty Publishing, a member of the School Specialty Family.

Send all inquiries to:
School Specialty Publishing
8720 Orion Place
Columbus, OH 43240-2111

ISBN 0-7696-6049-5

2 3 4 5 6 7 8 QPD 13 12 11 10 09

Science Essentials Grades 5–6
Table of Contents

The **scientific method** is the way scientists learn and study the world around them. You become a scientist when you try to find answers to your questions by using the scientific method.

Asking questions and coming up with answers is the basis for the scientific method. When you begin a science project, you begin with a question that you have. The educated guess you make about this question is called a **hypothesis**.

After you have asked the question and made an educated guess, you have to perform tests to determine whether or not your hypothesis is right. To test your hypothesis, you must follow a **procedure**, which is the name given to the steps you take in your experiment or fieldwork. Your experiment or fieldwork should give you information that can be measured. It is important to conduct your test multiple times and use as many test subjects as possible to make sure your results are consistent before you draw your conclusion.

Your **conclusion** describes how your **data**, or results you received from your experiment, compare to your hypothesis. A disproved hypothesis is just as important as a proven hypothesis because it gives important information to others. Your conclusion should also include any new questions that arise as you are doing your experiment.

Refer to this model sheet whenever filling out a lab sheet. It will guide you as you record your information.

QUESTION	What is this experiment about? What are you trying to discover? The question you write in this section must be specific, focusing on the exact concept of the experiment.
MATERIALS	List the items you use for the experiment, including the product names. Be specific in the amounts needed and used, as this may have an effect on the final outcome of the experiment.
PROCEDURE	The procedure is like a recipe. It tells step-by-step how to do the experiment. Someone completely unfamiliar with the subject should be able to read and follow the procedure and be successful with the experiment. Remember that in an experiment everything should be kept the same each time it is performed. This is called "controlling the variable."
DATA	The data is the numeric result of your experiment. This is often shown in a graph or chart to make the information clearer for the people seeing the results.
RESULTS	This section includes a detailed description of what you saw happening during the experiment. You will not tell why something happened, only what happened. Changes and patterns that take place during the experiment are also mentioned, since these may have an effect on the outcome.
CONCLUSION	What was discovered? This is the answer to the original question. The answer must be based on the results of the experiment, not on opinions.

The Scientific Method

Planning Your Investigation

A typical lab sheet looks like this.

QUESTION   (purpose of the experiment)

_____

_____

MATERIALS   (materials needed for the experiment)

_____

_____

PROCEDURE   Steps in your procedure:

1. _____

2. _____

3. _____

4. _____

5. _____

DATA

_____

_____

RESULTS   Record observations and/or collect data.

_____

_____

_____

CONCLUSION

_____

_____

_____

The animal kingdom can be divided into two main groups. Animals with backbones are called **vertebrates** and those without are called **invertebrates**.

It's All in the Name! Every living thing is given a scientific name made from two Greek or Latin words. The first is the *genus* name, and the second is the *species*.

human = *Homo sapiens*
dog = *Canis familiaris*
cat = *Felis domesticus*

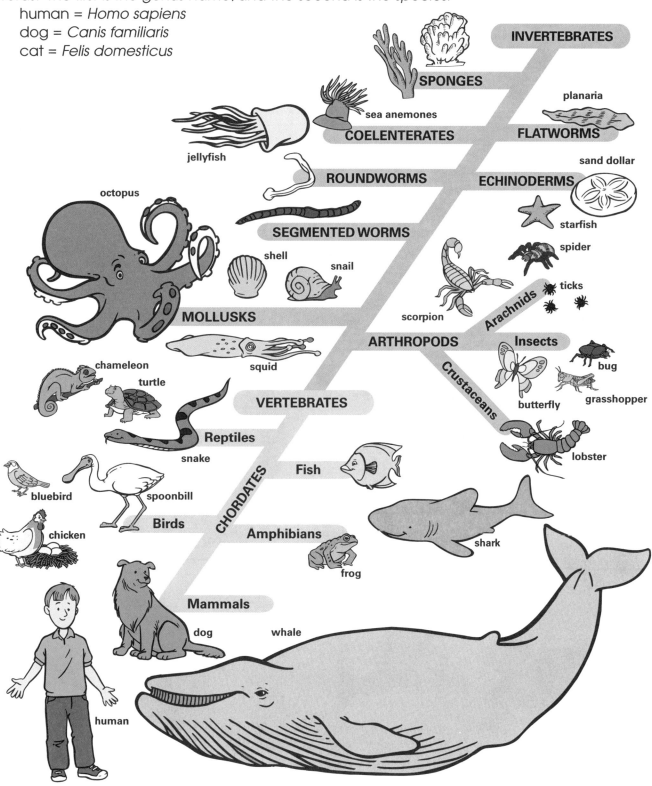

Name _____

Vertebrates are animals with backbones. Animals without backbones are called **invertebrates**. At the bottom of the page are pictures of both kinds of animals.

Directions: Write the name of each animal under the correct heading below.

VERTEBRATES	INVERTEBRATES
1. _____	1. _____
2. _____	2. _____
3. _____	3. _____
4. _____	4. _____
5. _____	5. _____

Vertebrates and Invertebrates

The animal kingdom is divided into two main groups—invertebrates and vertebrates. An invertebrate is an animal without a backbone. A vertebrate is an animal with a backbone. Only 4 percent of the approximately 1.5 million known species on Earth are vertebrates. Vertebrates can be divided into five categories, or types. The types are fish, amphibians, reptiles, birds, and mammals. Of the 4 percent of known species that are vertebrates, only a small fraction are mammals.

Look at the table below. Read the basic characteristics and examples of the five basic groups of vertebrates.

GROUP	CHARACTERISTICS	EXAMPLES
Fish	Most often a cold-blooded water creature with an elongated body and fins and gills	Sharks and bony fish such as trout, bass, and tuna
Amphibians	Most often a cold-blooded creature with young that live in the water and use gills to breathe and adults that are air-breathing	Frogs, toads, and salamanders
Reptiles	Most often an animal that crawls or moves on the ground on its belly; has a bony skeleton and is covered with scales or bony plates	Snakes, lizards, alligators, and turtles
Birds	Most often a warm-blooded animal that is covered with feathers, has hollow bones, and has forelimbs modified into wings	Robins, ostriches, ducks, and geese
Mammals	Most often a warm-blooded animal that feeds its young with milk; has skin and is often covered with hair; gives birth to live young	Humans, dogs, whales, platypuses, bats, and apes

While vertebrates are different in many ways, as shown in the table, they also have significant similarities. All of the animals use food to obtain and maintain energy. They all reproduce, give off waste products, and respond to the environment. Vertebrates also are bilaterally symmetrical. This means that the left and right sides of the body are alike. More advanced vertebrates have necks, while others are usually divided into a head and trunk.

The Animal Kingdom

Vertebrates and Invertebrates, cont.

Types of vertebrates are found throughout the world. Certain species are able to survive the polar freeze. Others can live in the tropics. All of these animals have responded to their environment by utilizing the world around them, using available food, water, and shelter. Often, animals will change over hundreds of years to adapt to changes that occur in their natural habitat; for example, growing a thicker or thinner coat of fur as a body covering.

Invertebrates are also found throughout the world. They are varied in characteristics. The invertebrates are often categorized into eight different groups. The following chart shows the different types, the characteristics, and examples of each.

GROUP	CHARACTERISTICS	EXAMPLES
Sponges	Vary in shape and size depending on environment; adult sponges live attached to items in the water and never move; they reproduce sexually and asexually	Sponges
Cnidarians	Hollow-bodied organisms with stinging cells; many have snake-like tentacles that capture food and help them move	Coral, jellyfish, and sea anemones
Flatworms	The simplest type of worm; most are parasites; others live in fresh- or saltwater	Tapeworms and flukes
Roundworms	Found almost everywhere in the world; most are free-living in the soil; more complex than the flatworm; a parasite	Nematodes and hookworms
Annelids	Most are free-living and live in the soils; some, such as leeches, are parasitic; complex enough to have systems for circulating blood, sensing stimuli, reproduction, and movement	Earthworms and leeches
Mollusks	Soft bodies generally, but not always; covered with a hard shell; has a special fold of skin called the *mantle*; a foot aids in movement and capturing prey	Clams, squid, and snails
Echinoderms	Live in oceans and are covered in spines, which are actually bony plates of the skeleton	Sea stars and sand dollars
Arthropods	1 million known species of arthropods on earth; external skeletons, jointed legs	Insects, crabs, and crayfish

Directions: Use the reading selection on pages 9 and 10 to answer the following.

1. What is a vertebrate? Give three specific examples. _____

   _____

   _____

2. What is an invertebrate? Give three specific examples. _____

   _____

   _____

3. What are the five groups of vertebrates? _____

   _____

4. What is meant by bilaterally symmetrical? _____

   _____

5. Define the word *backbone*. _____

   _____

6. Define the word *parasite*. _____

   _____

7. What is meant by cold-blooded and warm-blooded? _____

   _____

   _____

8. What is the mantle on a mollusk? _____

   _____

Concept Mapping Invertebrates

Remember that invertebrates are animals that have no backbone. Learn about them by completing a concept map of invertebrates.

Directions: To complete the map, write one of the subgroups from the box in an empty oval. Then, branch off of each subgroup and write group names. An example is done for you. You may want to include sketches.

WORD BANK   sponges   cnidarians   mollusks   segmented worms
                flatworms   arthropods   roundworms   echinoderms

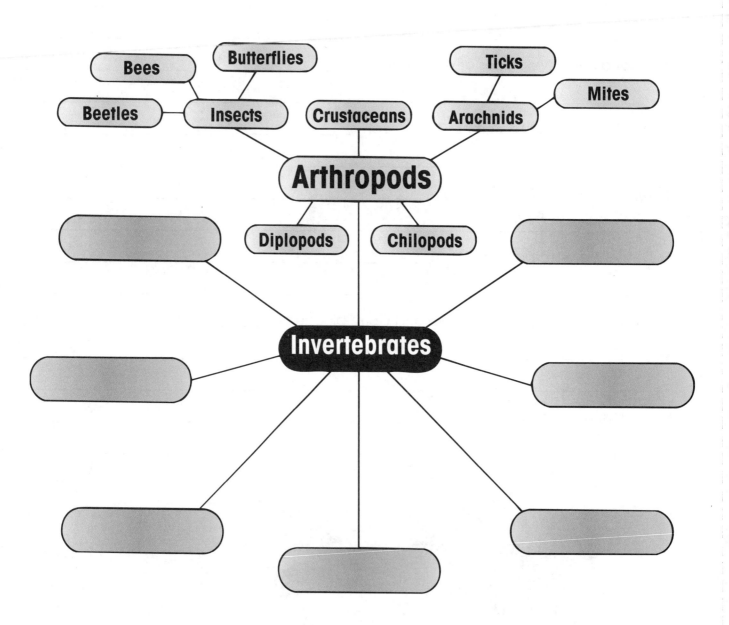

Directions: Complete the chart to show how the different classes of vertebrates are alike and how they are different.

	FISH	AMPHIBIANS	BIRDS	REPTILES	MAMMALS
Body covering					
Warm- or cold-blooded					
Lungs or gills					
Born alive or hatched					
Habitat					
Name one example					

Most scientists divide all living things into five groups, called kingdoms. Two of the largest are the Animal Kingdom and the Plant Kingdom.

Directions: Using the information from the reading selection on pages 9 and 10, complete the Venn diagram below. Compare and contrast characteristics of vertebrates and invertebrates. Be sure to include physical similarities as well as habitats and other habits.

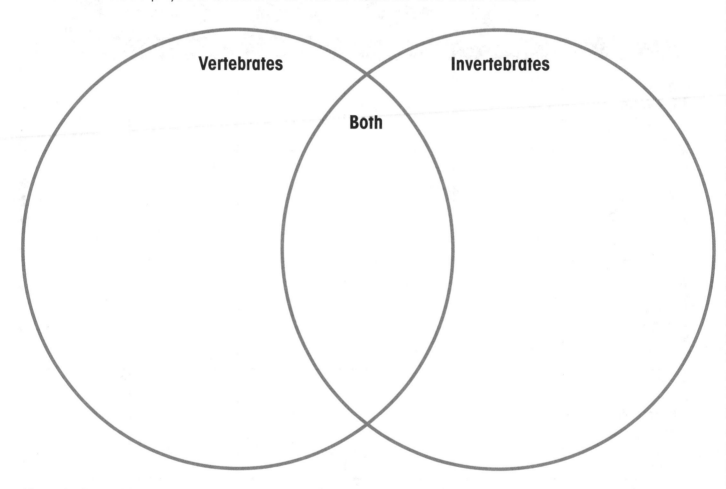

Vertebrates — Both — Invertebrates

Use what you have written in the diagram to write a paragraph about vertebrates and invertebrates. Focus on one aspect of the creatures.

_____

_____

_____

_____

_____

_____

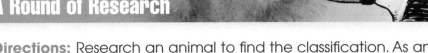

A Round of Research

Directions: Research an animal to find the classification. As an example, use the following taxonomy for a brown squirrel.

Kingdom *Animalia*, or "animal"

Phylum *Chordata*, or "has a backbone"

Class *Mammalia*, or "has a backbone and nurses its young"

Order *Rodentia*, or "has a backbone; nurses its young; and has long, sharp front teeth"

Family *Scuridae*, or "has a backbone; nurses its young; has long, sharp front teeth; and has a bushy tail"

Genus *Tamiasciurus*, or "has a backbone; nurses its young; has long, sharp front teeth; has a bushy tail; and climbs trees"

Species *hudsonicus*, or "has a backbone; nurses its young; has long, sharp front teeth; has a bushy tail; and has brown fur on its back and white fur on its underparts"

NAME OF MY ANIMAL

Kingdom _____

Phylum _____

Class _____

Order _____

Family _____

Genus _____

Species _____

The Animal Kingdom

Animal Characteristics Recall

Name _____

Directions: Circle the correct answers.

1. The system of classification for plants and animals is called
    a. hieroglyphs.
    b. taxonomy.
    c. respiration.

2. Which of the following is not a category for the system used to classify animals?

    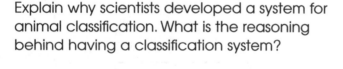
    Kingdom   Phylum   Class   Order   Neighbor   Family   Genus   Species

3. The majority of animals on Earth are
    a. invertebrates.
    b. vertebrates.
    c. old.

4. Animals with a backbone are called vertebrates.

    true or false

Directions: Answer the following using complete sentences.

Explain why scientists developed a system for animal classification. What is the reasoning behind having a classification system?

_____

_____

_____

_____

_____

_____

_____

_____

_____

Name _____

Arthropods are animals with segmented appendages. They are invertebrates as they have no backbones. Three of the classes of arthropods are arachnids, insects, and crustaceans.

Directions: Identify the animals below by placing **A** in front of the arachnids, **I** in front of the insects, and **C** in front of the crustaceans.

_____ 1. grasshopper

_____ 2. mite

_____ 3. brine shrimp

_____ 4. wasp

_____ 5. bumblebee

_____ 6. scorpion

_____ 7. tick

_____ 8. spider crab

_____ 9. crayfish

_____ 10. butterfly

_____ 11. hornet

_____ 12. cockroach

_____ 13. lobster

_____ 14. water bug

_____ 15. hermit crab

_____ 16. barnacle

_____ 17. earwig

_____ 18. beetle

_____ 19. mole cricket

_____ 20. stinkbug

_____ 21. termite

_____ 22. dragonfly

_____ 23. ant

_____ 24. silverfish

_____ 25. louse

_____ 26. black widow spider

_____ 27. brown recluse spider

_____ 28. copepod

_____ 29. wood louse

_____ 30. fiddler crab

_____ 31. walking stick

_____ 32. damsel fly

_____ 33. cat flea

_____ 34. roach

_____ 35. tarantula

_____ 36. wolf spider

_____ 37. cricket

_____ 38. cicada

_____ 39. aphid

_____ 40. trap-door spider

_____ 41. orb weaver

_____ 42. locust

_____ 43. katydid

_____ 44. bedbug

_____ 45. orange garden spider

_____ 46. blue crab

The World of Arthropods

The largest percentage of animals in the world are arthropods. Arthropods are animals with exoskeletons and jointed appendages. They live in all parts of the world and in every type of habitat.

Directions: Look at the list of arthropods below. Print the names of insects in the square, the names of arachnids in the triangle, and the names of crustaceans in the circle.

 WORD BANK

tarantula	bee	mite	crab
lobster	butterfly	scorpion	wasp
beetle	shrimp	hornet	fly
grasshopper	cricket	crayfish	tick
garden spider	brown recluse	black widow	cicada
barnacle	louse	water flea	aphid
termite	ant	wood louse	flea
moth	firefly	gnat	mayfly

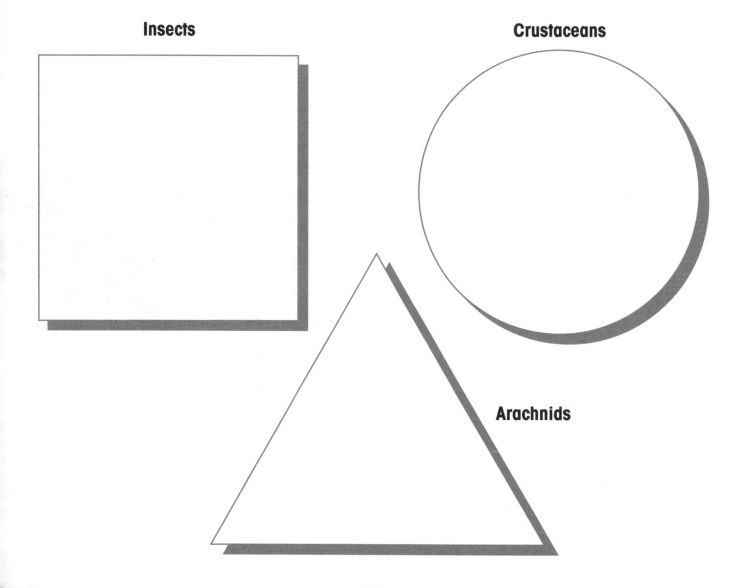

Insects

Crustaceans

Arachnids

Earthworms love to dig in soil. In this activity, you will observe earthworms and their role in mixing soil.

Directions:

1. Obtain earthworms from a bait shop or pet store.
2. Alternate layers of builder's sand, potting soil, and crushed leaves in the glass jar.
3. Place several earthworms in the jar. Add some chopped potatoes.
4. Place the jar in a dark, cool place or cover it with a cloth.
5. Remove the cloth and observe the conditions in the jar each day.

Materials
- one-gallon glass jar
- potting soil
- builder's sand
- chopped potatoes
- crushed leaves
- earthworms

DATE	OBSERVATIONS

How has the soil been changed by the earthworms' movements? _____

_____

_____

Of what value are earthworms to the soil in a garden or flower bed?_____

_____

_____

Snail Observations

Snails have a soft body which is usually covered with a coiled shell. Land snails live under logs and stones, on the edges of ponds and rivers, and in woods. In this activity, you will create a habitat for land snails and observe their behavior.

Materials
- clear gallon jar
- snails
- chlorine-free water
- aquarium plants
- aquarium sand or gravel
- magnifying lens

Directions:

1. Obtain some land snails, aquarium plants, and sand or gravel from a pet store.

2. Fill a clear gallon jar almost full with chlorine-free water.

3. Add the plants and snails to the jar.

4. Complete the observation chart below for two weeks.

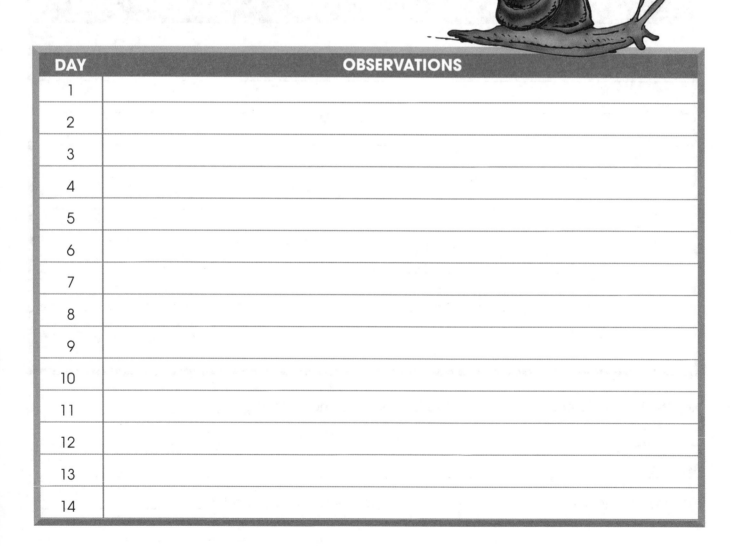

DAY	OBSERVATIONS
1	
2	
3	
4	
5	
6	
7	
8	
9	
10	
11	
12	
13	
14	

Have You Seen It?

We can see many living things when we are on the playground. A living thing that we might see is a grasshopper. A grasshopper is a good example of an insect. It represents a typical insect with the head, thorax, and abdomen. It has three pairs of legs and two pairs of wings. The grasshopper also has two antennae, two eyes, legs, a stomach, a heart, a mouth, and breathing holes called *spiracles*.

Directions: Look at the diagram below. Use the WORD BANK to write the correct parts of the insect in the diagram and under the correct heading below. Two words are not used for the diagram.

WORD BANK

eyes	wings	heart	mouth
spiracles	stomach	legs	antennae

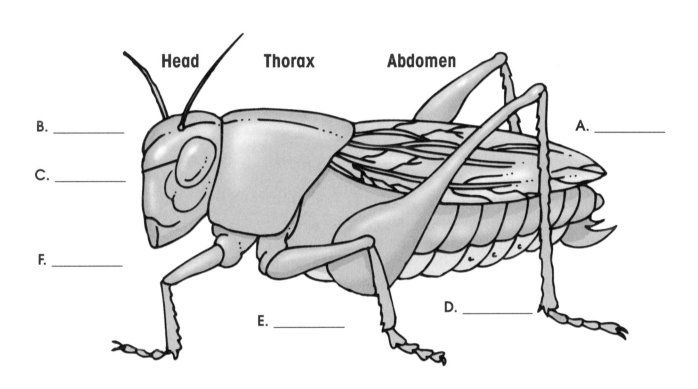

B. _____

C. _____

F. _____

A. _____

E. _____

D. _____

Head   Thorax   Abdomen

HEAD	THORAX	ABDOMEN
_____	_____	_____
_____	_____	_____
_____	_____	_____

PURPOSE
Describe how a frog, toad, or lizard uses its tongue to capture insects. Explain that animals have adaptations that assist them in survival.

MATERIALS
- party blower
- graph paper
- pencil
- 1 foot piece of string or ribbon
- 1 inch strip of Velcro

INTRODUCTION
Frogs are found throughout the world with the exception of Antarctica. They live in ponds, lakes, marshes, and other wetland areas. To capture insects, a frog uses its long, sticky tongue which is attached to the front of its mouth. The frog flips its tongue over and out and then draws it back into Its mouth after capturing the prey. This is an example of an adaptation that aids the frog in its survival. In this activity, each student has the opportunity to attempt to "capture" prey by using a simulated frog's tongue. Find out what your students already know about how a frog, toad, or some lizards capture food. Using pictures, explain that some animals have special adaptations that enable them to catch their food.

PROCEDURE
1. Unroll the party blower so that the end is in your hand.
2. Attach the "rough" piece of Velcro to the party blower by folding it over the end. (This is the frog's tongue.)
3. Make a loop with the string.
4. Attach the "soft" piece of Velcro to this loop by folding it over the end of the loop. This secures the Velcro on both sides of the string. (This is the "fly.")
5. Working with a partner, take turns pretending to be a "frog" and try to catch the "food" as your partner slowly dangles the string or "fly" in front of the party blower.
6. Predict how many flies you can catch in a minute. Record your estimate.
7. Have your partner count how many times you try to catch the fly in one minute and how many flies are actually caught. Make a graph to show the results.
8. Discuss the results. Are frogs and lizards better at catching insects than humans? Why?

QUESTIONS
1. How many flies did you predict that you could catch in one minute?_____
2. How many flies did you actually catch in one minute? _____
3. How many times did you try to catch flies in a minute? _____
4. On the back of the paper, make a bar graph to show the number of flies you caught and the number of attempts you made.
5. Explain why a frog's tongue is a special adaptation that helps in its survival.
6. Describe how you felt trying to catch "flies" with your constructed frog's tongue.

Name

A reptile is an animal that has dry, scaly skin and breathes using lungs. It is a vertebrate.

Directions: Complete the word grid by filling in the squares with the names of the reptiles below.

WORD BANK

adder	caiman	gavial	leopard frog	python
alligator	cobra	gecko	lizard	spring pepper
anole	corn snake	green toad	mamba	tuatara
boa	crocodile	iguana	newt	turtle
viper				

A L L   K I N D S   O F   R E P T I L E S

Marine Life

The oceans are teeming with living things.

Directions: Complete the word grid below to learn the names of some marine life.

WORD BANK

conch	eel	lobster	octopus	shrimp	starfish
coral	hermit crab	manatee	scallop	sponge	triton
dolphin	limpet	mussel	seal	squid	whale

M A R I N E L I F E

Mollusks

Mollusks are animals with soft, boneless bodies. Most of them have shells. Three of the most common classes of mollusks are bivalves, gastropods, and cephalopods.

Directions: Choose one of the mollusks below to research. Data collected on each example could include the following: size, habitat, description, uses of, and unusual characteristics or behaviors. Write the data in the chart below.

BIVALVES
oyster, clam, scallop, mussel, cockle, ark, angel wing, jewel box, jingle, ox heart

GASTROPODS
land snail, abalone, conch, slug, sea slug, limpet, sea snail, moon snail, cone shell, murex, olive, cowrie, whelk, bonnet, periwinkle

CEPHALOPODS
squid, octopus, nautilus, cuttlefish

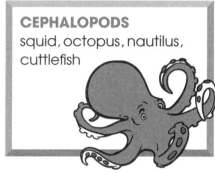

Mollusk I will research (Circle one):   bivalve   gastropod   cephalopod

Name of mollusk: _____

TYPE OF DATA	
Size	
Habitat	
Description	
Uses of	
Unusual characteristics or behaviors	

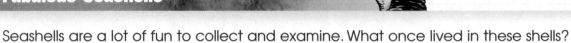

Fabulous Seashells

Seashells are a lot of fun to collect and examine. What once lived in these shells?

Directions: Learn the names of some shells by completing the word grid below.

WORD BANK

clam	cowrie	moon	periwinkle	triton
conch	jingle	murex	scallop	tulip
cone	limpet	nerite	scotch bonnet	wentletrap
coquina	margin	olive	slipper	whelk

F A B U L O U S S E A S H E L L S

Echinoderms

Echinoderms are marine animals. The term *echinoderm* is derived from two Greek words, *echinos* meaning "spiny" and *derma* meaning "skin."

Directions: In a group, research the echinoderms listed below. Look for these special terms as you research your animals.

 WORD BANK

radial symmetry
arms
stomach
rays

tube feet
water canals
suction cups
eyespot

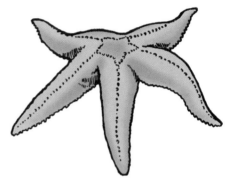

ECHINODERM	CHARACTERISTICS, BEHAVIORS, HABITATS, USES
Starfish	
Sand Dollar	
Sea Urchin	
Sea Lily	
Sea Cucumber	
Brittle Star	

Some Sharks to Study

Sharks live in oceans throughout the world. They are one of the most feared sea animals.

Directions: Choose one of the sharks below to research. Fill in some interesting facts about the shark.

 WORD BANK

angel shark	basking shark
blue shark	bull shark
cat shark	cookie-cutter shark
dwarf shark	frill shark
great white shark	hammerhead shark
horn shark	lemon shark
leopard shark	mako shark
tiger shark	

SHARK DATA	
Shark Name	
Size	
Description	
Habitat	
Behaviors	
Other	

What Can You See?

PURPOSE

Define the advantages of eye location on the side of the head or eye location on the front of the head.

MATERIALS

- 2 bathroom tissue cardboard tubes
- ruler
- elastic string
- black felt
- hole punch
- scissors
- paper and pencil

INTRODUCTION

All animals with eyes have adapted to life with their eyes placed in specific locations. Fishes that need to know precise directions and distances have eyes on the front of their heads for binocular vision. These fishes tend to be hunters, or predators. Fishes which are prey and must be ready to flee from danger tend to have eyes located on the sides of their heads. While these fishes lack binocular vision of predators, they have a greater field of vision and can see more angles for an early warning of the prospective attackers which may lurk nearby. Eye location is also important for other animals, including the world of mammals. For example, the eyes of a rabbit are set to the sides (greater field vision) but the fox has eyes on front of its head (binocular vision).

PROCEDURE   MAKING AN EYE PATCH

1. Cut out a 2-inch circle from black felt. Punch two holes in the felt. Thread a piece of elastic string through each hole, then tie the string to secure it to the patch.
2. Tie the ends of the string together to wear the patch over one eye.

FINDING THE TARGET

1. Draw a bull's eye target on a sheet of paper.
2. Hang the target on a wall.
3. Place a cardboard tube in front of one eye and the eye patch over the other eye.
4. Look at the target through the tube. At the same time, touch the bull's eye with a pencil. Draw a small "X."
5. Remove the eye patch and the tube.
6. Hold a tube in front of each eye with one hand. At the same time, try to touch the bull's eye with the pencil. Draw a small "X."
7. Compare your results.

QUESTIONS

Answer these questions on a separate sheet of paper.

1. Which way is easier to touch the bull's eye?
2. Which arrangement is more like a predator that needs to judge distances accurately?
3. Which arrangement is more like prey that needs to see in different directions?

Animal Adaptations and Behavior

Animals of all kinds have a lot of interesting ways in which they adapt to their environment and in which they behave.

Directions: To learn about some of these adaptations and behaviors, match the animals and adaptations or behaviors below.

Column I

1. _____blue jay

2. _____bobcat

3. _____woodpecker

4. _____crow

5. _____tree frog

6. _____heron

7. _____hornet

8. _____eagle

9. _____turkey

10. _____screech owl

11. _____robin

12. _____cicada

13. _____opossum

14. _____gray fox

15. _____big brown bat

Column II

a. A bird that builds a nest called an aerie

b. A large game bird that rests in trees at night

c. A blue-colored bird that squawks loudly when disturbed

d. This bird drills holes in trees in search of insects for food.

e. A fox that prefers to live in woodlands and often climbs trees

f. The males of this type of insect make loud sounds on warm summer evenings.

g. A large-eyed bird that searches for food at night

h. A marsupial that sometimes avoids danger by "playing dead"

i. An amphibian that has stick pads on its feet to help it climb trees

j. An all-black bird that caws

k. A wild cat that catches its prey by pouncing on small animals

l. A furry mammal that has a wingspan of about 12 inches

m. A long-legged wading bird that nests in flocks

n. A stinging insect that builds a paper nest

o. A red-breasted bird whose arrival signals the beginning of spring

Animal Adaptations

Animals have adapted to climate changes, changes in food supply, and changes in landforms in order to survive.

Directions: Choose three of the animals listed below that have had to adapt their lifestyles in order to survive. Research them and write about them.

 human   flying squirrel   owl
koala   giant panda   deer
pelican   polar bear   sloth
giraffe   chimpanzee
camel   hummingbird

1. Animal _____

   Vertebrate or invertebrate _____

   Special adaptations _____

   _____

   _____

   _____

2. Animal _____

   Vertebrate or invertebrate _____

   Special adaptations _____

   _____

   _____

   _____

3. Animal _____

   Vertebrate or invertebrate _____

   Special adaptations _____

   _____

   _____

   _____

Beak Pick-Up

Name _____

Birds have adapted over many years to help them survive in their environment and get the food they need.

Directions: Simulate various kinds of bird beaks. Using the different "beaks," try to gather food. Decide what type of beak is best for picking up what types of food.

1. Use each beak to try picking up each "food item."

2. Notice which beaks are better for the various items and think about why.

3. Record your observations or opinions in the chart.

Materials
- a clothespin
- a toothpick
- a spoon
- gummy worms
- packaging foam nuts
- scissors
- chopsticks
- a marble
- raisins

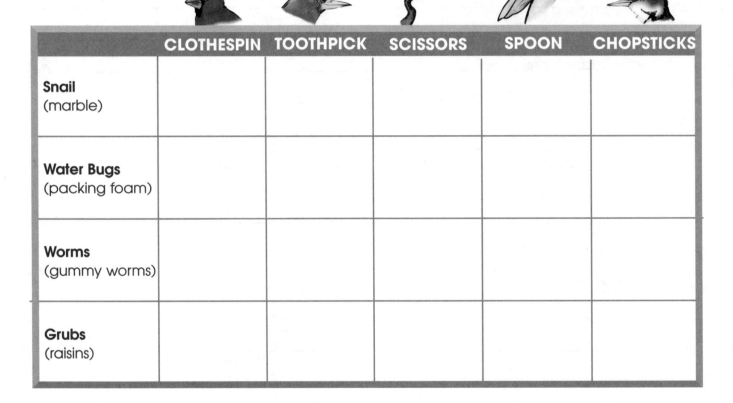

	CLOTHESPIN	TOOTHPICK	SCISSORS	SPOON	CHOPSTICKS
Snail (marble)					
Water Bugs (packing foam)					
Worms (gummy worms)					
Grubs (raisins)					

1. What food was the easiest to pick up with what tools? Explain why.

_____

_____

2. Think about other animals. Give three examples of ways they have adapted or changed to accommodate getting food or living in a changing environment.

_____

_____

Name

Animals adapt so they can survive in certain conditions. One special way that some animals have adapted is **camouflage**. Using camouflage helps many animals survive in their environment. They are not readily visible to their predators.

Directions:

1. Think of an animal that relies on camouflage to help it survive. Draw the animal below.

2. Explain how the camouflage specifically helps the animal.

_____

_____

3. List important things to consider about camouflage.

a._____

b._____

c._____

My Animal

Name _____

Directions: Choose one animal to research and/or observe. This can be a small animal such as a squirrel or bird. As you do research and make observations, think of ways the animal uses the environment to help get its needs met.

Draw the animal.	**Draw or list the food resources the animal relies on.**
Draw or list the water resources the animal relies on.	**Draw or list the shelter the animal relies on.**

Describe special adaptations the animal may have experienced throughout its species' existence.

_____

_____

_____

_____

_____

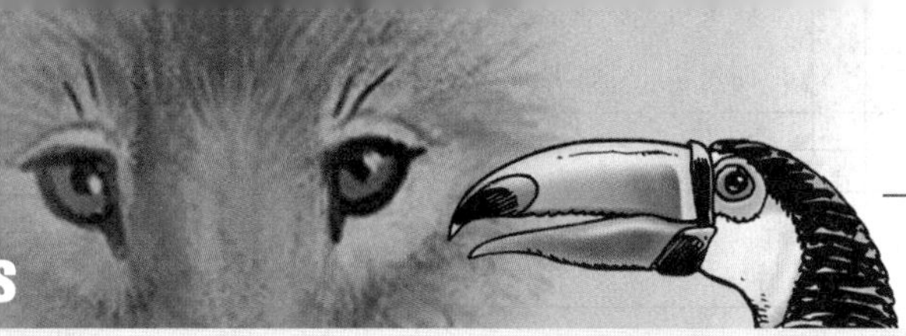

Animal Adaptations

Directions: Create a "new" animal. Use the following questions while thinking of the new animal. In the chart below, draw pictures or describe the animal and its characteristics.

NEW ANIMAL	
What is the name of the new animal?	
What is the weather like in the animal's habitat?	
What kind of shelter does the animal use?	
What does this animal eat? Where is the food found?	
Does the animal have any predators? If so, what are they?	
What behaviors show that this animal adapted to its environment?	

Now, draw the new animal, including its natural environment.

Name _____

Directions: Circle the correct answers.

1. Natural selection is the process by which organisms that are best suited for their environment are successful in living and reproducing.

   true or false

2. One adaptation animals have made to hide by blending in with their surroundings is called

   a. sense of smell.

   b. camouflage.

   c. eating more.

3. Many animals have ways to defend themselves. Which of the following is NOT a way they protect themselves?

   a. hiding

   b. color

   c. senses

   d. spray/taste

   e. food

Directions: Answer the following using complete sentences.

1. What are some ways wildlife use their environment to live and survive?

   _____

   _____

2. Compare and contrast how humans and animals make use of their environment for survival. Use the Venn diagram.

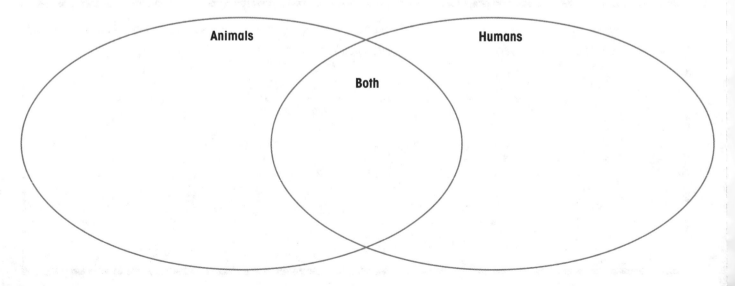

Animals   Humans

Both

Endangered Animals

An endangered animal is one whose population is so low that it runs the risk of becoming extinct.

Directions: Unscramble the names of the endangered animals below. The circled letters will then spell out the name of an endangered animal from Borneo.

L A O K A   __ ◯ __ __ __

G U A J A R   __ __ __ __ ◯ __

A M U P   __ __ ◯ __

A N T E A M E   __ __ ◯ __ __ __ __

T I G A N D A P A N   __ __ ◯ __ __ __   __ __ __ __

U C I V A Ñ   __ __ __ ◯ __ __

H E T H A C E   __ __ __ __ ◯ __ __

I T C A O   __ __ ◯ __ __

G H P O O R N R N __ __ __ ◯ __ __ __ __ __

Print the name of the secret endangered animal below.

__ __ __ __ __ __ __ __ __

From a reference book, find some interesting facts about this endangered animal.

_____

_____

_____

_____

_____

_____

_____

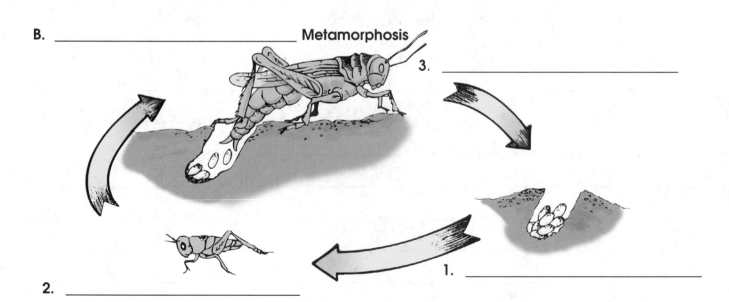

Metamorphosis

Name _____

Certain animals go through big physical changes as part of their development. There are two kinds of change: an incomplete metamorphosis and a complete metamorphosis. A **complete metamorphosis** means the organism goes through four stages of growth and can look very different from the adult organism. An **incomplete metamorphosis** means the change in the organism is not complete—meaning the young may resemble the adult.

Directions: Look at the cycles below. Label the stages of complete and incomplete metamorphosis. Use the words from the WORD BANK.

WORD BANK

complete	adult	larva	nymph
incomplete	egg	pupa	

A. _____ Metamorphosis

4. _____

1. _____

3. _____

2. _____

B. _____ Metamorphosis

3. _____

1. _____

2. _____

Fascinating Fruit Flies

Here's an easy way to observe the stages of the life cycle of a fruit fly.

Directions:

1. Set out some very ripe bananas in a jar.
2. Leaving the open jar close to a trash can, let it sit.
3. After a day, you should be able to see fruit flies around the jar.
4. Draw your observations below. Seal the jar.

Materials
- a jar with lid
- a piece of nylon panty hose (large enough to cover jar top)
- ripe bananas
- a trash can

5. Over a two-week period, fruit flies will reproduce. Draw your observations of each stage.

6. What stages did you see the fruit fly go through? Draw and label them.

The Animal Kingdom

Brine Shrimp Exploration

Name _____

Set up an aquarium for raising brine shrimp, also called sea monkeys. Brine shrimp are related to crabs and lobsters in a group commonly known as **crustaceans**.

Directions:

1. In the morning, begin by combining 4 tablespoons of rock salt with 1 gallon of water.

2. Pour the solution into the cake pan. Add 1 teaspoon of dried brine shrimp eggs.

3. Cover the pan with cardboard, leaving a small area for light to come through.

Materials
- a glass cake pan
- rock salt
- water
- dried brine shrimp eggs
- cardboard

Brine shrimp should be hatched in a semiwarm environment and will hatch within 24–48 hours. Check the eggs every 8–12 hours or at the end of the first day and the beginning of the second day. Draw observations of the stages of growth in the chart below.

BRINE SHRIMP LIFE CYCLE		
Cyst	**Nauplii**	**Adult**

Through the observations, I learned these things about the life cycle of brine shrimp.

1. _____

2. _____

3. _____

4. _____

Compare and Contrast

Directions: Answer the questions that follow.

1. Compare and contrast the life cycles of the fruit fly and the brine shrimp using the Venn diagram.

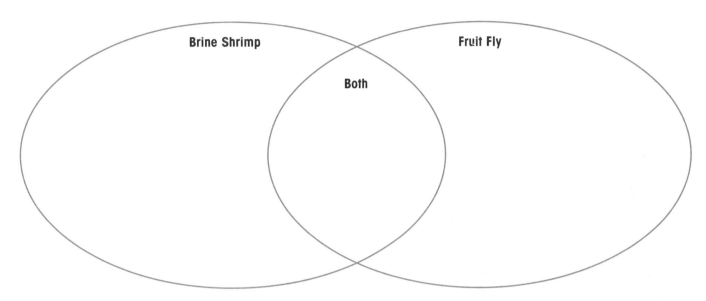

Brine Shrimp   Fruit Fly

Both

2. Using the information you have organized in the diagram, write a paragraph describing the similarities and differences of the life cycles.

_____

_____

_____

_____

_____

_____

3. How does a human life cycle compare with the life cycles in the diagram above?

_____

_____

_____

_____

_____

Name _____

Your body is made of many systems which work together. These systems work in groups.

Directions: Use the words from the WORD BANK to label the different body systems in each group.

 WORD BANK

skeletal	muscular	digestive
respiratory	circulatory	urinary
nervous	sensory	endocrine

MOVEMENT GROUP

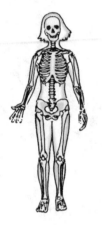 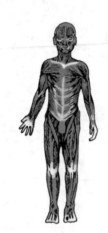

_____ _____

CONTROL GROUP

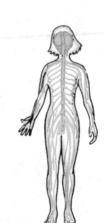 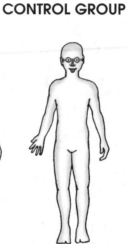 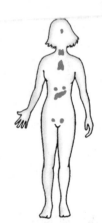

_____ _____ _____

ENERGY GROUP

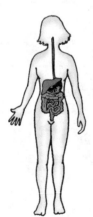 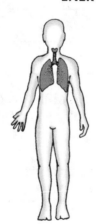 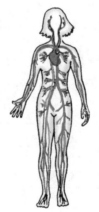 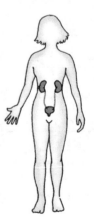

_____ _____ _____ _____

Your Body Parts

Directions: Use the words from the WORD BANK to label all these parts of your body.

WORD BANK

forehead	nose	cheek	hip
chest	forearm	palm	instep
abdomen	thumb	thigh	sole
calf	heel	shoulder	shin

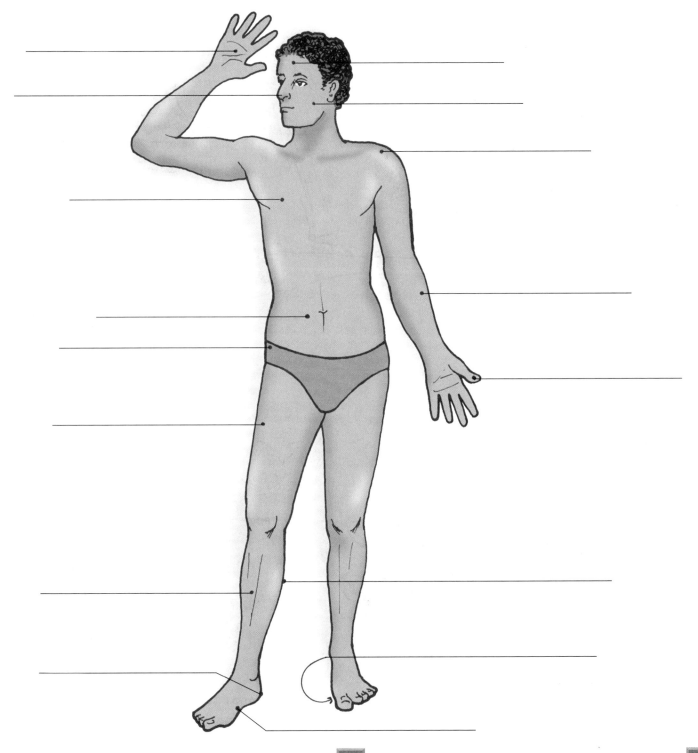

The Human Body

Name

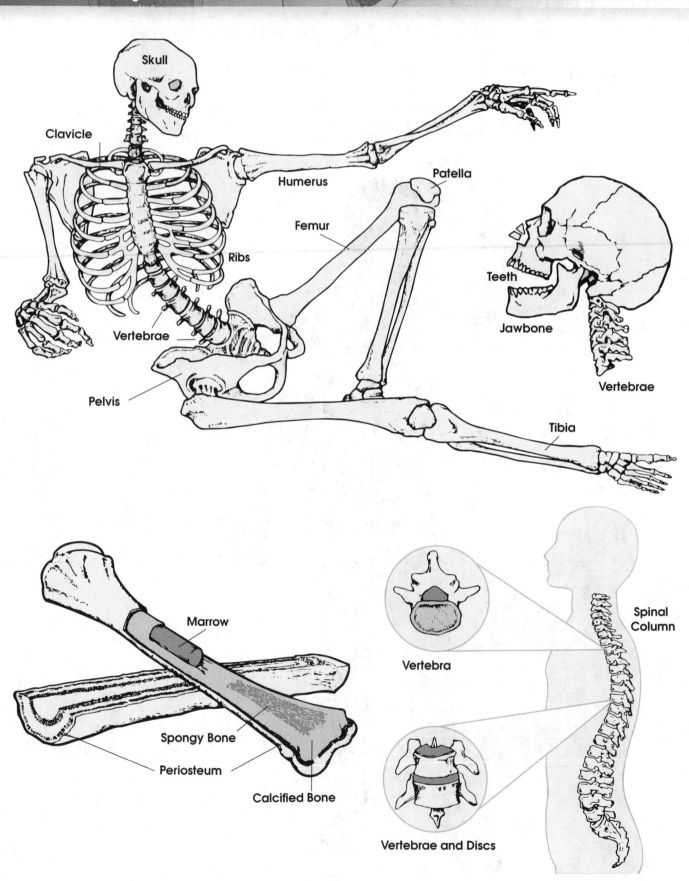

Skull

Clavicle

Humerus

Patella

Femur

Ribs

Teeth

Jawbone

Vertebrae

Vertebrae

Pelvis

Tibia

Marrow

Spongy Bone

Periosteum

Calcified Bone

Vertebra

Vertebrae and Discs

Spinal Column

Meeting Places

The place two bones meet is called a **joint**. Joints allow us to bend, twist, and turn our bodies. The human body has several different types of joints. Each allows a different kind of movement.

Directions: Read the descriptions below. Then, write examples of the joints below each description.

Hinge Joints — These joints can only move in one direction, like a door hinge. One bone works against another. Movement is back and forth on one plane.

*Examples:*_____

Ball-and-Socket Joints — These joints provide us with swinging and rotating movements. Make a fist with one hand. Cup the fingers of the other. Put your fist inside the cupped hand. You can turn your fist (the ball) in any direction within your cupped hand (the socket).

*Examples:*_____

Saddle Joints — These joints move in two directions, back and forth, up and down or in rotation.

*Examples:*_____

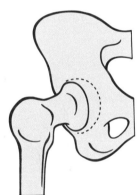

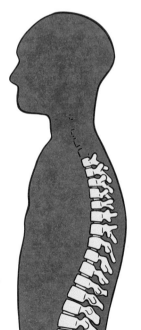

Sliding Joints — In a sliding joint, several bones next to one another bend together in limited gliding motion.

*Examples:*_____

Pivot Joints — These joints give us a rotating motion.

*Examples:*_____

Fixed Joints — With these types of joints, bones are fused together and permit no movement.

*Examples:*_____

What part of your body can move forward, backward, side to side, and around on top of a vertical axis and is not one of the above?

_____

The Human Body

Name _____

Directions: Label the bones of the hand and foot.

WORD BANK

Common Name (*Scientific Name*)

digits (*phalanges*)   instep (*metatarsals*)
wrist (*carpals*)   digits (*phalanges*)
ankle (*tarsals*)   palm (*metacarpals*)

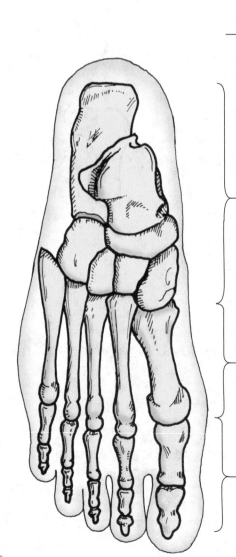

Directions: Label the different arm bones and regions.

WORD BANK upper arm   ulna   humerus
lower arm   radius

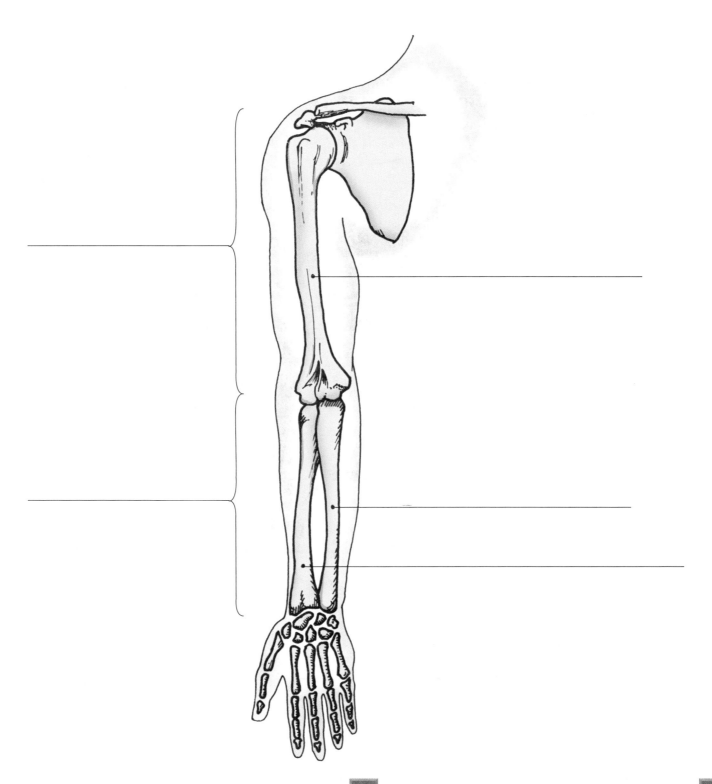

Name

Directions: Your teeth are made up of a number of layers. Label the layers and outside parts of the tooth below.

WORD BANK

| neck | root | crown | dentin |
| cementum | enamel | pulp | root canal |

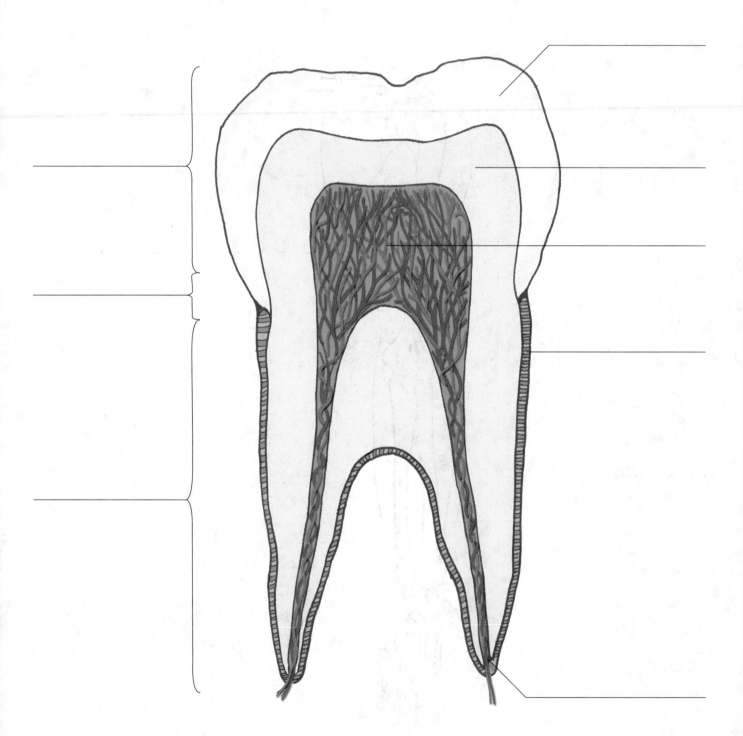

Four Kinds of Teeth

You have four kinds of teeth in your mouth.

Directions: Label the adult teeth pictured below.

 WORD BANK   canines   bicuspids   incisors   molars

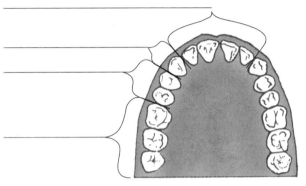

Adult upper

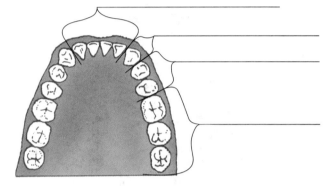

Adult lower

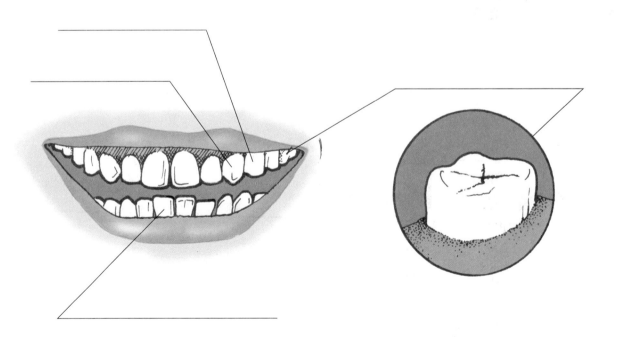

The Human Body

Name _____

Directions: Use the WORD BANK to complete the puzzle.

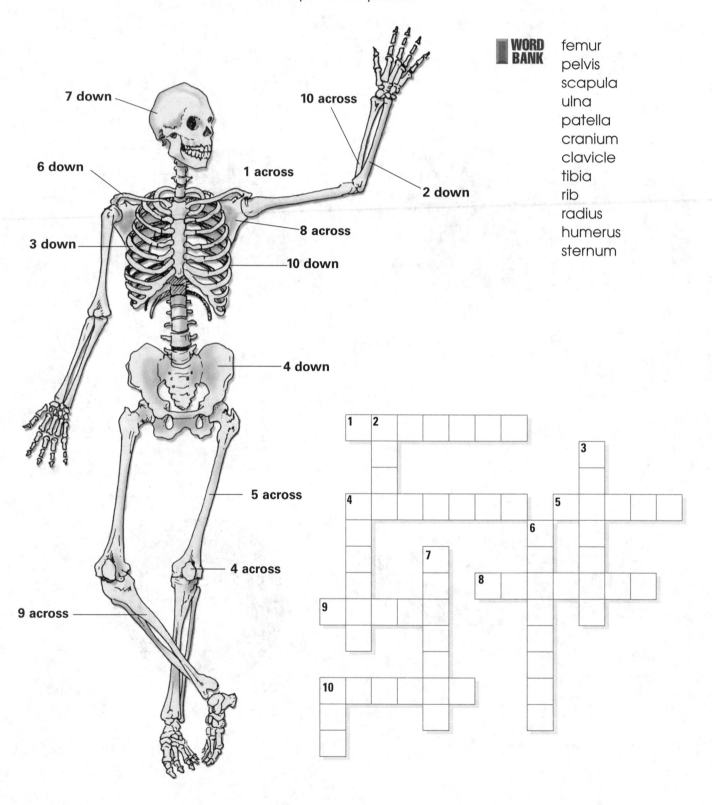

7 down
10 across
6 down
1 across
2 down
3 down
8 across
10 down
4 down
5 across
4 across
9 across

WORD BANK
femur
pelvis
scapula
ulna
patella
cranium
clavicle
tibia
rib
radius
humerus
sternum

The Supportive System

The bones are the body's **supportive system**. They are usually divided into two major groups–bones of the middle (skull, backbone, and ribs) and bones of the arms and legs (including the shoulder and hip bones). When you were born, your skeleton was made of soft bones called **cartilage**. As you grew, most of that cartilage turned into bone. However, all people still have some cartilage in their bodies. Our noses and our ears are cartilage, and there are pads of cartilage between sections of the backbone that acts as cushions.

Bones do more than just support the body. The center of the bone, called **bone marrow**, makes new blood cells for our body. Bones are also a storage house for important minerals like calcium and phosphorous.

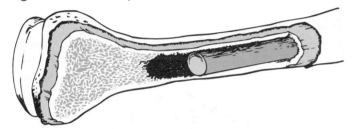 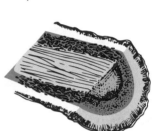

Directions: Answer the questions below. Use a science book or an encyclopedia, if necessary.

1. What are the main functions of the skeletal system?

   _____

   _____

   _____

   _____

2. What is the largest bone in your body?_____

3. What is the smallest bone in your body?_____

4. What do bones first develop as?_____

5. What does bone marrow do?_____

6. Do all bones have real bone marrow?_____

7. What is the outer layer of a bone called?_____

8. Where two bones meet is called a_____ .

Fascinating Fact! Did you know that a giraffe has the same number of vertebrae in its neck as you?

The Human Body

Muscle Man

There are hundred of muscle groups in your body.

Directions: Label these muscles that appear on the surface of your body.

WORD BANK

Common Name (*Scientific Name*)

chest muscles (*pectorals*)   thigh muscles (*quadraceps*)
calf muscles (*gastrocnemius*)   shoulder muscles (*deltoids*)
head muscles (*sternocleidomastoids*) stomach muscles (*inter coastals*)
biceps   triceps

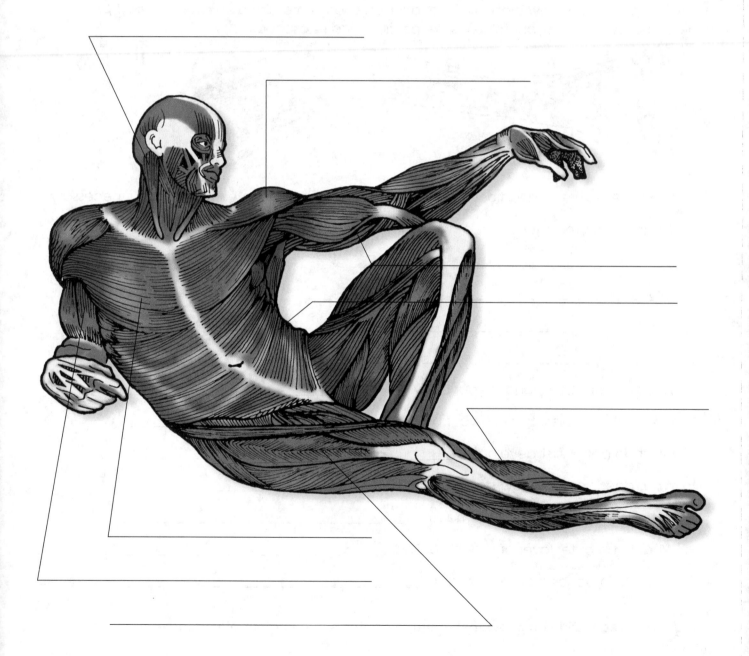

Name _____

Skeletal muscles are attached to the skeleton by means of **tendons**.

Directions: Label the parts of the arm pictured below.

WORD BANK

tendons   shoulder blade
biceps muscle humerus
radius   ulna

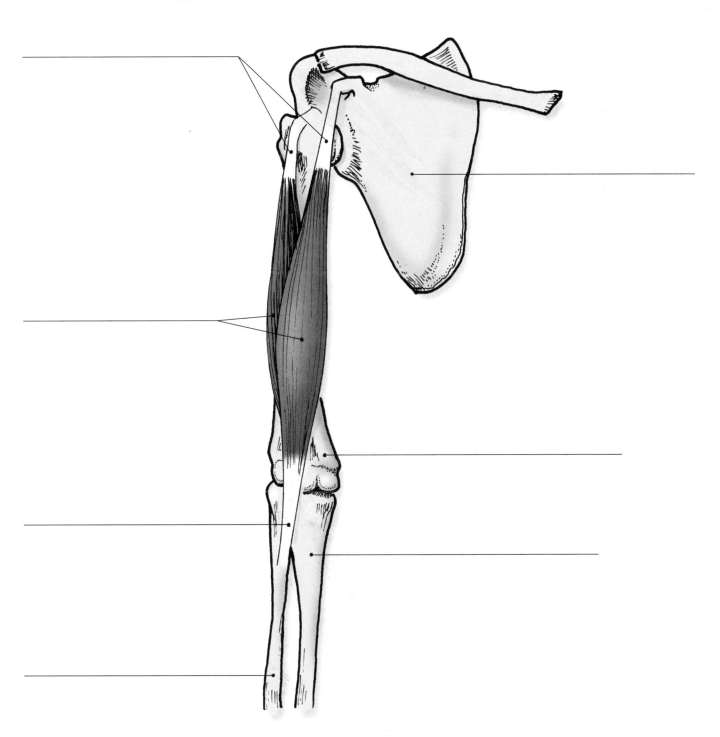

Name _____

Directions: Label the three different kinds of muscles in section **A**. Give an example of the kind of work they do. Label the muscle parts in section **B**.

 WORD BANK

skeletal muscles
tendon
muscle fiber
muscle group
cardiac muscles
smooth muscles

These muscles can make your heart beat.
These muscles can move your bones.
These muscles can move food in your stomach.

A.

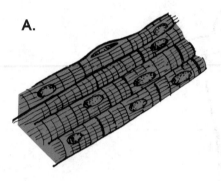  

Kind of Muscle

_____   _____   _____

Kind of Work

_____   _____   _____

Muscle Parts   _____

B.

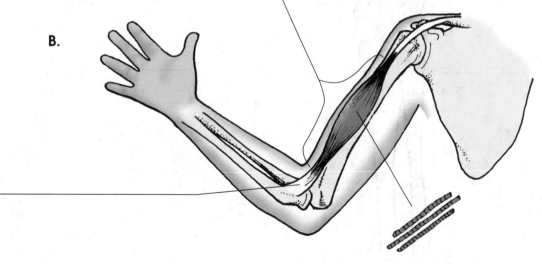

_____

_____

Name _____

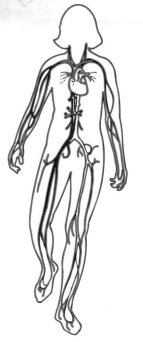

Directions: Read the information below. Underline the two main functions and the main organ of the circulatory system. Then, answer the questions. The **circulatory system** is responsible for transporting materials throughout the body and for regulating body temperature. The heart is vital to the circulatory system. It pumps blood to all parts of the body. The blood then carries nutrients and other important materials to the cells. Blood also carries waste products away from cells to disposal sites like the liver, lungs, and kidneys.

The circulatory system also acts as a temperature control for the body. Warmer blood from the center of the body is brought to the surface to be cooled. On a cold day, the blood vessels contract very little allowing little blood to flow through. This is why skin might appear pale, or even blue. However, in hot weather, blood vessels widen and more blood is able to flow through them to increase the loss of heat. Thus, your skin looks pinker and feels warmer.

1. What are the two main functions of the circulatory system? _____

   _____

2. The blood carries important nutrients to the _____

3. Blood carries _____ away from cells and to the_____,

   _____ , and_____ .

4. Warmer blood is brought from the_____of the body to

   the _____of the body to be cooled.

5. In cold weather, why does your skin appear pale, or even blue? _____

   _____

A "HEARTY" EXPERIMENT

You will need: a tennis ball and a watch with a second hand.

Hold the tennis ball in your stronger hand and give it a hard squeeze. This is about the strength it takes your heart muscle to contract to pump one beat. Squeeze the ball as hard as you can and release it 70 times in 1 minute.

Record how your hand feels. _____

Conclusion: _____

_____

The Human Body

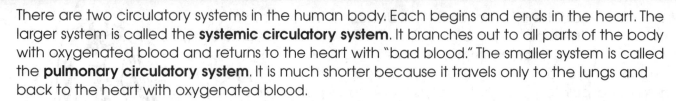

Name

There are two circulatory systems in the human body. Each begins and ends in the heart. The larger system is called the **systemic circulatory system**. It branches out to all parts of the body with oxygenated blood and returns to the heart with "bad blood." The smaller system is called the **pulmonary circulatory system**. It is much shorter because it travels only to the lungs and back to the heart with oxygenated blood.

Blood vessels that carry blood to the heart are called **veins**. Those that carry it away are called **arteries**. Blood from the systemic circulatory system flows from the **superior** and **interior vena cavas** into the **right atrium**, then into the **right ventricle** and out through the **pulmonary arteries** to the lungs. At the same time, blood from the lungs enters the atrium from pulmonary veins, drops into the **left ventricle**, is pumped into the body's largest artery, called the **aorta**, then flows into blood vessels that carry it to various parts of the body.

Directions:

1. Color the systemic circulatory system red.
2. Color the pulmonary circulatory system gray.
3. Draw blue arrows to show the flow of the systemic circulatory system.
4. Draw black arrows to show the flow of the pulmonary circulatory system.
5. Label the parts of the circulatory system listed in the WORD BANK. If a number in parentheses follows a part, label it that many times.

 WORD BANK

aorta
superior and inferior vena cava
right and left atriums
right and left ventricles
pulmonary veins (2)
arteries leading from aorta
pulmonary arteries (2)

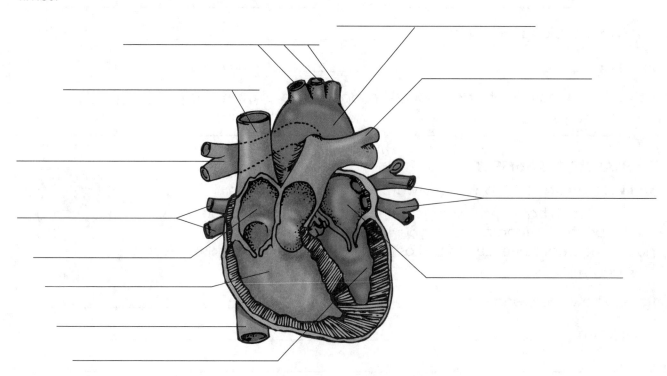

Directions: Draw red arrows on the arteries showing the flow of blood away from the heart.

Directions: Draw blue arrows on the veins showing the flow of blood back to the heart.

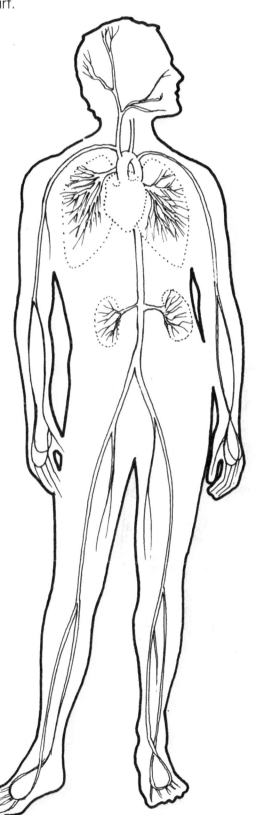

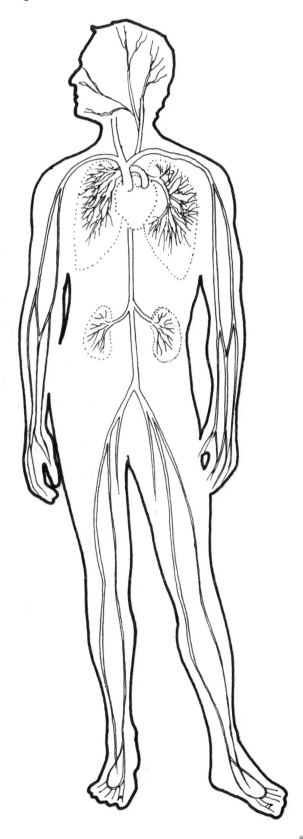

Name _____

Directions: Label the parts of your heart.

WORD BANK

left atrium	right atrium	vena cava
left ventricle	right ventricle	aorta
pulmonary artery	pulmonary veins	

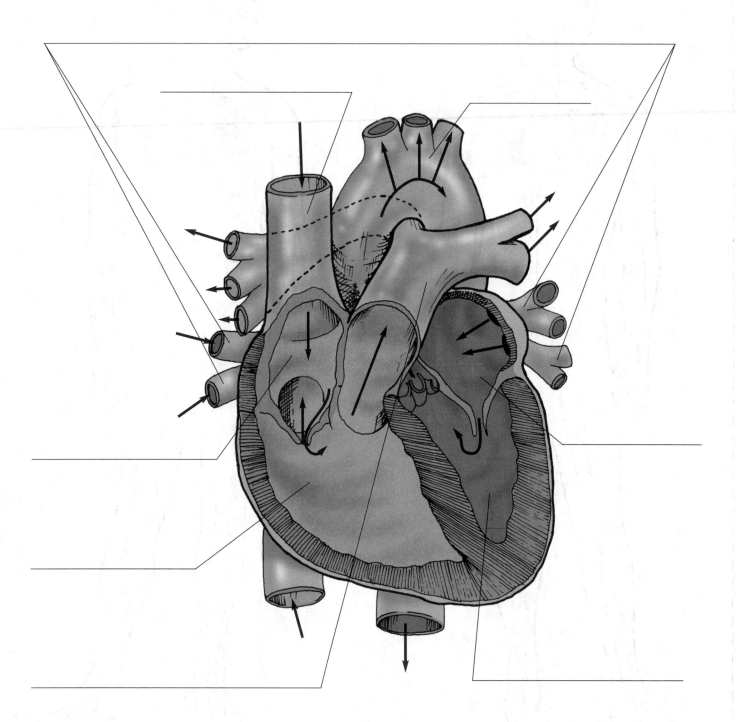

Name _____

Directions: Use the WORD BANK to complete the puzzle.

WORD BANK
lungs
heart
liver
kidneys
aorta
right atrium
right ventricle
left ventricle
left atrium
pulmonary vein
artery

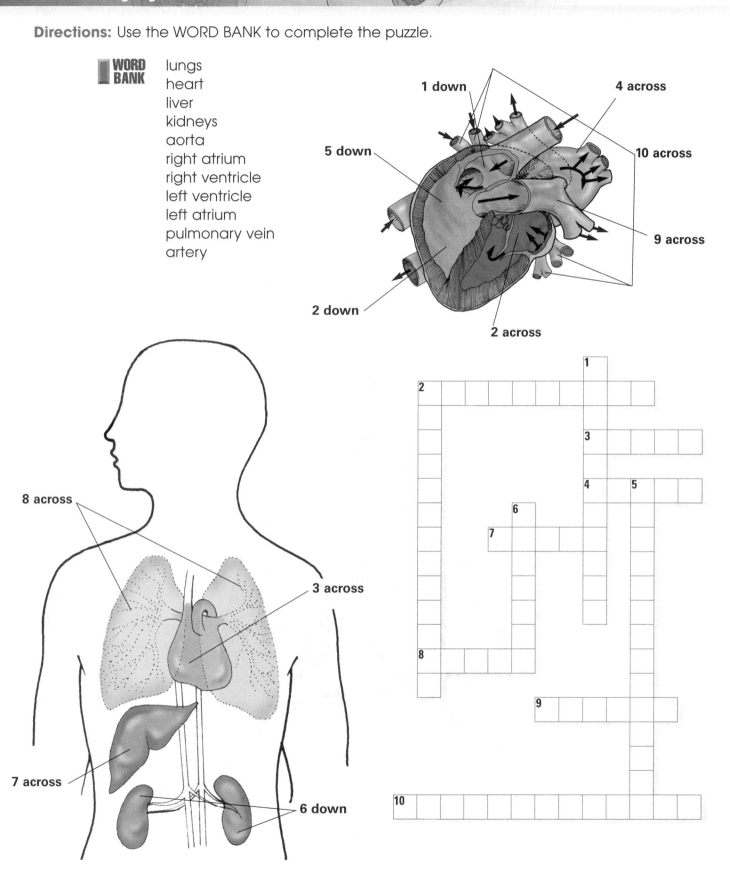

1 down
4 across
5 down
10 across
9 across
2 down
2 across

8 across
3 across
7 across
6 down

Name _____

Directions: Label the parts of your **respiratory system**.

WORD BANK

Common Name *(Scientific Name)*

throat *(pharynx)*   voice box *(larynx)*
windpipe *(trachea)*   lung cover *(pleura)*
bronchial tube   diaphragm

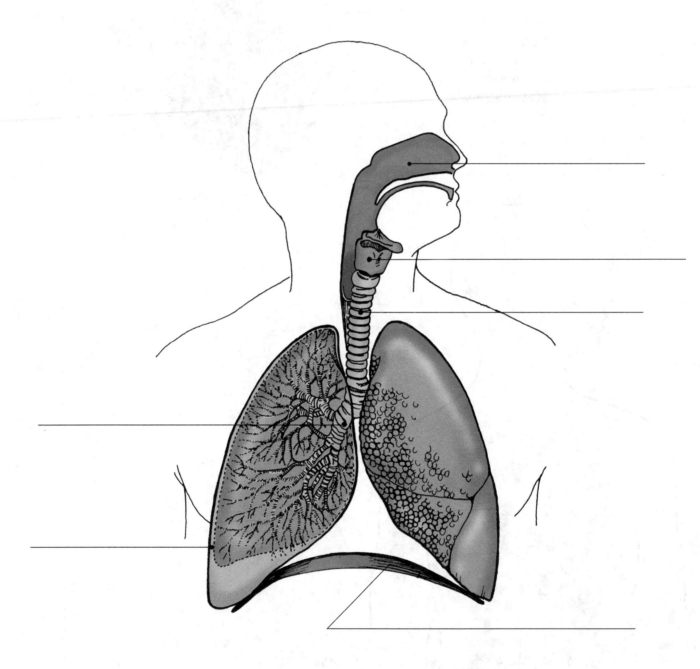

Name _____

Directions: Label the parts of your lungs.

WORD BANK

trachea   bronchial tube
pleura   alveoli
bronchiole   capillaries
right lung   left lung

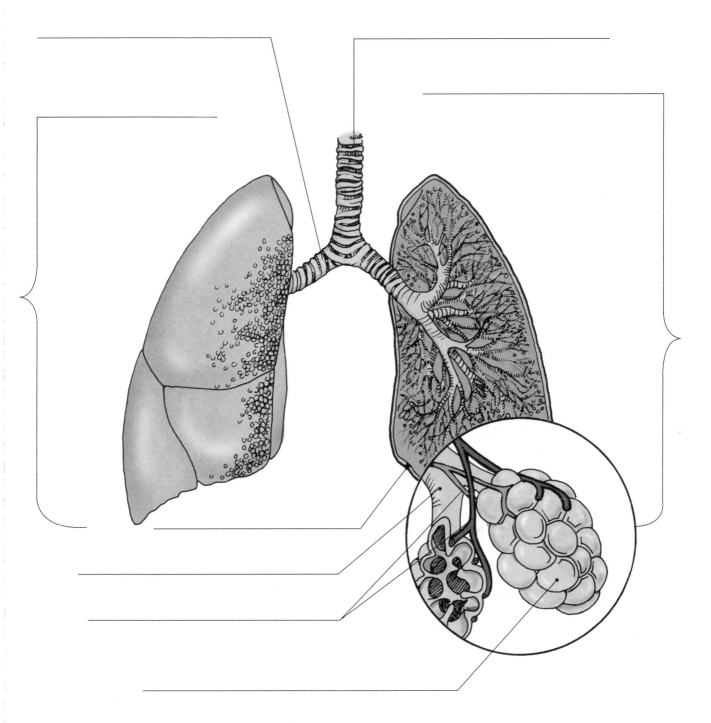

The Human Body

Name _____

Directions: Use the WORD BANK to complete the puzzle.

WORD BANK

diaphragm	bronchial tube	trachea	capillaries
alveoli	lung	larynx	
bronchioli	pleura	pharynx	

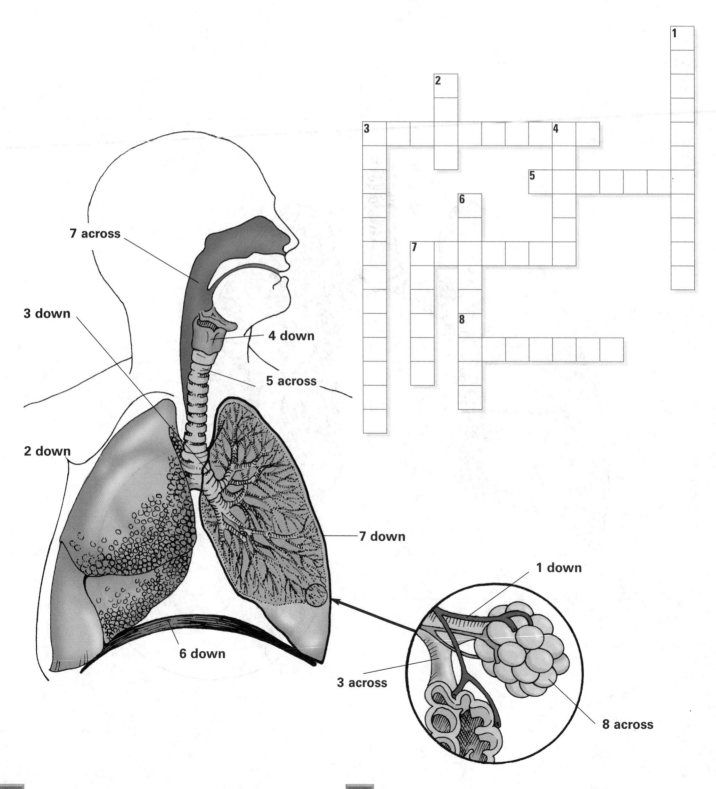

7 across

3 down

4 down

5 across

2 down

7 down

1 down

6 down

3 across

8 across

Breathing and Heart Rates

QUESTION How does exercise affect a person's breathing and heart rates?

PREDICTION You will be counting the number of breaths you take and the number of times your heart beats in 15 seconds. How do you think the two rates will be affected if you exercise? Write your prediction on the record sheet.

MATERIALS
- stopwatch
- cardboard tube

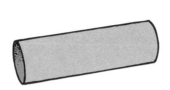

PROCEDURE Work with a partner.

1. Sit quietly for three minutes. At the end of three minutes, breathe normally and count your breaths for 15 seconds. Record the number of breaths you took. Have your partner listen with the cardboard tube to your heartbeat for 15 seconds. Write how many heartbeats there were.

2. Walk around the room for two minutes. Then count your breaths for 15 seconds. Have your partner listen to your heartbeat for 15 seconds. Write the results on your record sheet.

3. Run in place very fast for one minute. At the end of the minute, count your breaths for 15 seconds. Have your partner listen to your heartbeat for 15 seconds. Write the results on your record sheet.

RESULTS Record your breathing and heart rates on the record sheet. Multiply each number by four to get the rate per minute.

CONCLUSIONS How does exercise affect a person's breathing and heart rates? Write your answer on the record sheet.

Although good health is not the same as physical fitness, regular exercise appears to influence how healthy a person is. How do you think exercise helps a person stay healthy? Write your answer on the record sheet.

The Human Body

Breathing and Heart Rates Record Sheet

QUESTION How does exercise affect a person's breathing and heart rate?

PREDICTION You will be counting the number of breaths you take and the number of times your heart beats in 15 seconds. How do you think the two rates will be affected if you exercise?

_____

_____

RESULTS Record your breathing and heart rates below.

	Breaths in 15 Seconds	Breaths Per Minute	Heartbeats in 15 Seconds	Heartbeats Per Minute
Sitting quietly				
After walking				
Sitting quietly				

CONCLUSIONS How does exercise affect a person's breathing and heart rate?

_____

_____

Although good health is not the same as physical fitness, regular exercise appears to influence how healthy a person is. How do you think exercise helps a person stay healthy?

_____

_____

_____

_____

Name

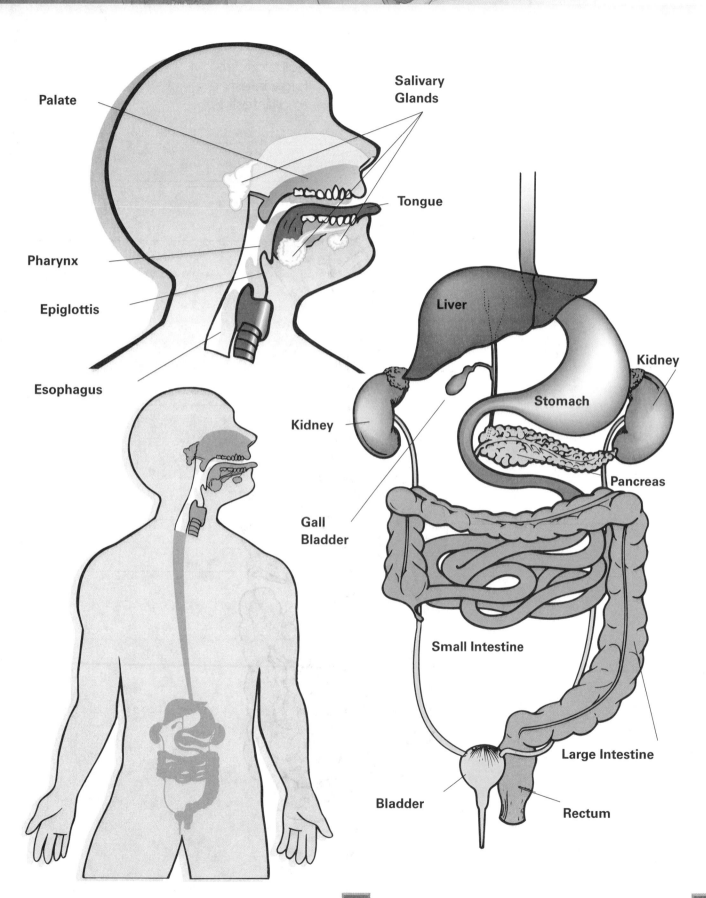

Palate

Salivary
Glands

Tongue

Pharynx

Epiglottis

Liver

Kidney

Stomach

Esophagus

Kidney

Gall
Bladder

Pancreas

Small Intestine

Large Intestine

Bladder

Rectum

The Human Body

Name

Directions: Label the parts of your **digestive system**.

WORD BANK

pancreas   liver   gall bladder
stomach   mouth   large intestine
esophagus   teeth   small intestine
salivary glands   anus

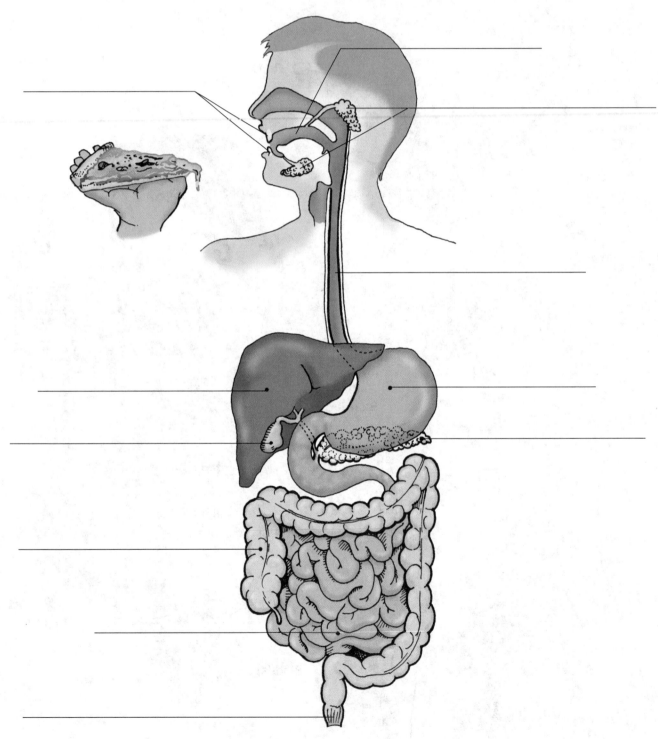

The main part of the digestive system is the **alimentary canal**, a tube which starts at the mouth, and travels through the body ending at the anus.

Directions: Label the parts of the alimentary canal.

WORD BANK

anus   small intestine   esophagus
mouth   large intestine   stomach

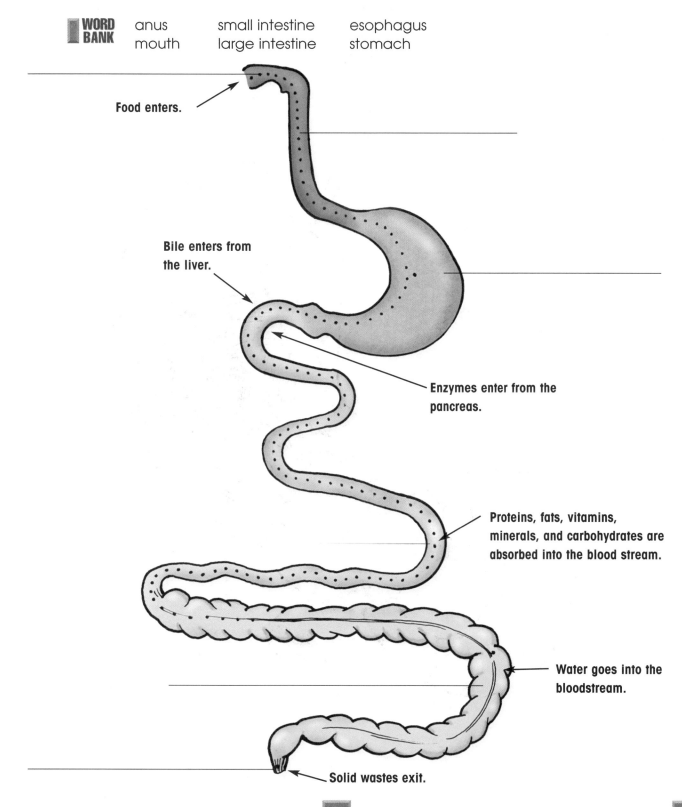

Food enters.

Bile enters from the liver.

Enzymes enter from the pancreas.

Proteins, fats, vitamins, minerals, and carbohydrates are absorbed into the blood stream.

Water goes into the bloodstream.

Solid wastes exit.

The Human Body

The **stomach** is the widest part of the alimentary canal. The stomach has three layers of muscles which allow it to contract in different directions. The contracting motion mashes food and mixes it with digestive juices.

Directions: Label the parts of the stomach and the tubes leading into and out of the stomach.

WORD BANK

sphincter	duodenum	mucous membrane
muscle layers	esophagus	

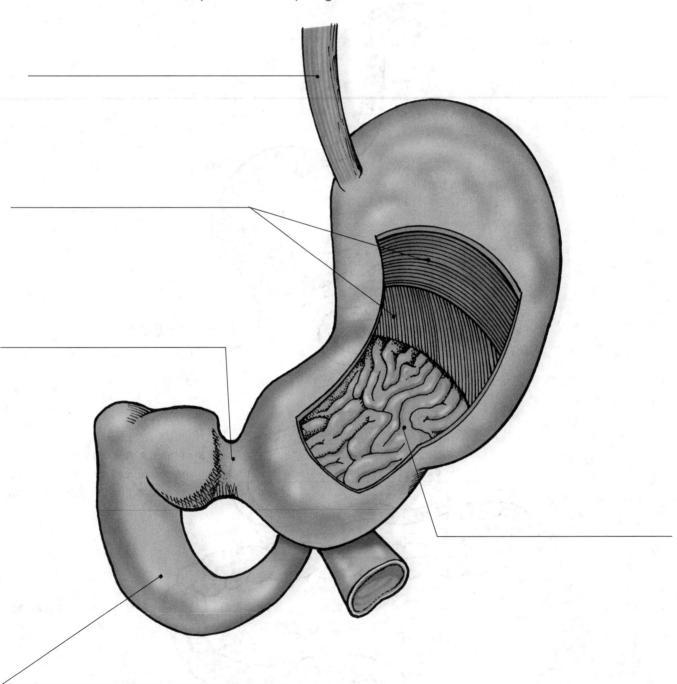

Name _____

Directions: Label the parts of the digestive system located in and around the mouth.

WORD BANK

teeth   tongue   palate
epiglottis   esophagus   salivary glands
pharynx

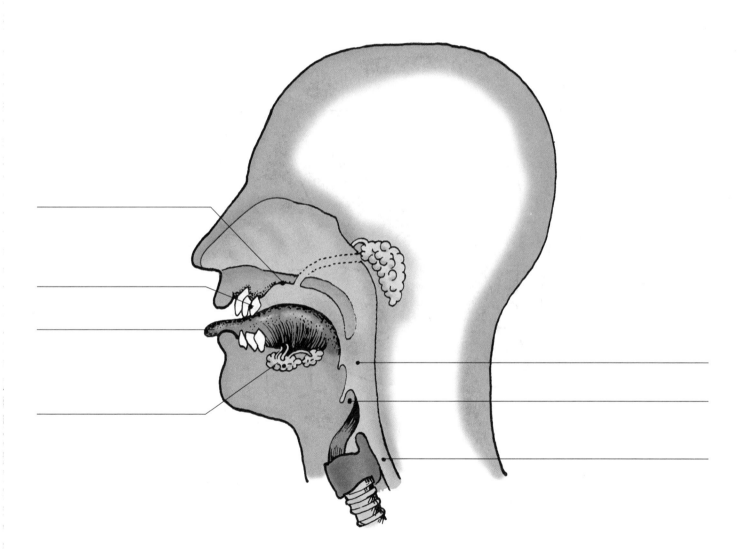

Name _____

Directions: Label these organs that aid in the digestion of the food you eat.

WORD BANK

liver   pancreas   gall bladder
bile duct   duodenum

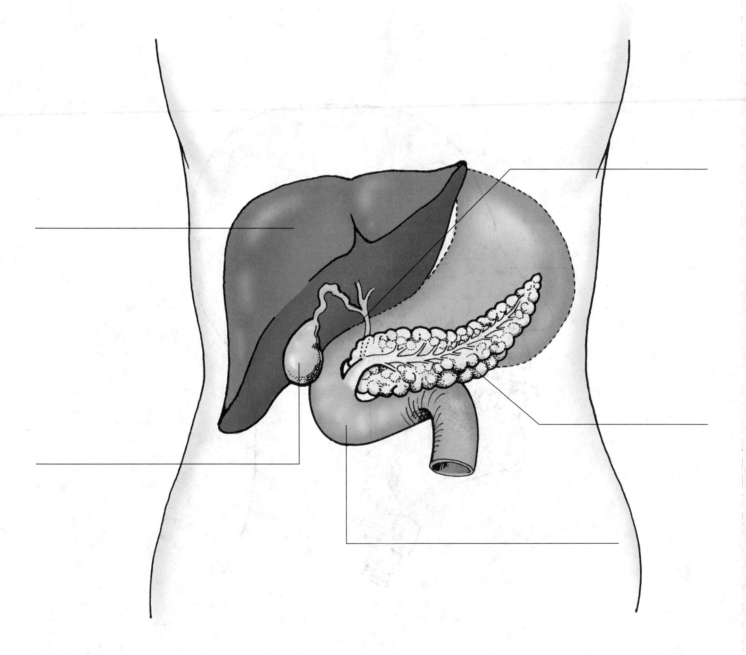

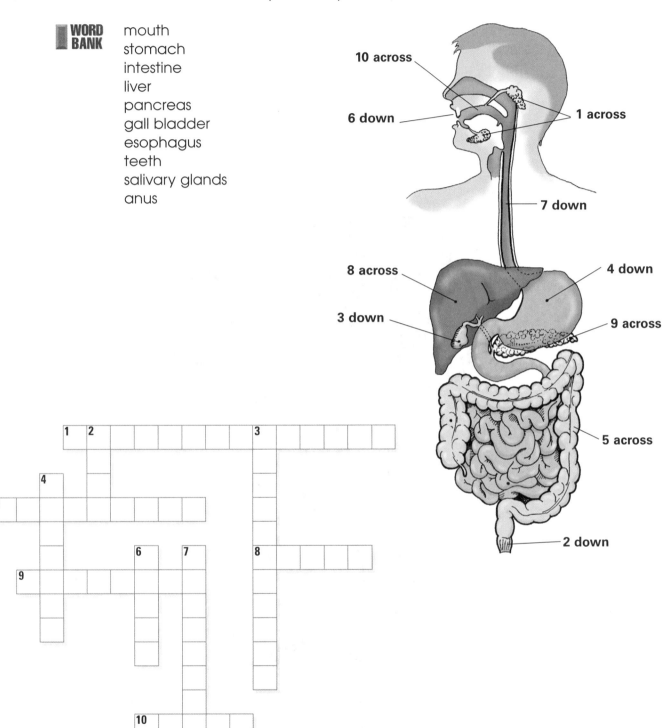

Name

Directions: Use the WORD BANK to complete the puzzle.

WORD BANK
- mouth
- stomach
- intestine
- liver
- pancreas
- gall bladder
- esophagus
- teeth
- salivary glands
- anus

10 across

6 down

1 across

7 down

8 across

4 down

3 down

9 across

5 across

2 down

The Human Body

Blood Scrubbers

Directions: Label the different parts of your body's **urinary system**.

WORD BANK

vein   artery   ureter
kidney   bladder   urethra
muscle

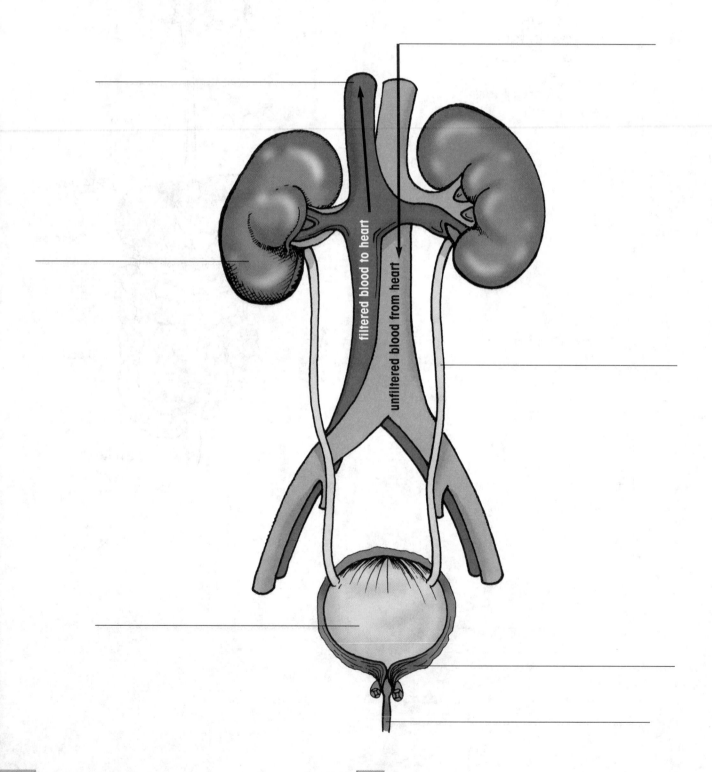

filtered blood to heart

unfiltered blood from heart

Name _____

The important job of removing bodily wastes is performed by the skin and the organs of the **urinary** and **respiratory systems**.

Directions: Label the excretory organs.

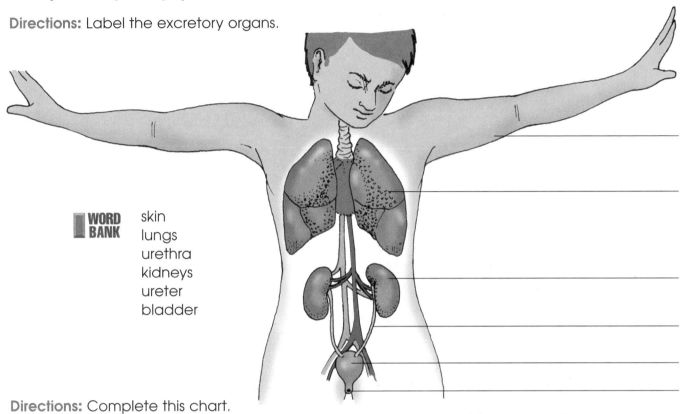

WORD BANK
skin
lungs
urethra
kidneys
ureter
bladder

Directions: Complete this chart.

FUNCTION	EXCRETORY ORGANS			
	Kidneys	**Lungs**	**Skin**	**Bladder**
Removes water				
Brings oxygen to blood				
Removes salt				
Stores urine				
Removes carbon dioxide				
Produces urine				
Removes body heat				

The Human Body

The Body's Communication System

Your body's **central nervous system** is made up of two parts: the **brain** and the **spinal cord**. The rest of the system consists of nerves coming from the brain and the spinal cord. These nerves are called **sensory nerve cells** and **motor nerve cells**. A stimulus causes your sensory nerve cells to carry messages from your skin and sense organs to your brain.

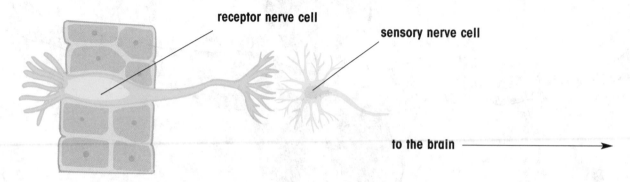

receptor nerve cell

sensory nerve cell

to the brain →

Imagine you see a bee coming to sting you. Your sensory nerve cells carry this message to your brain. Your brain is the control center that interprets the message. Motor nerve cells carry the message (Run!) back from the central nervous system to the muscles. Your response (running) then occurs.

Directions: Listed below are different kinds of stimuli. Write how you would respond to each stimulus in the Response column.

Example: Stimulus — Feel pain in chest   **Response** — Dial 9-1-1.

STIMULI	RESPONSE
Smell of burning food	
Bad odor from outside	
Sit on sharp object	
Traffic light turns green	
Bathtub overflowing	
Dog darts in front of car	
Pitcher throws ball at you	
Gale force wind blowing	

Fascinating Fact! Did you know your nervous system contains more than 10 billion nerve cells?

Name _____

Directions: Label the parts of your **central nervous system**.

WORD BANK
brain   spinal cord   nerves
cerebrum   cerebellum   brain stem
nerve cell

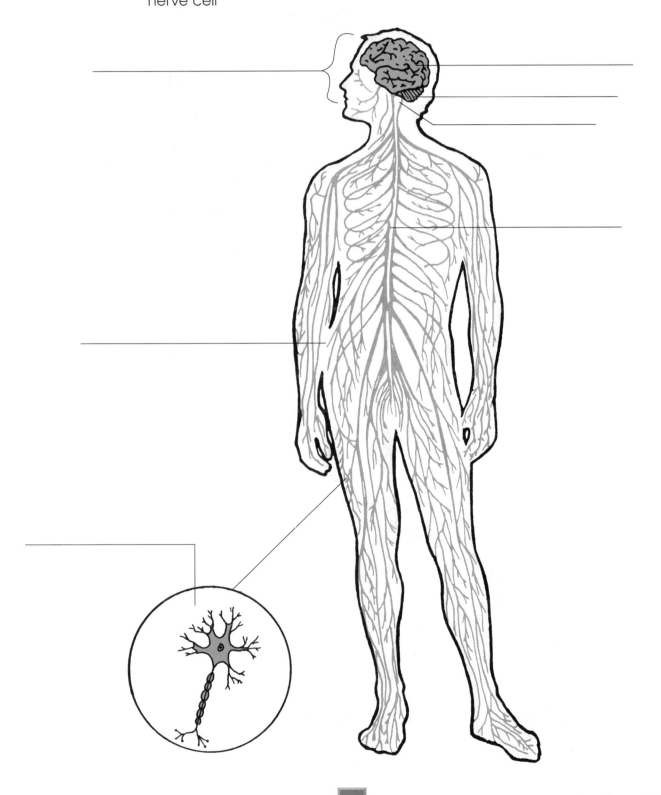

The Human Body

Name

Directions: Label the parts of a neuron.

WORD BANK   nucleus   axon   terminal fibers
dendrites   cell body

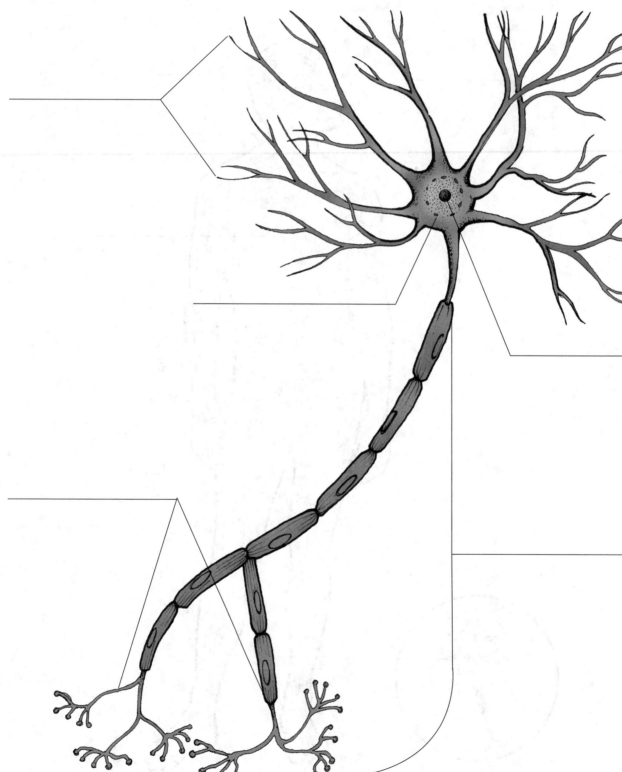

Name _____

Neurons act as "go-betweens" in the sending and receiving of impulses within the nervous system. The drawings below illustrate how impulses pass from one neuron to another.

Directions: Label the parts of the enlarged illustration.

WORD BANK
synaptic cleft   transmitting molecule
axon terminal   dendrite

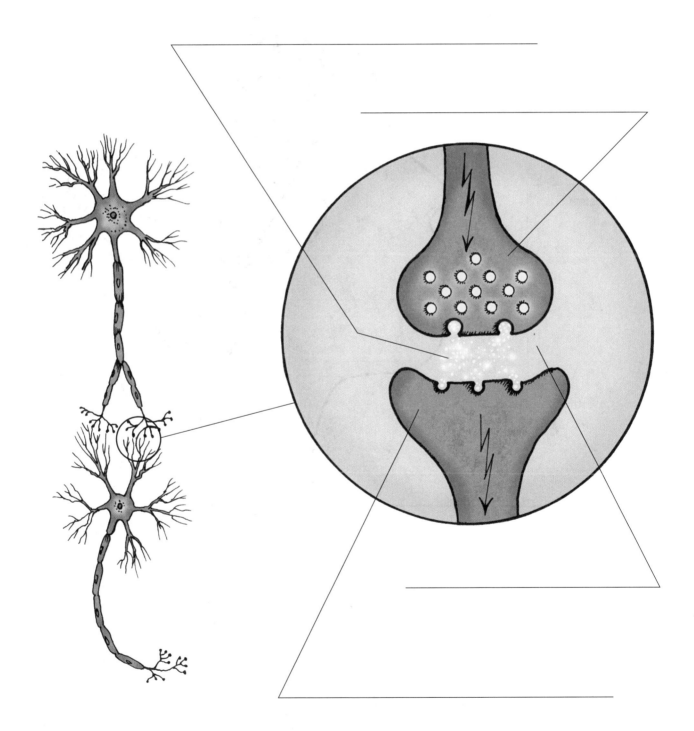

The Human Body

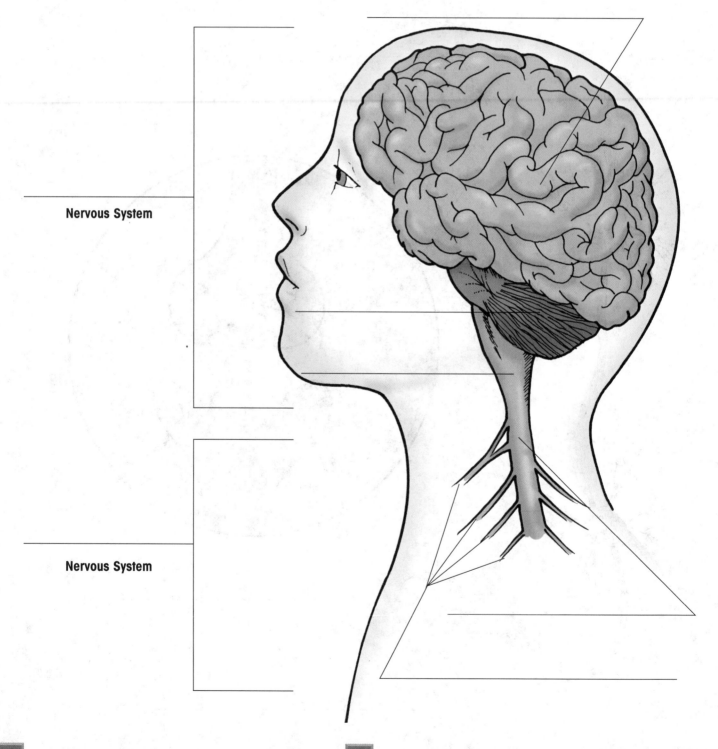

The Nervous System

Two of the nervous systems in the human body are the **central** and the **peripheral**.

Directions: Label these two systems and their parts.

WORD BANK

central	cerebrum	medulla	spinal cord
peripheral	cerebellum	spinal nerves	

Nervous System

Nervous System

Directions: Write the letter of each function next to its matching part. Draw a line from the pictured part of the nervous system to its function.

PARTS

1. _____ cerebrum
2. _____ cerebellum
3. _____ medulla
4. _____ spinal cord
5. _____ spinal nerves

FUNCTION

a. It controls balance and muscular coordination.

b. It controls thought, voluntary movement, memory, and learning, and also processes information from the senses.

c. They carry impulses between the spinal cord and body parts.

d. It controls breathing, heartbeat, and other vital body processes.

e. It relays impulses between the brain and other parts of the body.

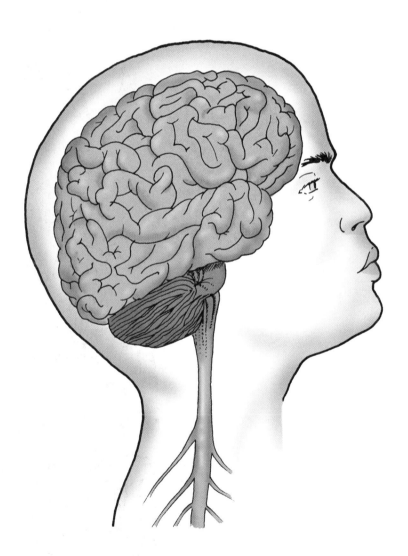

The Human Body

Name _____

The **autonomic nervous system** works almost independently of the central nervous system. It controls the life-sustaining functions of the body, such as breathing, digestion, and heartbeat. These organs and muscle tissues work involuntarily.

Directions: Label these important parts of the autonomic nervous system.

WORD BANK

eye	trachea	heart	lungs
liver	gallbladder	stomach	pancreas
small intestine	large intestine	rectum	

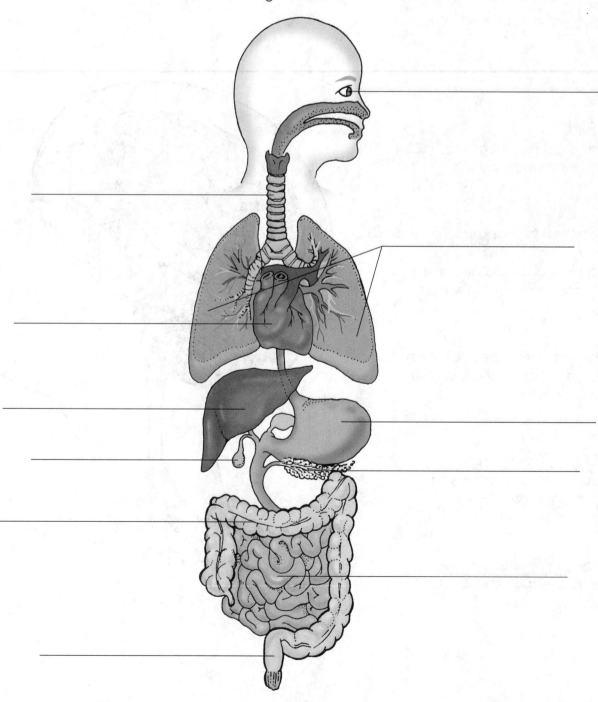

Directions: Use the WORD BANK to complete the puzzle.

WORD BANK

cerebrum	cerebellum	brain stem	spinal cord
dendrite	axon	nucleus	neuron
medulla			

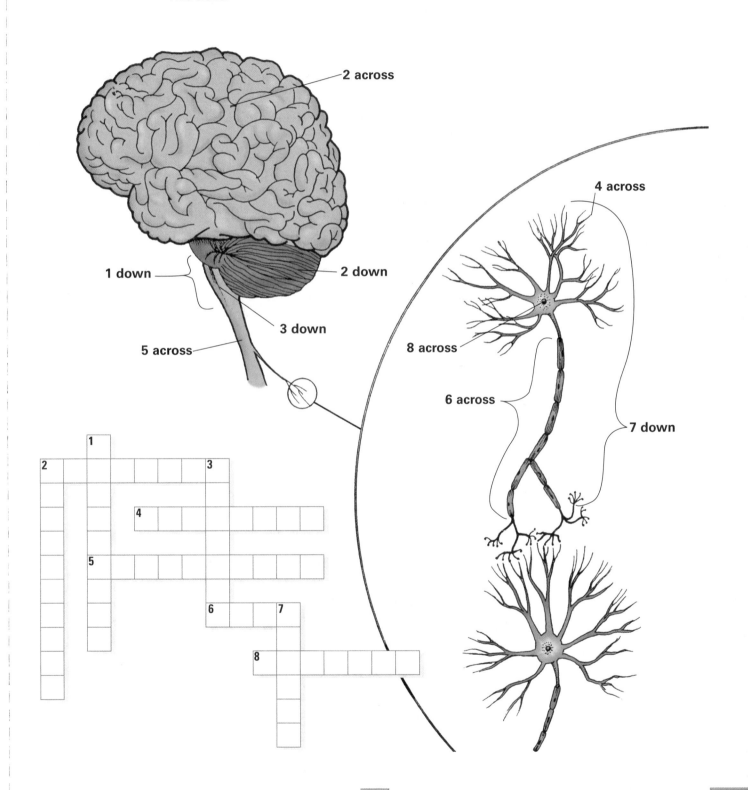

2 across

1 down

2 down

3 down

5 across

4 across

8 across

6 across

7 down

The Human Body

Name _____

The **endocrine glands** help control many of your body's functions.

Directions: Using the words from the WORD BANK, label the glands of the endocrine system.

 WORD BANK

thyroid gland   pituitary gland   pineal gland   pancreas
adrenal glands   ovaries (female)   testes (male)

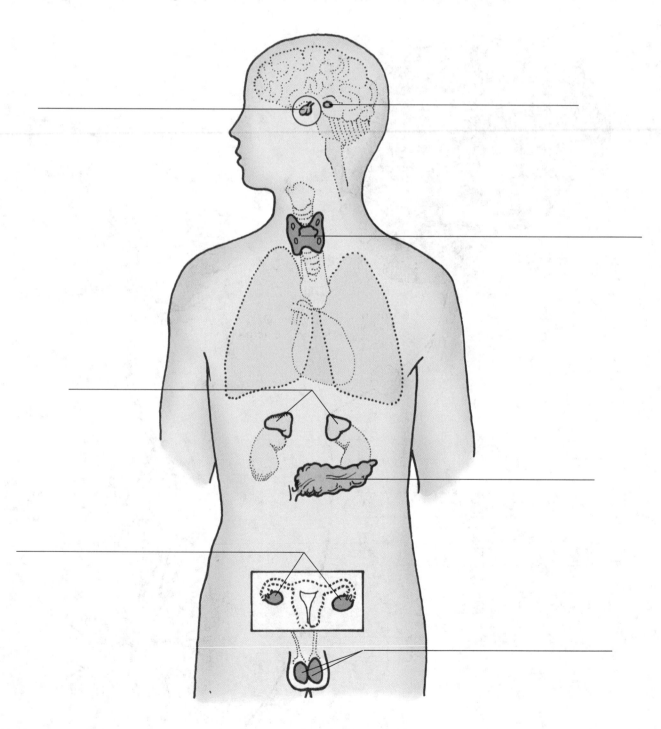

Name _____

Directions: Draw a line from the name of the gland to its picture.
Draw a line from the picture of the gland to its function.

GLAND

thyroid •

pituitary •

parathyroids •

adrenal •

thymus •

ovaries •

pancreas •

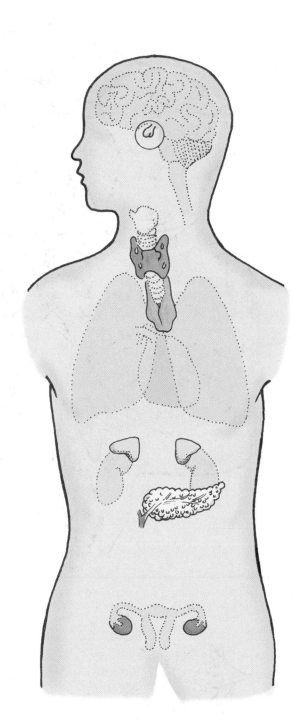

FUNCTION

• Controls other glands and body growth.

• Control the amount of calcium in your blood.

• Controls the rate that food is turned into energy.

• Helps the body's immune system to recognize and reject germs.

• Affects kidneys and helps when you are excited, angry, or frightened.

• Controls the body's use of glucose.

• Produce female characteristics and initiate female bodily functions.

The Human Body

Name _____

Your brain gets information from outside your body through many different sense organs.

Directions: Label the different sense organs and the nerve cell pictured on this page.

WORD BANK

eye
ear
tongue
receptor nerve cell
sensory nerve cell
nose

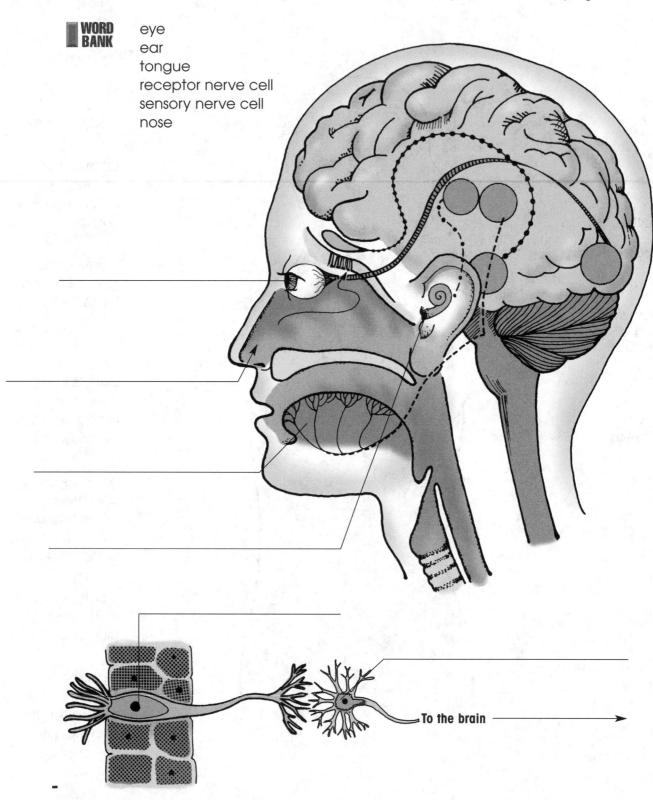

To the brain →

The Senses

QUESTION What observations can I make with each of my senses?

MATERIALS a piece of candy in a wrapper

PROCEDURE Complete the table using your senses.

What to Do	Observations	Sense Used	Organ Used
Look at the piece of candy in the wrapper.			
Hold the candy in its wrapper.			
Hold the candy in its wrapper up to your nose.			
Listen as you open the candy wrapper.			
Hold your nose and place the candy in your mouth.			
Let go of your nose and move the candy around in your mouth.			
Listen as you move the candy around in your mouth.			
Feel the candy in your mouth.			
Look at someone else as he or she eats candy.			
Listen as he or she eats candy.			
Listen to the wrapper as you crinkle it up to throw it away.			

Directions: Answer the questions.

1. Did looking at the piece of candy help you decide what it would taste

   like? _____ Why or why not? _____

2. Which sense do you think you rely on the most? Why? _____

   _____

The Human Body

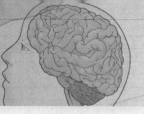

Map Your Tongue

The human tongue is a sense organ that has a very high nerve cell density. It is uniquely suited to taste, but not all of the nerve cells sense the same taste. Some recognize sweet, some identify sour, and others sense saltiness. Because of this, there are "regions" on the tongue.

Directions: Do the following experiment with a partner to locate the taste regions on your tongue.

MATERIALS

- cotton swabs
- lemon juice
- measuring spoons
- small piece of paper
- cups of water
- sugar
- salt

PROCEDURE

1. Prepare three paper cups for the taste test.
2. Add 1/2 tsp. sugar to first cup and label it "sugar."
3. Add 1/2 tsp. salt to the second cup and label it "salt."
4. Add enough lemon juice to the third cup so it is 1/8 full.
5. Add water to each cup so each is about 1/4 full.
6. Soak one end of a cotton swab in a random cup so no pattern is established.
7. Gently place the swab on the center, sides, and tip of your partner's tongue to find where the taste is sensed.
8. Record where the taste is sensed.   Test 1, Cup _____
9. Repeat the test with the remaining cups, using a new cotton swab each time. Remember to record the results.

   Test 2, Cup _____   Test 3, Cup _____
10. On another piece of paper, make a drawing of the tongue and label the regions as "sweet," "salty," and "sour."

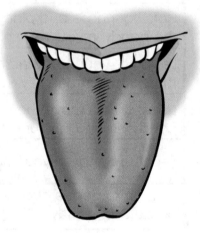

QUESTIONS

1. Where does the tongue have high nerve density? _____

2. What did you learn about the nerve cells in the tongue? _____

   _____

   _____

3. What other nerve cells have unique functions? _____

   _____

   _____

Directions: Label the parts of your nose.

nostril   olfactory nerve   brain
nasal passage   receptor cells

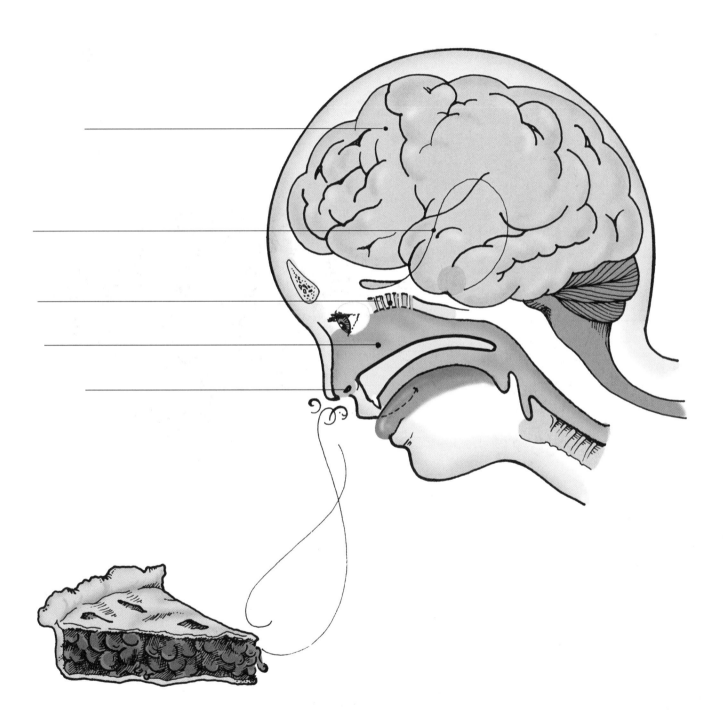

The Human Body

Your Ear

Directions: Label the parts of your ear.

WORD BANK

auditory canal
hammer
stirrup
semicircular canals

auditory nerve
oval window
eardrum
anvil

cochlea
eustachian tube
wax gland
auricle

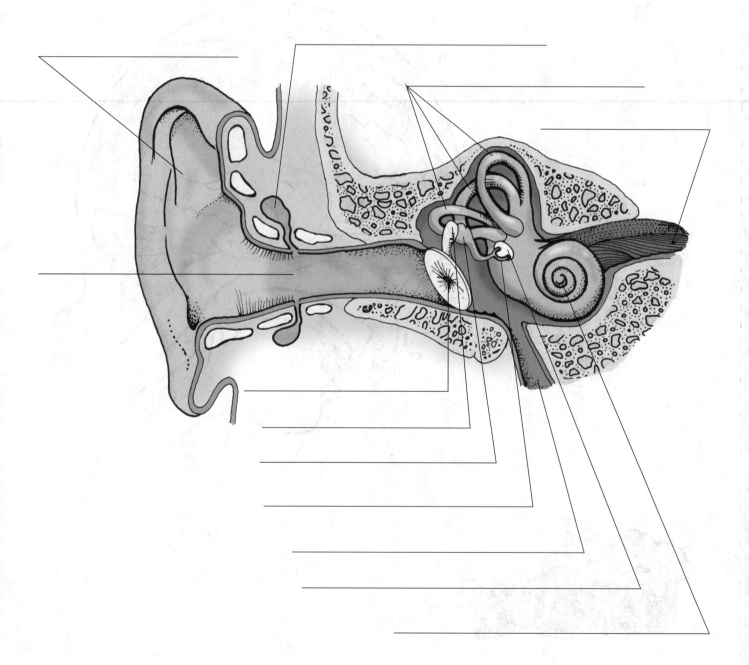

Ear, Nose, and Throat Connection

Your ears, nose, mouth, and throat are all connected to each other.

Directions: Label the parts in the picture below.

WORD BANK

windpipe   epiglottis   food tube
eustachian tube   nasal passage   roof of the mouth

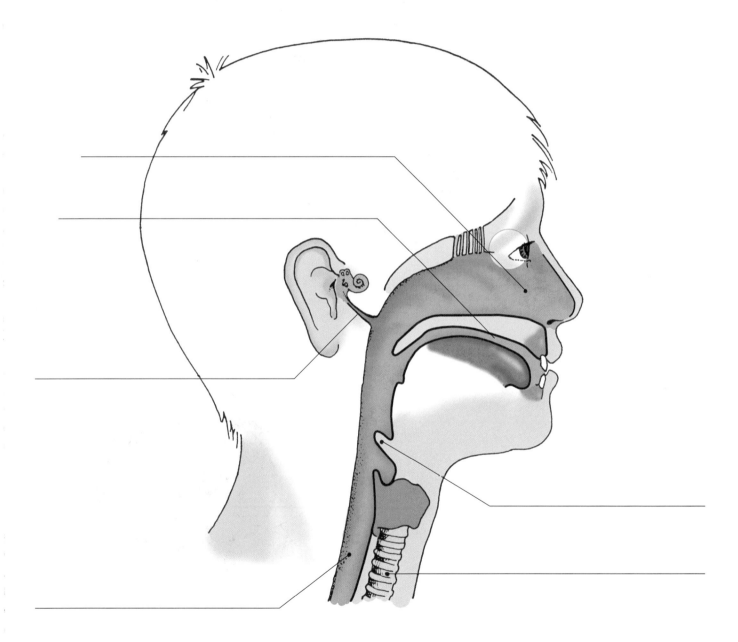

The Human Body

Name _____

Directions: Label the parts of your eye pictured below.

WORD BANK   optic nerve   retina   lens   sclera
             iris   cornea   pupil

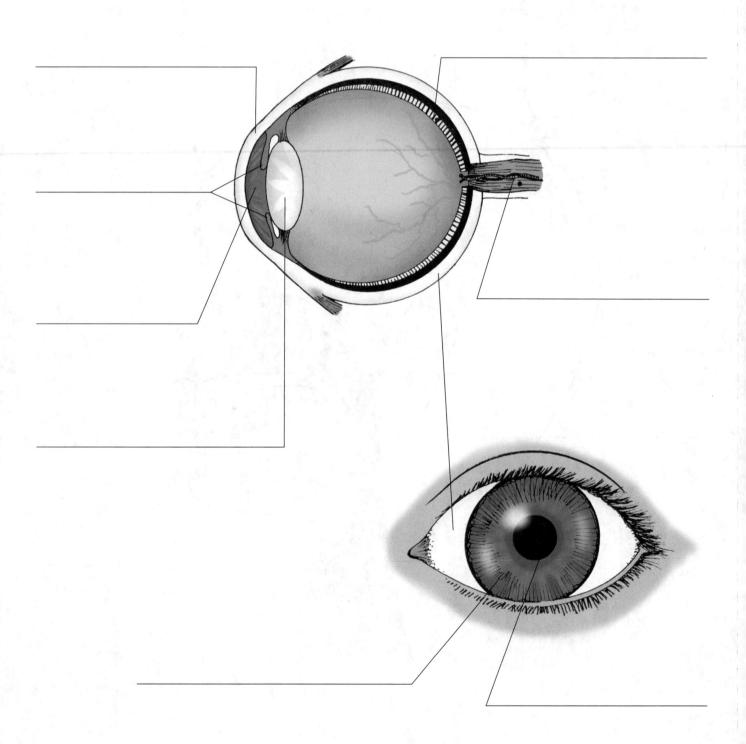

Name

Your eyes gather the rays of light coming off an object. They change the light rays into nerve impulses, but your brain interprets these impulses and "draws" a picture of the image.

Directions: Label the parts of this "Eye-to-Brain Connection."

 WORD BANK

image   cornea   lens   upside-down image

retina   optic nerve   visual cortex

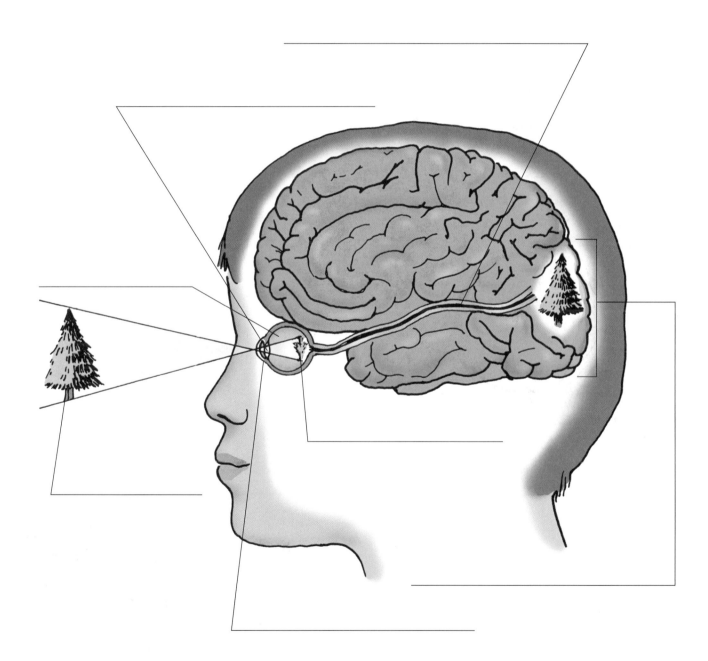

The Human Body

Ear and Eye Review

Directions: Use the WORD BANK to complete the puzzle.

WORD BANK

cornea
semicircular canals
auditory nerve
lens
retina
optic nerve
sclera
stirrup
cochlea
anvil
auricle
eardrum
pupil
hammer
iris

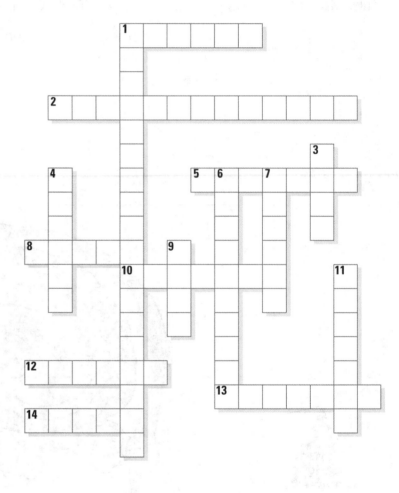

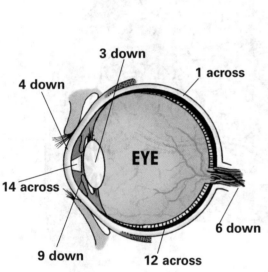

EYE

3 down
4 down
1 across
14 across
6 down
9 down
12 across

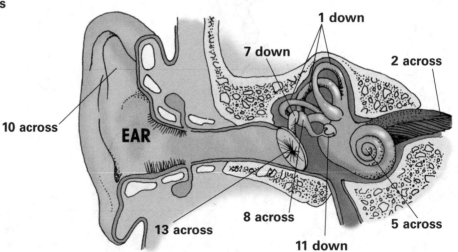

EAR

1 down
7 down
2 across
10 across
8 across
5 across
13 across
11 down

Skin Deep

Your skin is made up of many layers. These layers contain hairs, nerves, blood vessels, and glands.

Directions: Label these layers and other parts using the words from the WORD BANK.

 WORD BANK

epidermis	dermis	fat layer	hair muscle
fat cells	hair	oil gland	blood vessel
sweat gland	pore	nerve	

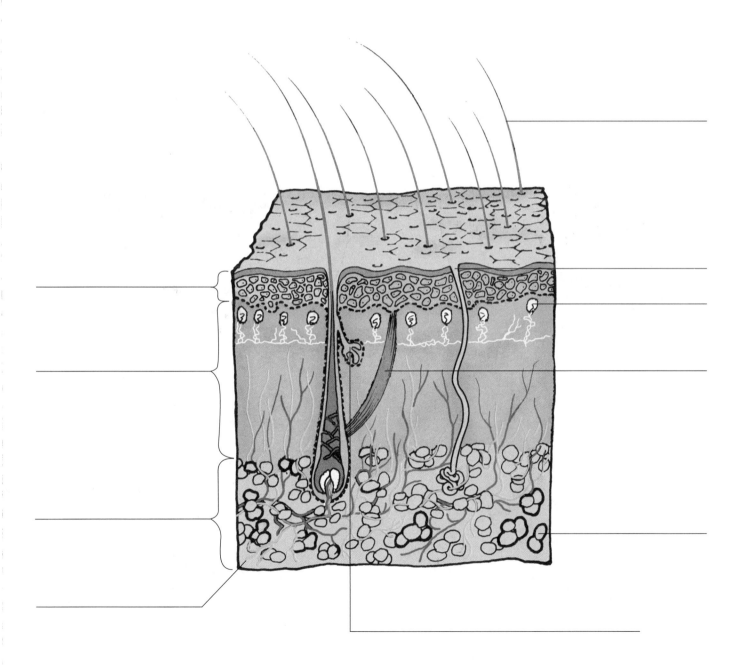

Sweaty Palms and Goose Bumps

Your body has its own air conditioning system. On cold days, your skin has a way to keep in your body's warmth. On hot days, your skin can cool you off.

Directions: Label the two pictures either **warm day** or **cool day**. Label the parts of the skin using the words from the WORD BANK.

 WORD BANK

closed sweat pore	open sweat pore
relaxed muscle	contracted muscle
sweat gland	blood vessels
goose bump	sweat

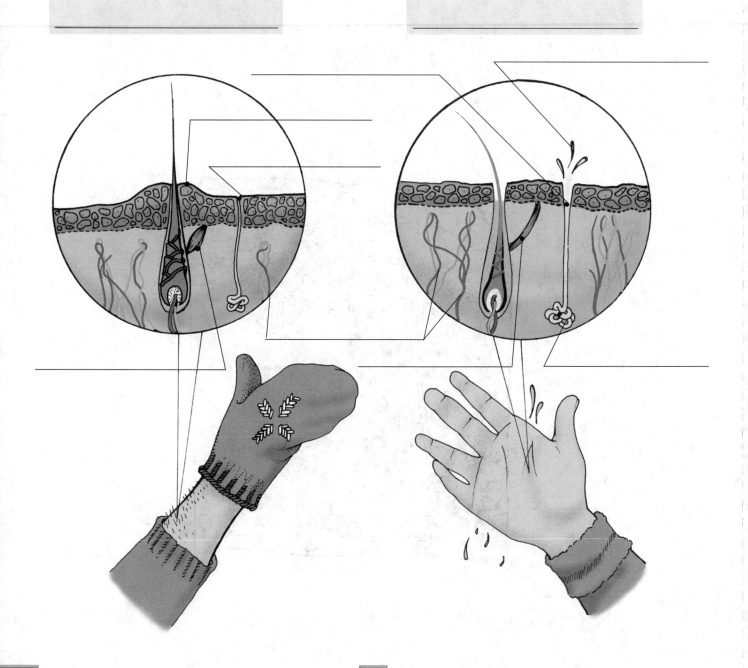

Body Tissues

Many of the body's organs are made of a variety of tissues working together. There are four kinds of tissue: **connective**, **epithelial**, **muscle**, and **nerve**. Each has a specialized function.

Directions: Study the pictures and read the descriptions. Write the name of each tissue beneath its description. Then, label the tissue parts in each picture.

 WORD BANK

connective tissue	epithelial tissue	muscle tissue
nerve tissue	collagen	fibroblast
nerve fiber	cell nucleus	cell

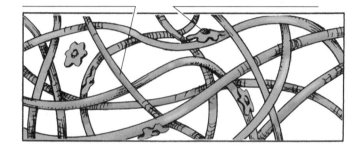

Composed of relatively few cells and surrounded by larger amounts of nonliving material. Supports and connects other tissues.

_____

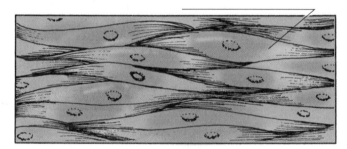

Made up of cells that can contract and relax. Allows the body to make internal and external movements.

_____

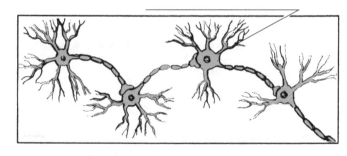

Specialized cells which carry electrical signals between the brain and other parts of the body.

_____

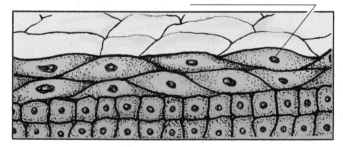

Tightly packed cells which form a covering for the skin and line the hollow internal organs.

_____

The Human Body

Fingerprints

The ridges in fingertips form unique patterns. No two people have the same pattern, not even identical twins. The ridges on fingers form three main groups of patterns – the **arch**, the **loop**, and the **whorl**.

arch

loop

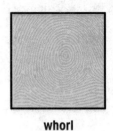

whorl

Directions: Make a record of your own fingerprints on the chart below by

a. placing the side of your fingertip on an inkpad and rolling your finger from one side to the other.

b. then placing the side of each inked finger on the chart and rolling it softly to leave a clear, crisp print.

c. labeling each print using the examples at the top of this page as a guide.

Right Hand

THUMB	INDEX	MIDDLE	RING	LITTLE

_____ _____ _____ _____ _____

Left Hand

THUMB	INDEX	MIDDLE	RING	LITTLE

_____ _____ _____ _____ _____

Your Toenails and Fingernails

Nails are a specialized part of your skin that protect the ends of your toes and fingers.

Directions: Label the parts of the nails below.

WORD BANK   bone   dead nail   nail root
                nail bed   fatty tissue

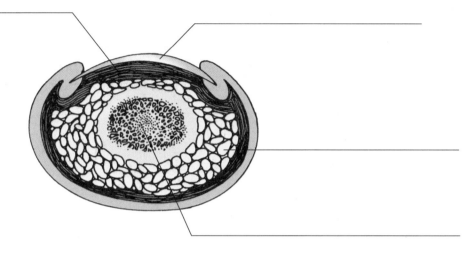

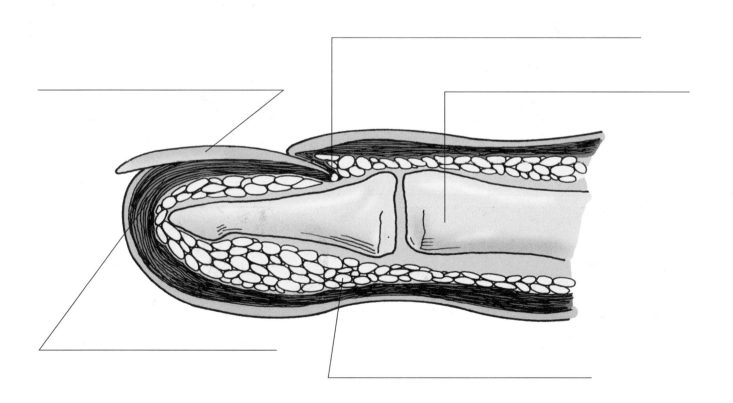

The Human Body

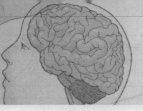

Name _____

The purpose of the male and female **reproductive system** is to create new life. From the time of conception, a single cell divides and keeps on dividing until it forms the six trillion cells of a human newborn baby. This development takes nine months.

Directions: Beneath each picture, write the matching description from the WORD BANK of a baby's development.

 WORD BANK

Fully developed with organs that can function on their own.
Develops tiny arm and leg buds, and its heart begins to beat.
Ears, eyes, nose, fingers, and toes are formed.
Can survive birth with special care.
First movements felt and heartbeat can be heard with a stethoscope.
Has recognizable human features and sex can be determined.

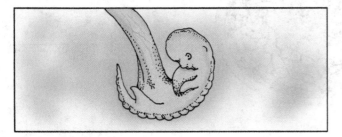

4 weeks _____

_____

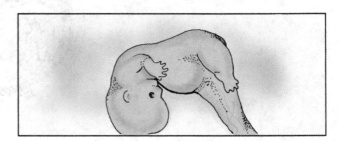

8 weeks _____

_____

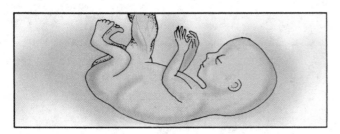

3 months _____

_____

4–6 months _____

_____

7 months _____

_____

9 months _____

_____

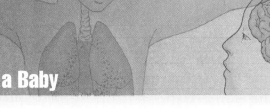

Birth of a Baby

When a baby is fully developed within the uterus, a hormone in the pituitary gland stimulates the muscles of the uterus. These muscle contractions signal the beginning of labor. The opening to the uterus, the cervix, gradually enlarges to allow the baby to pass through. The amniotic sac that surrounds the baby will break, releasing a gush of amniotic fluid. After the baby is born, the placenta separates from the wall of the uterus and is pushed out by more muscle contractions.

Directions: Study and label the diagram of the birth of a baby.

 WORD BANK   birth canal   placenta   uterus   umbilical cord

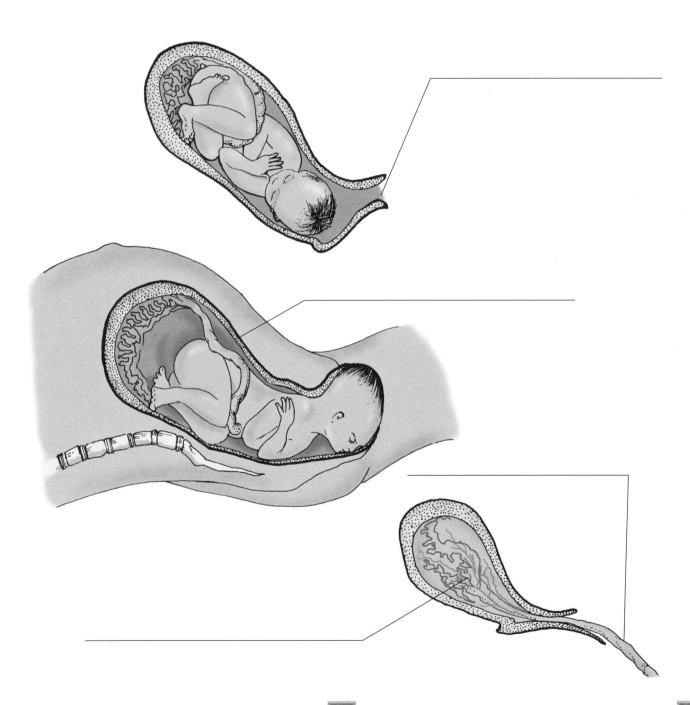

The Human Body

Human Body Recall

Directions: Circle the correct answers.

1. The human body has numerous systems that work together.

   true or false

2. One system accounts for about half of the body's weight. It is the
   a. cellular system.
   b. digestive system.
   c. muscular system.

3. The circulatory system
   a. holds the body up.
   b. protects the internal organs.
   c. pumps blood throughout the body.

4. The skeletal system
   a. holds the body up, provides structure for the muscles, and protects the inner organs.
   b. takes food and transfers it into something the body can use.
   c. gives the body the energy it needs to run races.

5. The respiratory system involves which important function?
   a. walking
   b. eating
   c. breathing

Directions: Answer the following question using complete sentences.

Think about how the different body systems work together. Explain how having a cold might affect various systems of the body.

_____

_____

_____

_____

_____

_____

_____

_____

Human Body Review

Directions: Use the WORD BANK to complete the puzzle.

WORD BANK

alimentary canal	amniotic	fracture	testes	bladder
palm	hinge	alignment	tendons	pelvis
humerus	skeleton	cervix	epidermis	enamel
pulse	pituitary	excretory	sebum	
pancreas	genes			
pressure point	adrenal			
heart	ovaries			

ACROSS:

1. Outer layer of skin
4. The blood pump
6. Stores urine
10. The "bite" is the _____ of the teeth
11. Opening to the uterus
12. Boney structure
13. The inside of the hand
14. Controls body growth and other glands
17. A break in a bone
20. Rhythm of the heart creates a _____
21. Female sex glands
22. Determine human traits

DOWN:

1. Waste removal system
2. Outer layer of the tooth
3. Upper arm bone
5. Gland that goes to work when we are excited, angry, or frightened
7. Fluid surrounding fetus
8. Long food tube
9. Joint found in elbow
12. Oily substance given off by the sebaceous gland
13. Gland which controls the body's use of glucose
15. Place by or beside a wound to stop bleeding
16. Muscles are attached to the skeleton by _____
18. Male sex glands
19. Framework of bones that supports lower part of abdomen

The Human Body

Name _____

Directions: Make an **X** in the correct box to show to which system/systems each organ belongs. One is done for you.

ORGANS	SYSTEMS						
	Digestive	Respiratory	Urinary	Reproductive	Circulatory	Nervous	Endocrine
Bladder			X				
Brain							
Heart							
Ovaries							
Liver							
Pancreas							
Kidney							
Spinal Cord							
Lungs							
Small Intestines							
Diaphragm							
Mouth							
Nerves							
Testes							
Thyroid Gland							
Arteries							
Esophagus							
Cerebellum							

GREGOR MENDEL

The history of and continuing developments in the study of **genetics** (the study of how parents and offspring have similar and different traits) is filled with complicated and technical information. Many important scientists have contributed their research and knowledge to fill a vast number of books about genetics. But Gregor Mendel, a humble Austrian-born botanist and monk, is the man known as the "Father of Genetics."

Born in 1822, Gregor Mendel was considered a brilliant student. He entered the Augustinian monastery in 1843. While in the monastery, he studied science and mathematics, hoping to be a teacher. Although he failed the teacher examination, perhaps because of test-taking stress, Gregor taught at a local high school for about fourteen years.

Mendel also spent time doing scientific experiments. The work he is most recognized for is his work with the simple pea pod plant and the forming of his theories on heredity, or the passing on of traits from parent to offspring. Mendel chose the pea plant for several logical reasons. First, the pea plant produces a fairly large number of seeds. Second, this plant can be easily cross-pollinated. And third, the plant has several obvious contrasting characteristics that can be easily studied.

He carefully studied seven traits of the pea plant, including seed shape, seed color, flower position, pod shape, seed coat color, stem length, and pod color. Mendel discovered, after making sure the plants he was using were pure, that crossing two pure plants with the same traits did not guarantee that those traits would show in their offspring. He discovered that if there were different traits in the plants' history, those traits might eventually show.

Because of this research, the terms **recessive traits** and **dominant traits** are part of genetics study. Recessive traits are traits that do not show, although they exist in the genes of the offspring. Dominant traits are those traits that physically show in the offspring. This theory holds for plants as well as other living things.

PEA POD EXPERIMENT

1. Mendel crossed yellow and green peas.

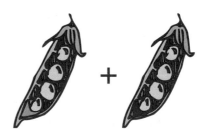

2. Only yellow pea pods were produced.

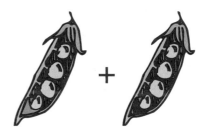

3. When Mendel crossed the yellow offspring, he got both yellow and green.

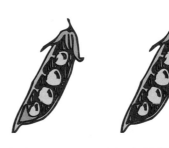

Genetics

GREGOR MENDEL, continued

Mendel presented his findings to a meeting of the Association for Natural Research in 1865. They published the report in a newsletter the following year. Many of his peers believed Mendel had simply done research into successful hybridization. The hard work and findings of the scientist went largely unnoticed until the very early 1900s, when scientists realized he had, in fact, studied the heredity of certain characteristics as they are passed on from parent to offspring.

Of course, Mendel did not have the technology to find out how the traits are passed on. But his work set the stage for researchers who studied genetics. Simply stated, they discovered thread-like parts, called **chromosomes**, in the nucleus of each cell. Each chromosome has tiny units all along its length. These are called **genes**, and they carry the information that determines the traits of an organism. Because of the way cells divide and join during reproduction, offspring end up with half of the mother's chromosomes and half of the father's.

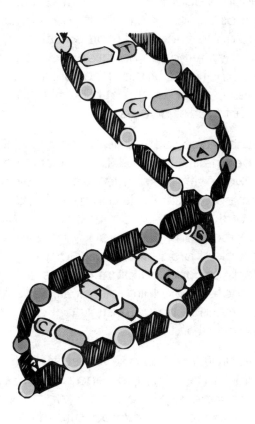

You may ask why this is significant to you. Have you ever wondered why you have the hair or eye color you do? Is it the same or different from that of your parents, brothers, or sisters? This question can be answered using Mendel's theories about dominant and recessive genes. These characteristics are passed on through your genes. A perfect example of the truth in Mendel's research is if you have red hair and the only other person in your family had red hair was a great-great-grandfather. Other traits, such as the ability to roll your tongue, the way your ear lobes are attached to your head, and your skin tone, are passed on through genetic material as well.

Directions: Use the selection on pages 103–104 to answer the following questions.

1. What does the study of genetics involve? _____

   _____

   _____

   _____

2. What is meant by the term *dominant trait*? _____

   _____

   _____

   _____

3. What is meant by the term *recessive trait*? _____

   _____

   _____

   _____

4. What is heredity? _____

   _____

   _____

   _____

5. Who is considered the "Father of Genetics"? How did he get that title? _____

   _____

   _____

   _____

6. What kind of plant did Mendel use to study heredity? Why do you think he used this
   particular plant?

   _____

   _____

   _____

   _____

Boy or Girl?

In most animals, including humans, gender is determined by the chromosomes inherited from the parents. If an organism inherits two **X** chromosomes, it will be female. If the organism inherits an **X** and a **Y** chromosome, it will be male.

Directions: You can show the chances of having a female or male offspring by doing the activity below.

MATERIALS

- 2 lima beans
- pencil
- black permanent marker
- paper

PROCEDURE

1. Mark one lima bean with a **Y** on one side and an **X** on the other side. Mark the other lima bean with an **X** on both sides.

2. Shake the lima beans in your hands, and drop them gently onto a desk or table. Record the results on your paper.

3. Repeat Step 2 nine more times and record the information. Write your **XX** results and your **XY** results over 10, for example, **XX** = $\frac{6}{10}$

Father										
Mother										

QUESTIONS

1. Write about the results of your experiment. Talk about the probability of the offspring being male or female. What factors might have an effect on the results of such an experiment? Are the results guaranteed? Why would people want to know such information?

_____

_____

_____

_____

2. Explain why there is a 50 percent chance that an offspring will be female.

_____

_____

_____

_____

Inherited Traits

All kinds of traits are inherited: the shape of your nose, the color of your hair, the shape of your body. Many of these traits cannot be changed. Your inherited characteristics are inborn and make you the way you are. Other traits, such as intelligence, personality, and learned abilities, may be inherited to a certain extent but are greatly influenced by your environment and your attitudes toward them. Your mother may have been a talented soccer player and your father a world-class wrestler, but you will not be either unless you choose to put in many long hours of practice.

Which of the following characteristics are inherited? Which of the following characteristics can be changed by your behavior?

Directions: Mark a **U** beside the things that cannot be changed and a **C** beside the things that can be changed.

1. _____ your ability to learn spelling words

2. _____ the shape of your feet

3. _____ your ability to ice skate

4. _____ the shape of your teeth

5. Now think about yourself and some of the characteristics you have—things you can change and things you cannot change. Write two paragraphs describing yourself in terms of the characteristics you have thought about.

_____

_____

_____

_____

_____

_____

_____

_____

6. Why do you think it is important to know whether a trait is inherited?

_____

_____

_____

Studying Traits

QUESTION   Why do people look different?

PREDICTION   Work with a partner. Look at the activities described below. Which traits do you think you two share? Write your prediction on your record sheet.

PROCEDURE   Do the activities described below.

1. Can you roll up the edges of your tongue? rolled not rolled	**2.** Do you have a widow's peak? widow's peak no widow's peak	**3.** Is the last segment of your thumb straight? straight curved
4. Do you have free earlobes? free attached	**5.** Is your hair naturally curly? curly straight	**6.** Do you have dimples? dimples no dimples
7. Do you have a cleft in your chin? cleft no cleft	**8.** Fold your hands. Which thumb is on top?	**9.** What color are your eyes?

RESULTS   Fill out the data table on the next page.

Recording Your Data

QUESTION   Why do people look different?

PREDICTION   Work with a partner. Look at the activities described below. Which traits do you think you two share?

_____

_____

RESULTS   Fill out the data table.

	Myself	**My Partner**
Tongue roller (rolled or not rolled)		
Hairline (widow's peak or no widow's peak)		
Thumb (straight or curved)		
Earlobe (free or attached)		
Hair (curly or straight)		
Dimples (yes or no)		
Cleft chin (yes or no)		
Thumb fold (left or right)		
Eye color (brown, blue, green, black, hazel)		

CONCLUSION   Why do people look different?

_____

_____

Why do children who have the same parents often look different?

_____

_____

Genetics

Designer "Genes"

There are more than 40,000 **genes** that determine traits each person has. These traits, such as, dark hair, blue eyes, etc., are inherited from parents. There are two strengths of traits: **dominant** - being the strongest, and **recessive** – being the weakest.

Directions: Place checks in each chart to show who would have the dominant and/or recessive genes in each category.

D = Dominant Trait   R = Recessive Trait

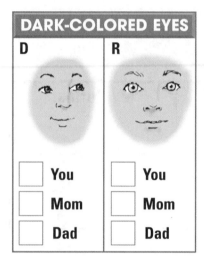

DARK-COLORED EYES

D	R
☐ You	☐ You
☐ Mom	☐ Mom
☐ Dad	☐ Dad

BLOND HAIR

D	R
☐ You	☐ You
☐ Mom	☐ Mom
☐ Dad	☐ Dad

DIMPLES

D	R
☐ You	☐ You
☐ Mom	☐ Mom
☐ Dad	☐ Dad

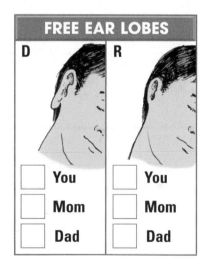

FREE EAR LOBES

D	R
☐ You	☐ You
☐ Mom	☐ Mom
☐ Dad	☐ Dad

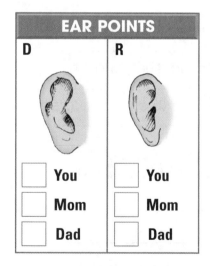

EAR POINTS

D	R
☐ You	☐ You
☐ Mom	☐ Mom
☐ Dad	☐ Dad

Name _____

D = Dominant Trait　　　　**R = Recessive Trait**

CAN ROLL TONGUE

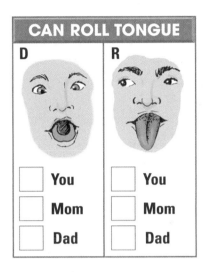

D	R
☐ You	☐ You
☐ Mom	☐ Mom
☐ Dad	☐ Dad

CAN FOLD TONGUE

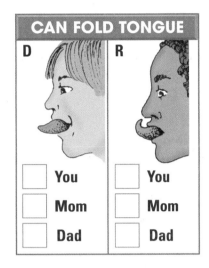

D	R
☐ You	☐ You
☐ Mom	☐ Mom
☐ Dad	☐ Dad

CLOCKWISE HAIR WHORL

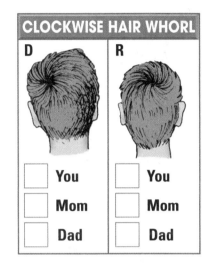

D	R
☐ You	☐ You
☐ Mom	☐ Mom
☐ Dad	☐ Dad

WIDOW'S PEAK

D	R
☐ You	☐ You
☐ Mom	☐ Mom
☐ Dad	☐ Dad

TURNED-UP NOSE

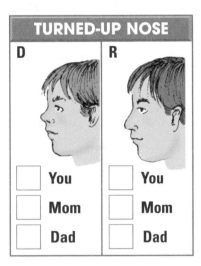

D	R
☐ You	☐ You
☐ Mom	☐ Mom
☐ Dad	☐ Dad

DARK HAIR

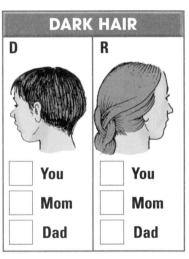

D	R
☐ You	☐ You
☐ Mom	☐ Mom
☐ Dad	☐ Dad

FRECKLES

D	R
☐ You	☐ You
☐ Mom	☐ Mom
☐ Dad	☐ Dad

HAIR ON MIDDLE FINGERS

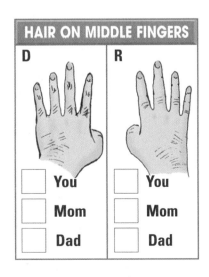

D	R
☐ You	☐ You
☐ Mom	☐ Mom
☐ Dad	☐ Dad

BENT LITTLE FINGER

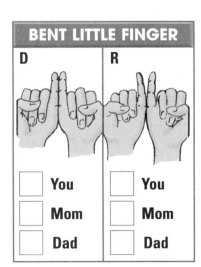

D	R
☐ You	☐ You
☐ Mom	☐ Mom
☐ Dad	☐ Dad

Genetics

The mirror in your bathroom gives you a reflected image of what you look like. You look the way you do because of your cells and genes. Although we don't really know how many cells make up a human body, it is estimated that our bodies contain 50–100 trillion cells. A **cell** is the basic unit of a living thing that performs all of the functions of life. Each cell contains a special unit called a gene. A **gene** is an inherited unit of genetic material found within a cell that determines a trait. Some of the traits we inherit can be seen while others cannot. Traits we can see include the color of our hair and eyes, the shape of our noses, and our build.

You inherited your genes from your parents. Your parents inherited their genes from their parents, and so on. Genetic material is passed from one generation to the next. You get half of your genes from your mother, and half from your father. It takes at least two genes to determine a single trait—one comes from your mother and the other one comes from your father. If your mother has brown eyes and your father has blue eyes, then you inherit a gene for brown eyes from your mother and a gene for blue eyes from your father. But the gene for blue eyes is not as strong as the gene for brown eyes. We call this weaker gene a recessive gene. We call the stronger gene a dominant gene. Because the brown eye gene is stronger than the blue eye gene, you will have two brown eyes.

Directions: Use the information to answer the following questions.

1. What is a cell? _____

2. What is a gene? _____

3. What are some other traits not mentioned above that people inherit?_____

   _____

4. How many genes determine a single trait? _____

   From where do they come? _____

5. Why are there more people with brown eyes than blue eyes? _____

   _____

6. Curly hair is a dominant trait. If you inherited a gene for curly hair from your mother and a gene for straight hair from your father, would you have straight or curly hair? Why?

   _____

   _____

   _____

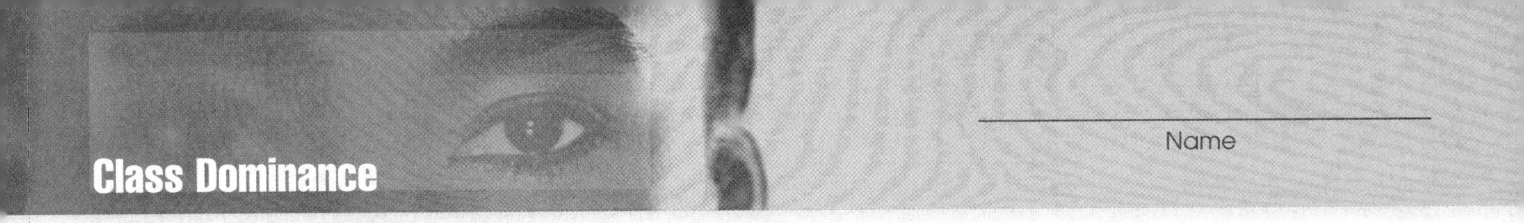

Name _____

QUESTION   What are some of the dominant traits in your class?

MATERIALS
- colored pencils
- a pencil

PROCEDURE
1. Survey the members of your class and fill in the chart below.
2. Then, answer the questions.

Class Trait Survey

Dominant Trait	Number of Students With Trait	Number of Students Without Trait
Brown eyes		
Dark hair		
Dimples		
Freckles		
Curly hair		
Dark eyebrows		
Bushy, thick eyebrows		
Turned-up nose		
Widow's peak		
Straight little finger		
Can roll tongue		
Free earlobes		
TOTAL STUDENTS:		

Directions: Answer the questions.

1. Did most of the students in your class display dominant traits? _____

   Why do you think this is? _____

2. Do you think the results would be different if you had surveyed the whole school? _____

   Why or why not? _____

Genetics

Have you ever stopped to think about which hand you use to brush your teeth, comb your hair, or wash your face? Scientists conducted experiments to find out which hand most of us prefer to use for different tasks. They found that about 90 percent of the population prefers to use their right hands, meaning they are right-hand dominant. This leaves about 10 percent of the population who are left-hand dominant. Only a few people can use both hands equally. These people are ambidextrous.

Exactly why people are right- or left-handed is a mystery. Some scientists believe that it is an inherited trait, such as eye color. Other scientists think that hand dominance is due to the way you developed before you were born and your environment. Still other scientists think that hand dominance is an inherited trait that is affected only by your environment.

Most people also have a dominant eye, a dominant ear, and a dominant foot. The graph shows that the right side is dominant for all the areas tested. However, it also shows that people who are right-hand dominant are not always right-side dominant when using their feet, ears, or eyes.

PERCENTAGE OF MEN AND WOMEN WHO USE THE RIGHT SIDE		
Body Part	**Men**	**Women**
Hand	86	77
Foot	77	86
Ear	55	65
Eye	73	69

Directions: Use the information to answer the following questions.

1. What does right-hand dominant mean? _____

   What percentage of people are right-hand dominant? _____

2. Until recently, left-hand dominant people were often made to write with their right hands. Do you think this could have affected the data collected? Why?

   _____

   _____

3. According to the graph, a higher percentage of women are right-side dominant than

   men in all of the areas except _____.

4. According to the graph, what percentage of men are left-hand dominant? _____

   left-foot dominant? _____

What's Your Dominance?

Name

QUESTION Do I have a dominant side?

MATERIALS
- a container of drinking water
- an empty paper-towel tube
- a tube of toothpaste
- a hand lens
- a ruler
- a book
- pants
- a ball
- a cup

PROCEDURE Perform the tasks shown below and mark the column that shows which side you use for each task.

Task Performed	Right Side	Left Side
Hand:		
Hand used to write your name		
Hand used to pour water into the cup		
Hand used to lift the cup to drink the water		
Hand used to take the cap off of the toothpaste		
Hand used to put toothpaste on a toothbrush		
Hand used to open a book		
Hand that is larger when you put your hands together		
Total: add the marks in each column for this section		
Eye:		
Eye used to look through the empty paper-towel tube		
Eye used to look at the book through the hand-lens		
Eye used to wink		
Eye that is more open when you squint		
Total: add the marks in each column for this section		
Foot/Leg:		
Foot that shoe is put onto first		
Leg that goes in your pants first		
Foot used to kick a ball		
Foot put down first when taking a step		
Foot that is longer when measured		
Total: add the marks in each column for this section		

Directions: Answer the questions.

1. Which hand is your dominant hand? _____ Which eye? _____

   Which leg or foot? _____

2. Were all of your marks in the same column? _____ Why do you

   think this is? _____

A Special Science Tool

The microscope is a necessary tool when observing tiny organisms in life science. In about 1590, two Dutch spectacle makers, Hans and Zaccharias Janssen, started experimenting with lenses. They put several lenses in a tube and made a very important discovery. The object near the end of the tube appeared to be greatly enlarged! They had just invented the compound microscope.

Other people heard of the Janssen's work and started work of their own. Galileo added a focusing device. Anthony Leeuwenhoek of Holland became so interested that he learned how to make lenses. By grinding and polishing, he was able to make small lenses with great curvatures. These rounder lenses produced greater magnification, and his microscopes were able to magnify up to 270 times.

Anthony Leeuwenhoek's new, improved microscope allowed people to see things no human had ever seen before. He saw bacteria, yeast, and blood cells. Because of his great contributions, he has been called the "Father of Microscopy."

Robert Hooke, an Englishman, also spent much of his life working with microscopes and improved their design and capabilities. He coined the word *cell* after observing cork cells under a microscope. He was reminded of a monk's cell in a monastery.

Little was done to improve the microscope until the middle of the 19th century, when great strides were made and quality instruments such as today's microscope emerged.

Directions: Use the words from the WORD BANK and a science resource book to help you label this microscope.

WORD BANK

eyepiece
fine adjustment
stage
mirror
body tube
objective
stage clips
diaphragm
coarse adjustment
arm
base
nosepiece

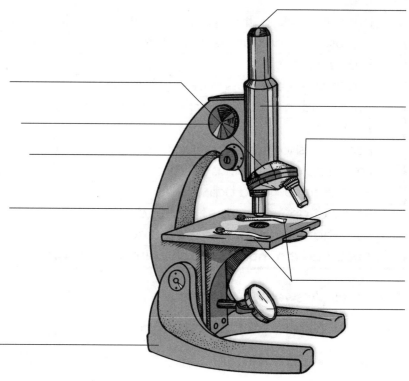

Animal and Plant Cells

QUESTION How does an animal cell compare to a plant cell?

PREDICTION Do you think an animal cell and a plant cell will share some qualities? Do you think they will be very similar or very different? Write your predictions on your record sheet.

MATERIALS

- microscope
- toothpick
- iodine
- onion
- two microscope slides
- two coverslips
- paper towels
- eyedropper
- reference sheet of animal and plant cells

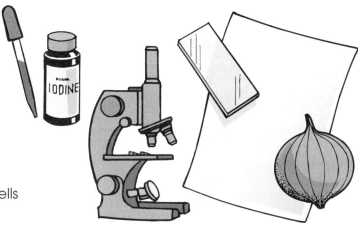

PROCEDURE

1. Put a drop of water on a slide. Peel a little of the transparent "skin" from an onion and put it on the drop of water.

2. Carefully place a coverslip over the onion skin. Put a drop of iodine at the edge of the coverslip. Put a small piece of paper towel at the opposite edge of the coverslip. The stain should spread beneath the coverslip. Examine the slide under the microscope.

3. Put a drop of water on the other slide. Using a clean toothpick, gently scrape the inside of your cheek. (Do not do this if you have sores in your mouth.) Place the soft material from your cheek in your drop of water.

4. Carefully place a coverslip over the cheek material. Put a drop of iodine at the edge of the coverslip. Put a small piece of paper towel at the opposite edge of the coverslip. The stain should spread beneath the coverslip. Examine the slide under the microscope.

5. Compare the cells to each other. Refer to your cell diagrams and try to identify the different structures.

RESULTS On your record sheet, draw the onion cell and the cheek cell. Look at the diagram on your reference sheet and try to identify the different structures on your drawings.

CONCLUSION How does an animal cell compare to a plant cell? Write what you found out on the record sheet.

QUESTION   How does an animal cell compare to a plant cell?

PREDICTION   Do you think an animal cell and a plant cell will share some qualities? Do you think they will be very similar or very different?

_____

_____

_____

_____

QUESTION   Draw an onion cell and a cheek cell. Label as many structures as you can.

Onion Cell   **Cheek Cell**

CONCLUSION   How does an animal cell compare to a plant cell?

_____

_____

_____

_____

_____

_____

Name _____

All living things are made of cells. Some organisms, such as the paramecium and the amoeba, have one cell, while others, such as the human, have millions of cells. Each type of cell has its own function. Plant cells have different functions than human muscle cells, for example. Look at the diagrams below and on the next page. They show similarities and differences between a plant cell and an animal cell. Be sure to read the descriptions of the parts of the cell.

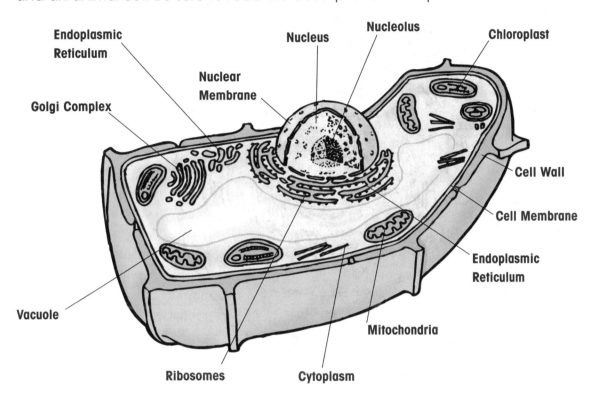

Ribosomes—where proteins are made

Golgi Complex—stores and releases chemicals

Cytoplasm—jelly-like substance within the cell

Nucleus—chromosomes are found here

Nucleolus—spherical body within the nucleus

Nuclear Membrane—holds nucleus together

Mitochondria—releases energy from the nutrients

Cell Wall—shapes and supports a plant cell

Vacuole—contains water and dissolved minerals

Chloroplast—food for plant cells is made here

Cell Membrane—controls entry into and out of the cell

Endoplasmic Reticulum—surface for chemical activity

Each small part of the cell is called an *organelle*. Each organelle has its own name and function. Many of the organelles in a plant cell are also in an animal cell.

Name

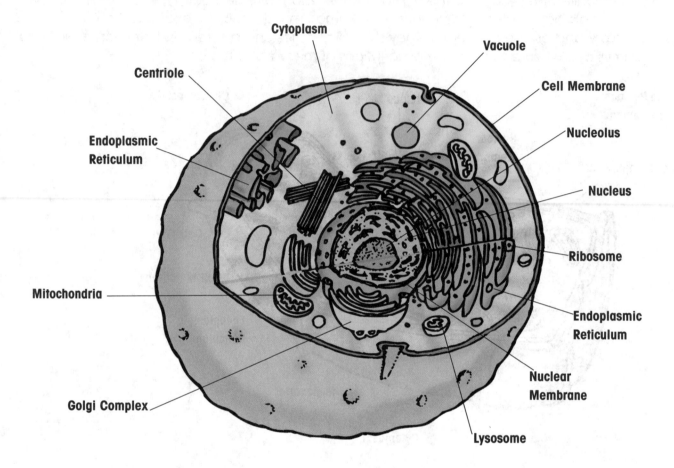

Cytoplasm
Centriole
Vacuole
Cell Membrane
Endoplasmic Reticulum
Nucleolus
Nucleus
Ribosome
Mitochondria
Endoplasmic Reticulum
Nuclear Membrane
Golgi Complex
Lysosome

Vacuole—contains water and dissolved minerals

Lysosome—digests large particles

Ribosomes—where proteins are made

Golgi Complex—stores and releases chemicals

Cytoplasm—jelly-like substance within the cell

Nucleus—chromosomes are found here

Nucleolus—spherical body within the nucleus

Nuclear Membrane—holds nucleus together

Cell Membrane—controls entry into and out of the cell

Mitochondria—releases energy from the nutrients

Endoplasmic Reticulum—surface for chemical activity

Centriole—structures involved in mitosis in animal cells only

Directions: Use the reading selection and the diagrams on pages 119–120 to define the following terms.

1. Ribosomes _____

   _____

2. Cytoplasm _____

   _____

3. Nucleus _____

   _____

4. Nuclear Membrane _____

   _____

5. Mitochondria _____

   _____

6. Cell Membrane _____

   _____

7. Golgi Complex _____

   _____

8. Vacuole _____

   _____

Directions: Now, use the words above to complete the following sentences.

1. The _____ holds the cell together.

2. The _____, organelles specific to green plants, contain the chemical chlorophyll, which permits a green plant to produce its own sugar.

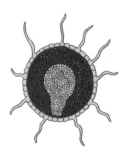

Directions: Look at the diagrams and descriptions of the animal and plant cells on pages 119–120.

1. Write about the differences that are obvious between the two cells. Think about why many parts are the same, and write about why you think that might be.

   _____

   _____

   _____

   _____

   _____

2. What might plants be like if their cells had no chloroplast? How might it make a difference?

   _____

   _____

   _____

   _____

   _____

3. Why do you think plant cells have cell walls instead of cell membranes? Why do you think animal cells have cell membranes instead of cell walls?

   _____

   _____

   _____

   _____

   _____

4. Do you think plant or animal cells use more energy to live? Why?

   _____

   _____

   _____

   _____

   _____

What Do You See?

Directions: Do the following experiment to see examples of a typical plant cell. Then, write about what you see.

MATERIALS

- eye dropper
- microscope
- tap water
- microscope slide and cover
- sample of *Elodea* (common waterweed)
- red onion skin also works well

PROCEDURE

1. Create a chart like the one to the right.
2. Put two drops of water on a microscope slide.
3. Tear a leaf from the waterweed, and place it in the water on the slide. Make sure it is lying flat.
4. Cover the leaf with the cover.
5. Place the slide under the microscope.

Cell Under Low Power	Cell Under High Power

OBSERVATIONS

1. Look closely at the leaf under the low power. Draw your observations and label the cell parts you can see.

2. Now, look at the leaf under high power. Draw what you observe.

3. Write about the differences between the two views of the cell.

_____

_____

_____

_____

Very Cheeky

Directions: Do the following experiment to observe human cheek cells. Then, compare the cheek cell with the plant cell observed on page 123.

MATERIALS

- compound microscope
- 2 glass slides
- 2 cover slips
- eye dropper
- methylene blue stain
- toothpick (flat type)
- water

PROCEDURE

1. Put a drop of stain on a slide, being careful as it will stain skin and clothing. Gently scrape the inside of your cheek with a toothpick.
   CAUTION: **Do not scrape hard enough to injure your cheek.**
2. Rub the toothpick in the stain. Break the toothpick in half and discard.
3. Cover the slide with a cover slip.
4. Locate the nucleus, cytoplasm, and cell membrane. Fill in the table below by putting a check mark in the box if the cell part can be seen.
5. Draw and label the nucleus, cytoplasm, and cell membrane of a cheek cell.
6. Refer back to the work done with the waterweed. Fill in the chart with the information about the *Elodea* cell.

NOTE: Lifting cells from a washed wrist by placing clear tape on the skin also works well.

Cell Parts	Cheek Cell Parts Present	*Elodea* Cell Parts Present
Cytoplasm		
Nucleus		
Chloroplast		
Cell Wall		
Cell Membrane		

1. Describe the shape of a cheek cell. Compare it to the shape and look of the waterweed cell.

   _____

2. Name the parts found in plant cells that are absent in animal cells. _____

   _____

3. Why do you think stains such as methylene blue are used when observing cells under the microscope?

   _____

4. Why don't animal cells have chloroplasts? _____

   _____

Plant Life

Plants are living things. They generally lack the ability to move, but they grow, reproduce, and respond to their environment. Plants share common characteristics with regard to their structure. Plants need certain things to grow: space, an appropriate temperature, light, water, air, nutrients, and time. One way that plants differ involves their vascular system. Plants can be categorized into two separate categories, vascular plants and nonvascular plants.

Vascular plants contain a system of tubes through their roots, stems, and leaves. Through this system, water and other liquid substances are carried throughout the plant. The movement through these tubes is called **capillary action**. This action allows the plants to grow and to provide nutrients to upper stems and branches that may be from a few inches to a hundred feet high. Plants in this group include all trees, grasses, ferns, weeds, and flowers. Thousands of vascular plants have been identified by scientists. Of these thousands of plants, about 95 percent bear flowers and are classified as angiosperms.

Nonvascular plants are not as abundant as vascular plants. Mosses and liverworts are common nonvascular plants. They are found growing in moist areas on soil or other vegetation. Aquatic plants such as algae are nonvascular. In nonvascular plants, food and waste are transported directly by the water that surrounds plants.

Most vascular plants contain the same basic parts. These parts are roots, stems, leaves, flowers, fruits, and seeds. The roots support the plant by holding it in the ground and absorbing water and other nutrients the plant needs to grow. Plants have one of two main root systems: a taproot system (like carrots) or a fibrous root system (like grass). In both of these systems, the roots bring water and nutrients to the plant.

Plant Life, cont.

Stems carry water and nutrients taken up by the roots to the leaves. The food produced by the leaves then moves to other parts of the plant. Leaves are the food-making factories of green plants. Leaves come in many different shapes and sizes. Leaves can be **simple**—made of a single leaf blade connected to the stem. They also can be **compound**, in which the leaf blade is divided into separate leaflets attached to the stem.

Leaves are designed to catch the light. They have openings to allow water and air to come and go. These openings are called **stomata**. Veins carry water and nutrients within the leaf. Leaves are where photosynthesis takes place. In this process, carbon dioxide and water with chlorophyll (the green pigment in leaves) and light energy are changed into glucose (sugar). The sugar that is produced through photosynthesis is the source of food used by most plants. **Photosynthesis** is a special process that occurs in green plants. Photosynthesis supplies food for the plant and oxygen for other forms of life.

Flowers are very pretty to look at, and they are the part of the plant that is responsible for reproduction. The stamen is the male part of the flower; it produces pollen. The pistil is the female part of the flower; it bears seeds. Pollination happens when a pollen grain is moved from the stamen to the pistil. Petals are important parts of the flower because they attract pollinators such as insects, birds, and bats. Humans, furry animals, and the wind also help flowers become pollinated.

Fruit is the ripened ovary of a plant containing the seeds. Many fruits help seeds spread. Many things we call vegetables are really fruits, such as tomatoes, cucumbers, and beans.

Each seed is a tiny plant called an **embryo**. With leaves, stems, and root parts, the seed waits for the right conditions to help it germinate and grow. Seeds are protected by an outer coating. This coat can be thin or thick. When it is thick, it can help the embryo survive tough conditions. Seeds are a plant's way of getting from one area to another.

Animal or Plant?

Most scientists divide all living things into five groups, called **kingdoms**. Two of the largest are the Animal Kingdom and the Plant Kingdom.

Directions: Compare these two kingdoms by using the chart below. Check the correct box or boxes next to each characteristic.

CHARACTERISTIC	PLANT	ANIMAL
Living organisms		
Formed from cells		
Cells have chlorophyll		
Makes its own food		
Gets food from outside		
Moves from place to place		
Has limited movement		
Can reproduce its own kind		
Depends on sun's energy		

Plants

Photosynthesis

Photosynthesis is a food-making process that occurs in green plants. It is the main function of the leaves.

Directions: With the help of a science book or the chart on page 149, complete the puzzle below.

ACROSS

1. Small green bodies that contain the green pigment chlorophyll
4. Gas that is released into the air as a by-product of photosynthesis
6. The escaping of water vapor from a leaf
7. Liquid obtained through the roots
8. Source of energy to power photosynthesis
9. Simple food made by photosynthesis

DOWN

2. The process by which green plants make food
3. One of the raw materials for photosynthesis is _____ dioxide.
5. Opening in the underside of a leaf

Name _____

Directions: Create the table shown below. Put a checkmark in the correct column(s).

CHARACTERISTIC	PLANT	ANIMAL
Made of cells		
Able to move from one place to another		
Able to produce its own food to supply its energy needs		
Relies on food that it eats to supply its energy needs		
Most reproduce through seeds		
Most reproduce through eggs		
Continues to grow and develop throughout its entire life		
Stops growing and developing as it gets older		
Obtains and uses energy to grow and develop		
Adapts to its environment		
Contains chlorophyll in its cells		

LEAFY OBSERVATIONS

You will need: green leaves of different sizes that come from different plants, a ruler

Directions: Create a chart like the one shown below.
To fill in the table, use words like *dark green, yellow green,* or *light green* to describe the color of each leaf. Sketch the shape of the leaf. Then, use your ruler to measure the lengths and widths of each leaf. Answer the following questions.

Color	Shape	Length	Top Width	Middle Width	Bottom Width

1. Did the size of the leaf seem to affect what color of green it was? Why do you think this is?

   _____

   _____

2. Were the leaves that came from the same plant the same color of green? Why do you think this is?

   _____

   _____

Name

Directions: Label the two root systems pictured below. Use the terms in the WORD BOX.

 WORD BANK

fibrous root system
taproot system

root hair cell
prop roots

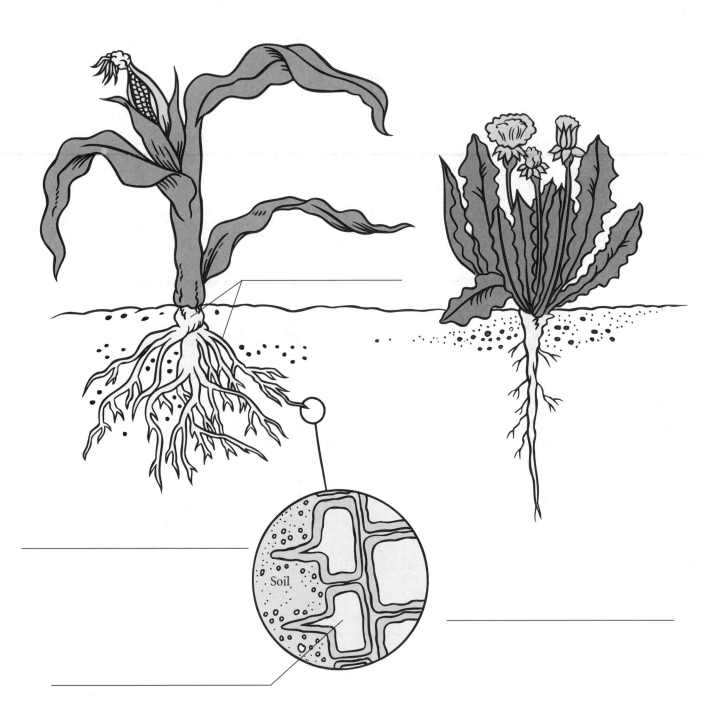

Soil

Inside a Root

Directions: Study the two views of a root shown below. Label the parts in both the top cross section and side cross section. Use the terms in the WORD BOX.

WORD BANK

| root hairs | root cap | root tip |
| surface layer | branch root | food and water carrying tissues |

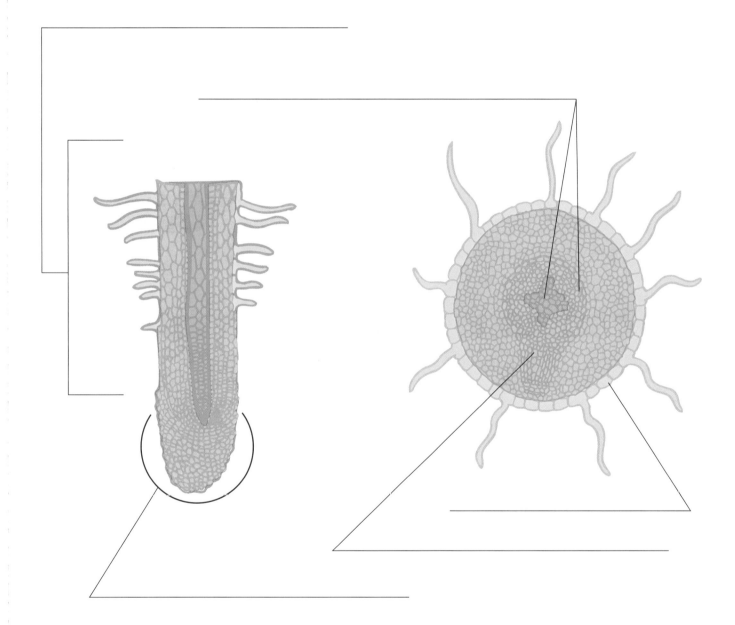

Side Cross Section

**Top Cross Section
of a Young Root**

Plants

Roots and Shoots

Plants develop from seeds. In this activity, you will measure the length of the roots and shoots of a plant as it develops from its seeds.

Directions:

1. Soak some dried lima beans in a jar of water overnight.

2. Place some wet paper towels in the bottom of a shallow pan or dish.

3. Arrange five of the soaked lima beans across the middle of the pan.

4. Cover with several thicknesses of wet paper towels.

5. Wrap the pan with plastic food wrap to prevent rapid evaporation of the water.

6. Each day, carefully uncover the beans and observe any growth of roots or shoots. Once growth begins, measure the lengths of the roots and shoots in inches.

7. Keep a record of your measurements and observations in the chart below.

Materials
- dried lima beans
- paper towels
- water
- shallow pans
- ruler
- jar
- plastic food wrap

DAY	OBSERVATIONS	LENGTH OF ROOTS	LENGTH OF SHOOTS
1			
2			
3			
4			
5			
6			
7			

What Color of Light Helps Plants Grow?

PURPOSE Recognize that some colors of light are more important for plant growth than others. Draw pictures and label plant parts that are affected by different colors of light.

MATERIALS

- bean seeds (lima or bush beans)
- colored cellophane (red, green, blue)
- 8 large drinking cups
- clear plastic bag
- rubber bands
- potting soil
- water
- pencils

PROCEDURE

1. Using a pencil, punch small holes in the bottoms of four cups.
2. Fill each cup three-quarters full with potting soil. Lightly pack the soil. Add water so that the soil is moist but not wet.
3. Place one bean seed, standing on end, into each cup.
4. Cover each cup with a plastic bag, and secure it with a rubber band.
5. Set aside and watch for plant growth.
6. When the tiny plants just start to emerge from the soil, remove the plastic bags.
7. Make covers for these cups by covering the remaining plastic cups with red, green, and blue cellophane or plastic wrap. Make one cover in each color. Keep one cup clear.
8. Measure and record the height of each plant.
9. Place the cover on each cup.
10. In four days, measure the height of the sprouts. Place the covers back on the plants as soon as the measurements are completed.
11. Continue the experiment to fill in the chart.

Color of Cover	4 Days	7 Days	11 Days	14 Days	17 Days	21 Days
Clear						
Red						
Blue						
Green						

Directions: Answer the questions on a separate sheet of paper.

1. Do all of the plants grow at the same rate?
2. Which of your plants grew the best?
3. Did a plant seem to grow poorly under a certain color of cellophane?
4. Why would it be difficult to grow plants in deep space?
5. Does this discovery have any meaning if pollution were to block out certain kinds of sunlight?

Name

PURPOSE Plant bean seeds and make observations about their growth. Observe plant structures such as the roots, leaves, stem, as a seed germinates.

MATERIALS

- paper towels
- water
- potting soil or dirt
- soaking solution
- resealable plastic bag
- 5-6 beans (lima, pinto, other store varieties)
- variety of seeds (pumpkin, sunflower, etc.)

INTRODUCTION This activity can be tied into *What Does Your Garden Need to Grow?* on page 136 since it requires the same materials. In this activity, you are making observations about the germination of seeds.

SETUP

1. Before planting, soak the beans for a few hours in a mixture of 1 quart of water to 1/2 oz. of bleach. *Note:* Bleach prevents mold from growing.
2. Plant some seeds in the soil and allow them to germinate. Watch for roots and stems to begin to grow. Do not let the stem break the soil. You want it as it exits the seed coat and begins to "right" itself in the soil. Remove from the soil and set aside for later observation.

PREPARATION

1. Collect some seeds such as pumpkin, sunflower, bean, corn. What do the seeds have in common?
2. Describe what you think the inside of a seed looks like.
3. Use the seeds that have been soaked.
4. Carefully split the bean along the seam in the seed coat and examine the seed parts. *Note:* Beans that have been soaked can be easily split with a fingernail. Also look at seeds you have germinated. What do you notice about the parts of the seed once it has started to germinate? Record your observations on the back of the lab sheet.
5. See the student lab sheet for further instructions. You can start extra plants for the next activity, *What Does Your Garden Need to Grow?*

PROCEDURE

1. Fold a paper towel into quarters and place it in the plastic bag so that the folded edge of the towel is along the bottom of the plastic bag.
2. In between the folds of the paper towel, place about 1 cup of soil.
3. Add water so the paper towel is damp.
4. Place beans in between the side of the plastic bag and the paper towel so that they are not touching each other.
5. Record your observations.

Day	Observations	Illustrations
1		
3		
5		
7		
_____		
_____		

Directions: Answer the questions that follow.

1. What did you first notice about the seed when it began to germinate?

_____

2. What direction was the plant facing when it began to emerge from the seed coating?

_____

3. Describe the changes that occurred once the plant broke through the surface of the soil.

_____

_____

What Does Your Garden Need to Grow?

PURPOSE Determine what conditions are needed for plants to grow.

MATERIALS
- bean seedlings
- water
- potting soil or dirt
- 5-6 beans (lima, pinto, other store varieties)
- shoe boxes
- milk cartons

INTRODUCTION Read either *The Plant Sitter* by Zion or *Plantpet* by Primavera as an introduction to this activity. Since you have already started growing your seeds as part of *How Does Your Garden Grow?* you will be anxious to determine what conditions are required to maintain healthy plants. To study these conditions, remove some seedlings from the plastic bags and replant them in the milk cartons.

DISCUSSION

1. Discuss what a plant needs to live.
2. Discuss how many or how much of each item a plant must have in order to survive. Is this the same for all types of plants?
3. See the student lab sheet for further instructions.
4. Using the chart provided, make and record observations about each of the four plants for two weeks.

PROCEDURE

1. Cut the tops off of four clean milk cartons leaving about 4 inches in height.
2. Poke holes in the bottom of each carton to allow water to drain.
3. Replant two bean plants in each carton.
4. Label each milk carton with the variables the plant will receive.
   - Milk carton #1: No water and no sunlight
   - Milk carton #2: Water but no sunlight
   - Milk carton #3: Water and sunlight
   - Milk carton #4: Saturate with water and sunlight.
5. Place cartons 1 and 2 under a shoe box.
6. Place carton 3 and 4 in direct sunshine. Keep the soil in Carton #4 very wet by watering it each day.
7. Make observations every day or two and record them on the chart.

	Carton #1	Carton #2	Carton #3	Carton #4
Day _____				
Day _____				
Day _____				
Day _____				
Day _____				
Day _____				

Directions: Answer the questions that follow.

1. Describe which plant grew best. Under what conditions did the plant grow?

   _____

   _____

   _____

2. In the beginning of the experiment, all plants were growing. Which plant was the first to physically change? What were the changes?

   _____

   _____

   _____

Plant Pipelines

How does a plant get its food? Thin tubes in the stem carry food from the leaf to the rest of the plant. Other tubes carry water and minerals from the roots to the leaves. Both kinds of tubes are found in bundles in the stem.

The tube bundles are arranged in two ways. A **monocot** plant has bundles scattered throughout the stem. A **dicot** plant has bundles arranged in a ring around the edge of the stem.

_____ _____

Dicot or monocot stem?
Label the two pictures above.

MATERIALS
- a drinking glass
- food coloring
- a stalk of celery
- water
- a knife
- an eyedropper

PROCEDURE   Put a few drops of food coloring in a glass of water. Trim off the bottom inch of the celery stalk. Place the celery in the water. Let it sit for 3–4 hours.

ANALYSIS

1. Describe what you see. _____

_____

2. Cut the stalk crosswise. Look at the cut end. What do you see?

_____

_____

_____

_____

3. What carried the water up the stalk? _____

4. What would happen if the stem of a plant were broken? Why?

_____

_____

_____

_____

Repeat this experiment using a white carnation in place of the celery. Watch what happens!

Growing Mold

PURPOSE
Recognize bread mold as a form of plant life by growing it in an activity. Explain what conditions are necessary for bread mold to form by observing activity results. Describe that mold spores are a common part of our environment by collecting them to begin the activity.

MATERIALS
- bread (no preservatives)
- spray bottle with water
- A-V marker or china marker
- 3 resealable plastic bags
- dark place for storage
- tape

INTRODUCTION
Fungi is a large division of nonvascular plants. Many people recognize that fungi includes puffballs and mushrooms. While some mushrooms are edible, most are not. What most people do not realize is that fungi includes molds. Bread mold is a common form of fungi growing on the occasional "bad bread." In this activity, you will collect mold spores from a room in your home or your classroom using pieces of bread. You will discover that mold develops more quickly in a dark, moist environment. *Note:* It is important to stress that mold can cause health reactions for some people. Growing mold must never be exposed to the atmosphere in order to limit the dispersion of spores and allergic reactions that could result. Care must be taken to keep the plastic bags closed from the beginning of the activity until they are discarded.

PROCEDURE

1. Using a slice of bread, wipe dust from surfaces around a room in your home or your classroom.

2. Cut the dusty bread into three pieces. Wet one piece with a light spray of water. It should not be soggy, just moist.

3. Using a permanent marker, label three plastic bags with your name.

4. Write the word "light" on one bag, "dark" on another bag, and "dark moist" on the third bag.

5. Place the plain pieces of dusty bread into the first two bags. Seal the bags.

6. Place the moist bread into the third bag which is labeled "dark moist." Seal the bag.

7. Tape the bags to secure the sealed openings to remind you not to open them.

8. Place the "light" bag on a shelf where it is exposed to light.

9. Set the "dark" and "dark moist" bags in a drawer or closet that should remain closed except for observations.

10. Carefully wash your hands after completing this activity.

11. On the chart below, record daily observations for five days.

Name _____

Day	Dry Bread in the Light	Dry Bread in the Dark	Moist Bread in the Dark
1			
2			
3			
4			
5			

Directions: Answer the questions that follow.

1. Which piece of bread had the most mold growth? _____

_____

2. Which piece of bread had the least mold growth? _____

_____

3. What conditions seem to favor the growth of mold? _____

_____

4. Are you more likely to find fungi growing in the sunlight or in the shadows? _____

5. If you were a mushroom grower, what conditions would you provide to grow your product for stores?

_____

Is Your Soil the Best or Is Mine?

PROCEDURE Define *clay*, *silt*, *sand*, and *humus* in terms of its physical appearance and characteristics by closely inspecting each sample during the activity.
• Determine which material can allow water to pass through more easily by observing the activity. Determine which material can hold more water.
• Create a soil with a water holding ability equal to its ability to let water pass through by evaluating the activity results and testing a mixture based on those results.

MATERIALS
• china marker or A-V pen
• five 16-oz. plastic drinking cups
• graduated cylinder
• sand, silt, clay, and humus soil samples
• six 8-oz. plastic drinking cups

• water
• stopwatch
• sharp pencil
• permanent marker
• magnifying lens

INTRODUCTION The water-holding ability of soil is an important characteristic. For a good rate of plant growth, the soil around a plant's roots must be able to hold water while being able to drain and not become soggy. Too much water or not enough water near the plant's roots will cause them to die. It is the relationship of sand, silt, clay, and humus that creates the ability of soil to let water pass through and to hold water in it. This activity asks which soils are best at holding water, which soils are best at allowing water to pass through, and then challenges the teams of students to create a mixture that holds as much water as it allows to pass through the soil.

PROCEDURE

1. Collect 5 large plastic cups (16 oz.). Carefully punch holes into the bottom of each one using a sharp pencil.

2. Fill each cup about halfway with material:
   • Cup 1: Fill the cup with sand. Label the cup "sand."
   • Cup 2: Fill the cup with clay. Label the cup "clay."
   • Cup 3: Fill the cup with silt. Label the cup "silt."
   • Cup 4: Fill the cup with humus. Label the cup "humus."
   • Cup 5: Set the cup aside for use later.

3. Record what you observed about each material. Describe how each material feels, smells, and looks.

Plants

Name _____

Sand	Clay	Silt	Humas

4. Carefully stack the cup with sand on top of small plastic cup.
5. Repeat Step 4 with each cup of material.
6. Fill a 8 oz. cup with water.
7. Using a stopwatch or clock with a second hand, start timing when the water is dumped into the container with the sand.
8. After three minutes, use the china marker or grease pencil to mark the level of the water in the lower cup.
9. Repeat Steps 6–8 with each cup of material.
10. Rank the materials from 1 to 4 as to which soil lets water pass through it.
    (Write the numeral 1 on the cup which allows the most water to pass through the soil.)
11. Rank the materials from 1 to 4 as to which soil holds more water.
    (Write the numeral 1 on the cup which holds the most water.).
12. Record your results on the chart by writing the name of the material in the space:

	Holds Water	Water Passes Through
Most		
Second		
Third		
Least		

FINDING THE PERFECT SOIL

13. Using the results from your investigation, consider which materials would hold exactly half of the water (4 oz.) poured into it.

14. Decide with a partner what proportion of sand, clay, silt, and humus to put into the fifth large plastic cup.

Sand	Clay	Silt	Humas

15. Fill the 8 oz. cup with water. Repeat the investigation by repeating Steps 7 and 8.

16. Using a graduated cylinder, measure the water collected in the cup.
    How much water drained through the soil? _____

17. Try a different proportion of materials if the test was unsuccessful.

Directions: Answer the questions that follow.

1. How close were you to allowing exactly 4 oz. of water to pass through the soil?

   _____

   _____

2. If you tried this investigation again, what ratio of materials would you use in your second soil mixture?

   _____

   _____

   _____

   _____

3. What proportion of materials do you think works the best?

   _____

   _____

   _____

Plants

A Seedy Start

All of the plants you see from your porch have something in common—they all need air, warmth, water, nutrients, and time to grow. Plants continue to grow throughout their entire lives. Just like humans, plants grow from a single cell and develop into a multi-celled organism. But most plants reproduce through seeds. The seed is protected by a hard outer coating called a **seed coat**. Inside the seed is a young plant, called an **embryo**. A seed also contains food the embryo needs to stay alive. Seeds can remain inactive for months, weeks, or even years. In fact, the oldest seed ever sprouted was inactive for 1,288 years before it sprouted into a lotus plant.

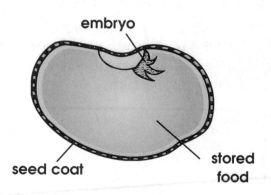

Seeds start to change in a process known as **germination**. A plant "hatches" from a seed. The seed absorbs water that causes the embryo to grow larger and "hatch" out of the seed coat as it splits open. This allows the baby plant, or embryo, to peek out and change into a sprout. The first part of the sprout to peek out is the roots. They are closely followed by the stem and leaves that push through the soil as the sprout develops into a seedling. The little seedling continues to stretch towards the sun's light that provides energy to help it grow and develop into a plant.

Directions: Use the information to answer the following questions.

1. What do all plants need? _____

    _____

2. How do plants reproduce? _____

    _____

3. What are the parts of a seed? _____

    _____

4. What happens when a seed germinates? _____

    _____

5. Which part of the embryo comes out of the seed first? _____

    Why do you think this is? _____

    _____

Sailing Seeds

We know how seeds grow into plants. But how do the seeds get from one place to another? Seeds travel in many ways.

Directions: Look below at the five ways that seeds travel. Tell how each seed moves.

1.

_____

_____

_____

_____

2.

_____

_____

_____

_____

3.

_____

_____

_____

_____

4.

_____

_____

_____

_____

5.

_____

_____

_____

_____

Plants

It's a lot of fun to watch plants grow from seeds. In this activity, you will discover the best conditions for the sprouting of radish seeds.

Directions:

1. Cut six pieces of paper towel to fit inside the jar lids.

2. Place one piece of paper towel inside each lid.

3. Count out 25 radish seeds for each lid. Carefully place them inside each lid.

4. Cover the seeds in each lid with another piece of paper towel.

5. Pour enough fresh water inside the first lid to thoroughly wet the paper towel.

6. Pour enough salt water inside the second lid to thoroughly wet the paper towel.

7. Pour enough vinegar inside the third lid to thoroughly wet the paper towel.

8. Label each lid with the name of the liquid.

9. Set the lids aside for about three days.

10. After three days, carefully remove the top paper towel and observe the seeds.

11. Record your observations in the chart below.

Materials
- 3 jar lids
- salt water
- fresh water
- vinegar
- paper towels
- scissors
- radish seeds

LIQUID	NUMBER OF SEEDS SPROUTED	OBSERVATIONS
Fresh Water		
Salt Water		
Vinegar		

What conclusions can you make from these results? _____

_____

_____

_____

Name _____

It's hard to believe that many of the big trees began as a seed. A tree seedling of an orange, lemon, lime, or grapefruit can be started in your very own classroom. Just follow the directions below.

Directions:

1. Prepare a mixture of potting soil and sand.

2. Punch several small holes in the bottoms of four cups. Label the cups as follows: #1—orange, #2—lemon, #3—lime, and #4—grapefruit.

3. Use the soil mixture to fill the cups about two-thirds full. Do not pack the soil in the cups.

4. Remove the whole seeds from a freshly cut orange.

5. Rinse the seeds in warm water.

6. Place several orange seeds in cup #1. Cover with one-half inch of the soil mixture. Water lightly and set in a warm place.

7. Repeat steps 4–6 with the lemon, lime, and grapefruit.

8. Check the cups each day. Do not allow the soil to dry out completely.

9. Complete the chart below to record your observations of how the seeds sprout.

Materials
- fresh seeds from oranges, lemons, limes, and grapefruits
- a knife
- potting soil
- sand
- 4 paper or plastic foam cups
- water

DATE	ORANGE	LEMON	LIME	GRAPEFRUIT

Name _____

Trees provide people with many wonderful foods. Choose one of the foods below. Complete the chart to show the different uses of and products made using the food. Then, design a poster that displays the different uses and products of the food. Food containers and food wrappers which list the selected food as an ingredient can be used on the poster. Bring a food product containing the food to school to help create a class display.

 WORD BANK

apple	orange	lemon	lime	grapefruit
pear	peach	plum	coconut	pecan
allspice	almond	apricot	avocado	cacao
cashew	cherry	chestnut	cinnamon	clove
date	fig	mango	nectarine	nutmeg
olive	pecan	pistachio	prune	walnut

FOOD _____

USES OF	PRODUCTS

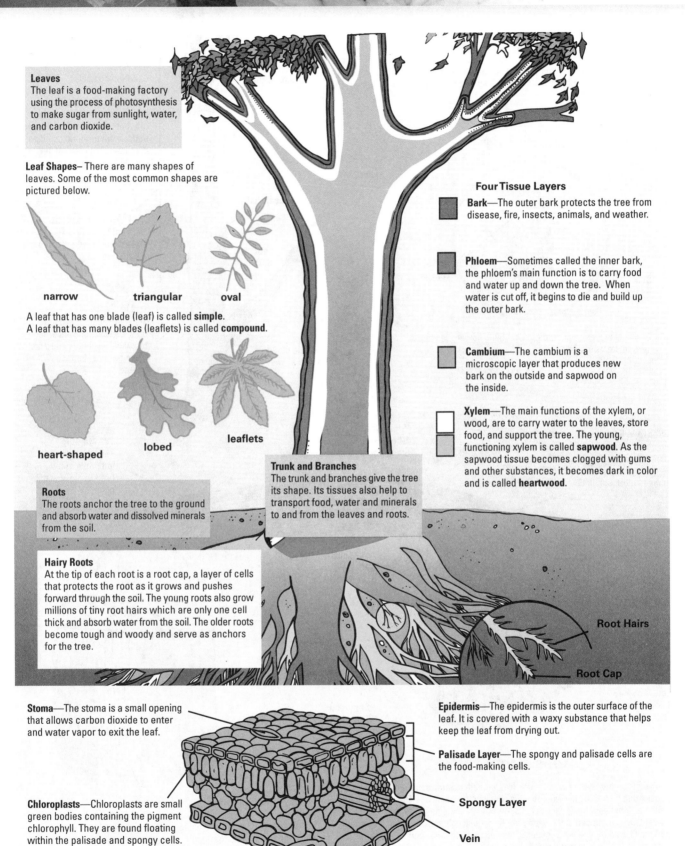

Leaves
The leaf is a food-making factory using the process of photosynthesis to make sugar from sunlight, water, and carbon dioxide.

Leaf Shapes— There are many shapes of leaves. Some of the most common shapes are pictured below.

narrow   triangular   oval

A leaf that has one blade (leaf) is called **simple**.
A leaf that has many blades (leaflets) is called **compound**.

heart-shaped   lobed   leaflets

Roots
The roots anchor the tree to the ground and absorb water and dissolved minerals from the soil.

Hairy Roots
At the tip of each root is a root cap, a layer of cells that protects the root as it grows and pushes forward through the soil. The young roots also grow millions of tiny root hairs which are only one cell thick and absorb water from the soil. The older roots become tough and woody and serve as anchors for the tree.

Trunk and Branches
The trunk and branches give the tree its shape. Its tissues also help to transport food, water and minerals to and from the leaves and roots.

Four Tissue Layers

Bark—The outer bark protects the tree from disease, fire, insects, animals, and weather.

Phloem—Sometimes called the inner bark, the phloem's main function is to carry food and water up and down the tree. When water is cut off, it begins to die and build up the outer bark.

Cambium—The cambium is a microscopic layer that produces new bark on the outside and sapwood on the inside.

Xylem—The main functions of the xylem, or wood, are to carry water to the leaves, store food, and support the tree. The young, functioning xylem is called **sapwood**. As the sapwood tissue becomes clogged with gums and other substances, it becomes dark in color and is called **heartwood**.

Root Hairs

Root Cap

Stoma—The stoma is a small opening that allows carbon dioxide to enter and water vapor to exit the leaf.

Epidermis—The epidermis is the outer surface of the leaf. It is covered with a waxy substance that helps keep the leaf from drying out.

Palisade Layer—The spongy and palisade cells are the food-making cells.

Spongy Layer

Chloroplasts—Chloroplasts are small green bodies containing the pigment chlorophyll. They are found floating within the palisade and spongy cells.

Vein

149

Plants

Trees Grow Taller

The end of each twig has a terminal bud with special cells that divide and make the twig grow longer. Each year's growth comes from a bud that contains the beginnings of a twig, leaves and flowers.

Inside a Bud

Bud Scales

Immature Leaves

Immature Stem

Scale leaves cover and protect young flowers, leaves, and stems inside the bud.

Lateral Bud

Terminal Bud
The terminal (leading) bud is protected from weather by thick, overlapping scales.

Terminal buds produce a hormone called *auxin* that prevents the growth of lateral buds. If the terminal bud dies or is removed, the lateral bud develops.

Leaf Bud

Leaf Scar

Last Year's Growth
Last year's growth extends from the terminal bud back to the scale scar.

Scale Scar
The scale scar, or growth rings, consists of lines around the twig that show where last year's terminal bud was located.

One-year-old side shoot formed by a lateral bud.

Increase in Growth
The neighboring trees were cut down or damaged, perhaps by a storm or disease. Thus, the tree has received more sunlight.

Growth Begins

Slow Growth
There is competition with neighboring trees for sunlight.

"V" Marking
This marking indicates that a branch grew at this point.

Decrease in Growth
This is probably due to drought or insects.

Normal Growth

Medullary Ray
This carries nutrients inward toward the center of the tree.

heartwood

sapwood

Heartwood
This helps to support the tree.

Sapwood
This carries water from the roots to the leaves.

Trees Grow Fatter

Each year, a new layer of wood forms just beneath the tree's bark. The tissue that causes this growth by dividing its cells is called the *cambium*. The new cells become xylem, and the layers of cells towards the outside of the tree become phloem. Cells produced in the spring are larger and lighter in color than the small, dark cells produced in the summer. These alternating dark- and light-colored cells make the rings in trees. Each ring represents one year of growth.

Xylem
Made of sapwood and heartwood.

Cambium
Makes new xylem (wood) and phloem (inner bark).

Phloem
Carries food made by the leaves to other parts of the tree.

Bark
Protects the tree.

Parts of a Flower

Most flowers have four main parts. Each of these parts consists of elements. These parts and elements are listed below. In this activity, you will display some of the parts of a real flower.

Materials
- one of the following kinds of flowers: daffodils, roses, lilies, tulips, irises, and phlox make good samples
- sharp cutting tool (adult supervision and help is required)
- paper towels
- heavy books or bricks
- construction paper or posterboard
- glue
- black marker

1. After you have collected a good flower sample, have an adult help you make a cross-section of the flower. This can be done by carefully slicing the flower using a sharp cutting tool.

2. Place the cross-section between several sheets of paper towels and press for several days with heavy books or bricks.

3. Carefully remove the paper towel. Attach the pressed flower to a sheet of construction paper or posterboard.

4. Cut out the labels below. Attach them to the construction paper or posterboard. Use a black marker to draw lines from the labels to the parts of the flower.

PETALS	SEPALS	POLLEN GRAINS
ANTHER	OVARY	FILAMENT
STAMENS	PISTILS	COROLLA
CALYX	OVULE	STYLE
STIGMA		

Each person in your classroom is an important part of what goes on in the classroom. Each person has a job to do, whether it is teaching, learning, or helping. Classrooms are busy and have many tools that are used to help students grow and learn.

Many plants are like that too. They have flowers that make seeds inside them. The flower has special things inside of it that help the seeds grow.

Directions: Look at the diagram and the chart below. Label and color the flower diagram using the information in the chart.

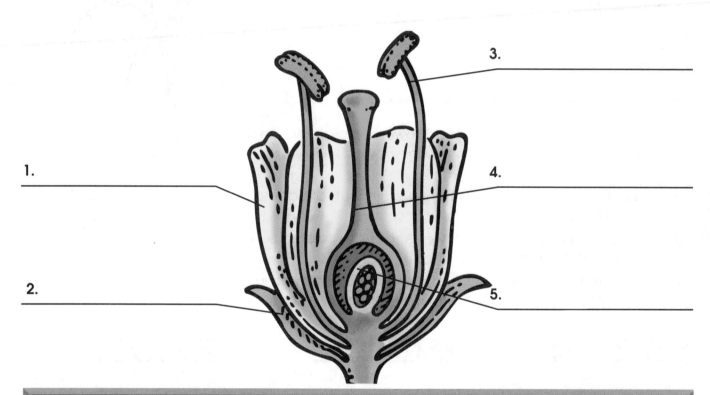

FLOWER PART	DESCRIPTION	COLOR
Pistil	A large center stalk, often shaped like a water bottle	Yellow
Stamen	Tall, thin stalk with a knobbed tip; it holds grains of pollen	Brown
Petal	Brightly colored and sweet-smelling leaves	Red
Sepal	Small, leaf-like part at the base of the flower	Green
Ovary	Ball-shaped part at the base of the pistil; this is where the seeds develop	Blue

Name _____

Use the words from the WORD BANK to complete the puzzle. Cross out each word as you use it. The remaining words will help you answer the riddle.

WORD BANK

petals	had	chlorophyll
ache	because	flower
sun	cotyledon	leaf
tap	it	an
ear	root	sugar
photosynthesis		

ACROSS

4. Deep-growing type of root
6. Beautiful, seed-making part of the plant
7. Brightly colored "leafy" parts of the flower
9. Large part of seed that supplies food
10. Sweet food made by the leaves

DOWN

1. Making food with the help of light.
2. Green food-making material in a leaf
3. Plant's "food factory"
5. Plant's anchor
8. Plants get their energy from the _____.

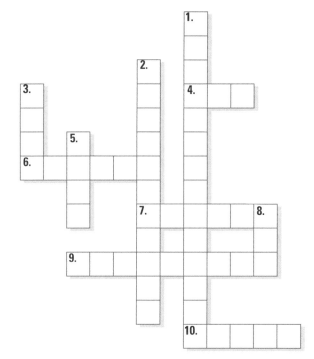

Riddle:

Why did the cornstalk go to the doctor?

_____

PLANTS

http://www.burpee.com
This page is the Burpee Seed homepage where students can find out more about growing plants from seeds.

http://www.plantamnesty.org/
This is the homepage of an organization dedicated to the proper use of plants in architecture. It is an excellent resource for information and speakers on this topic. It also displays humorous pictures of "bizarre yard-art architecture."

http://www.weather.com/activities/homeandgarden
The Weather Channel's homepage has a section on gardening that provides information on daily precipitation forecasts, soil treatments, and monthly planting maps for specific crops.

http://plantfacts.osu.edu
PlantFacts has merged several digital collections developed at Ohio State University to become an international knowledge bank and multimedia learning center. It includes a plant dictionary, how-to videos, a glossary, and frequently asked questions.

http://aggie-horticulturetamu.edu/kinder/sgardens2.html
This site offers activities and on-line games that cover the topics of soil, air, and water.

INTERTEBRATES

http://www.aqualink.com/marine/reef.html
This commercial site offers a number of excellent articles with valuable information regarding coral and the coral reef.

http://research.amnh.org/invertzoo/
This American Museum of Natural History site lists research and research staff involved in a variety of projects dealing with invertebrate zoology.

http://www.umesci.maine.edu/ams/inverts.htm
This site contains a listing of sites regarding invertebrates organized by phyla and by source.

http://butterflywebsite.com
This site offers facts, descriptions, and pictures of butterflies and moths.

http://www.kidport.com/RefLib/Science/Animals/Animal IndexInv.htm
This site contains an animal index of invertebrates. Students can click on pictures of invertebrate animals to learn more about them.

VERTEBRATES

http://netvet.wustl.edu/pix.htm
This is an electronic zoo that provides Web links to a variety of pictures and information about animals.

http://www.chebucto.ns.ca/Environment/NHR/index.html
This site is peppered with images to compliment its listing of the world of birds, butterflies and moths, and beetles.

http://pubs.usgs.gov/gip/dinosaurs/
This site, maintained by the United States Geological Survey, includes information and links to other sites about dinosaurs.

http://santaanazoo.org/
The home page for the Santa Ana Zoo includes links about their animals, history, calendar, and more.

http://sandiegozoo.org
The home page for the San Diego Zoo has numerous links including one on the Giant Panda Research Station.

http://www.neaq.org/
The home page for the New England Aquarium has links for news and events as well as research and conservation information.

THE HUMAN BODY

http://www.innerbody.com/htm/body.html
The educational site provides information on ten systems of the human body with simplified graphics for students.

http://odp.od.nih.gov/
This is the official site for the Office of Disease prevention at the National Institutes of Health. Offers other links to sites.

http://ificinfo.health.org/brochure/10kid2.htm
A site designed for children to help them choose healthful snacks and foods. It also gives suggestions on staying healthy through physical activity.

http://www4.tpgi.com.au/users/amcgann/body
This Web site was designed to help children learn about how our bodies work. There are 7 pictures to click on to learn about the major systems of the body: skeletal, muscular, circulatory, nervous, immune, digestive, and respiratory.

http://www.medtropolis.com/VBody.asp
This Web site is a virtual body tour that covers the brain, skeleton, heart, and digestive tract with games to organize each of the systems and shows a breakdown of the parts.

http://kidshealth.org/kid
This is an informative Web site with topics for kids—with links for dealing with feelings, staying healthy, everyday illnesses and injuries, and kids' talk, to name a few.

http://www.stcms.si.edu/hbs_student.htm
This is a Web site of human body systems where students can click on a system that leads them to related links.

The whole ecology of a given location on the earth can become unbalanced with the disappearance of just a single creature. This is because of a system called the **food chain**. The food chain is a concept that was developed by a scientist named Charles Elton. In 1927, he laid out the process by which plants get their energy from the sunlight, plant-eating animals get their energy from eating plants, and meat-eating animals get their energy from other animals. Seen in black and white, this looks very much like a chain, with its links all together.

Let's look at the food chain more closely. The food chain has four basic parts.

- The first part is the **sun**. The sun provides the energy for everything on the earth.

- The second part is known as **producers**. Producers are all green plants. They make their own food, and every organism is in part dependent on plants for the oxygen and/or food they need.

- **Consumers** are the third part of the food chain. Consumers are, very simply, every organism that eats something else, whether it is a **carnivore** (eats meat), an **herbivore** (eats plants), an **omnivore** (eats plants and animals), a **parasite** (relies on another living thing to provide food), or a **scavenger** (usually feeds on dead organisms).

- The fourth part of the food chain is **decomposers**. These organisms, such as fungi and bacteria, break down dead matter into important gases that are released back into the ground, air, or water. These "recycled" nutrients are then used by the producers in their growth process.

Look at the simplified food chain on the right. The sunlight helps the grass to grow, the rabbit eats the grass, and the fox eats the rabbit. Because the fox does not have a predator, it is the "top" of this food chain.

If something happens to the grass—perhaps a drought occurs—and the rabbits have less food, many may die. Without as many rabbits to eat, some of the foxes in the area may also die or leave the location. While this is a very simple look at the food chain (because rabbits do eat things other than grass), you can see that the disappearance of one element in the chain can have a lasting effect.

The term **food web** describes the many interlocking food chains in an area somewhere on the earth or in the water. Look at the food web below. Notice how the crops are eaten by humans, birds, aphids, and crickets or how the cricket is eaten by the chameleon and the frog. This shows very clearly how one food chain relies on another. It also shows how the failing of one element in a food chain might affect all living things in a location.

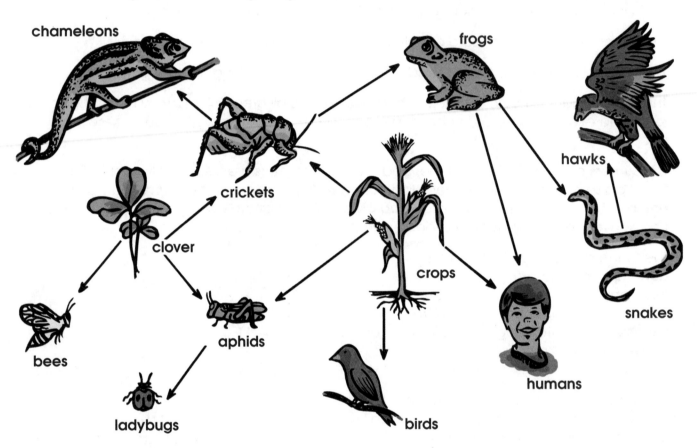

By breaking one link in an existing food chain, we run the risk of threatening all of the organisms above that one link, as well as other chains in a large food web. And this has happened many times. One example is the use of the pesticide DDT in the 1960s. This pesticide was very effective in helping to eliminate certain insects. But as it washed off the plants and out of the soil into the water supply, plankton and other small organisms took in the DDT. These organisms were then eaten by small fish, resulting in the fish having the DDT in them. Larger fish and birds ate the smaller fish, and the birds were affected. Birds such as the osprey and eagle developed very thin eggshells and became threatened. This is known as the *domino effect*.

Name _____

Directions: Use the reading on pages 155–156 to help define the following terms.

1. Consumers _____

   _____

2. Producers _____

   _____

3. Sun _____

   _____

4. Pesticides _____

   _____

5. Food chain _____

   _____

6. Food web _____

   _____

7. Domino effect _____

   _____

8. Energy _____

   _____

Directions: Now, answer the following questions.

1. What term means that the "death of one species in a food chain upsets the rest of the food chain"? _____

   _____

2. Look at the food web on page 156. Describe several different food chains in the web.

   _____

   _____

   _____

   _____

   _____

Chain Reactions Everywhere

Name ______________________

All organisms need food and energy whether they are in or above the water. Energy comes from many sources, and those sources are usually a part of a food chain. In the spaces below, create one marine food chain and one land food chain. Make sure the "links" in the chains are in sequential order.

MARINE FOOD CHAIN

LAND FOOD CHAIN

Consider the food chains you have recorded. Would a marine food web have as many elements in it as a land food web? Why or why not?

____

____

____

____

We eat food from many sources. We eat fruits, vegetables, meats, dairy, grains, and sweets. Most items that are part of our daily diet are made from natural sources such as potatoes, cows, and wheat plants. Each of those items needed energy to grow and mature so that they were ready to be producers or sources of the foods we eat.

For example, wheat plants get their energy to grow from the sun and the nutrients in the soil and water. Cows get their energy from the plants and grains they are fed. Those plants and grains grow like the wheat plant does, and they are all part of a food web.

Directions: Choose three of your favorite foods. Write the ingredients of the food, and trace a food chain to show where those ingredients came from.

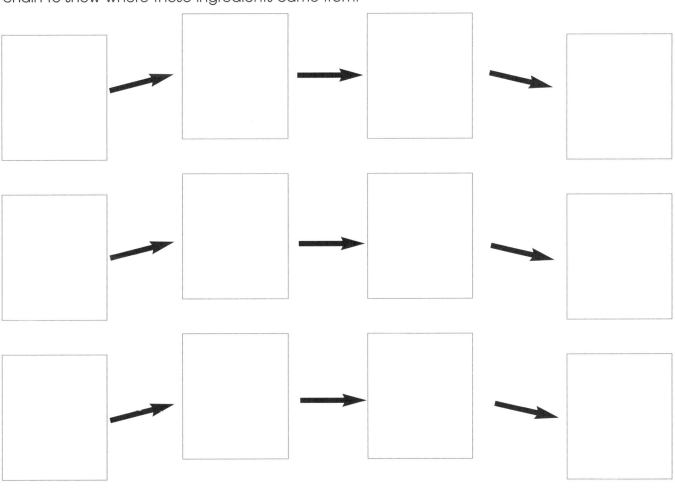

Is there an item in your diet that isn't made from something that grows naturally? Name it and explain where it comes from.

_____

_____

_____

_____

Shop Around

What happens when one organism in a food chain simply dies, becomes extinct, or leaves an area? How are the rest of the organisms in the food chain and food web affected? What types of repercussions might there be if two organisms disappear from a food chain or web?

These are the types of questions that some researchers and scientists must ask themselves. As the world changes and the atmosphere is affected by changes in the ozone layer and by the weather patterns on earth, this is what happens.

Directions: Study the food chain shown below, and answer the questions that follow.

1. Predict what might happen if the stream that the fish and frogs live in and around began to dry up. What effect might this have on the food web in the area?

   _____

   _____

2. If a large group of foxes came into the area and began eating the frog population, what might happen?

   _____

   _____

3. On a separate sheet of paper, create a new food chain showing how things might change if the frog and fish populations were depleted. Consider what might replace them in the chain and how it might have an effect on the larger food web. After drawing and labeling the new chain, write about the changes that would take place.

#	Symbol	Name	Mass	Electron configuration
1	H	Hydrogen	1.00794	1
88	Ra	Radium	(226)	2, 8, 18, 32, 18, 8, 2
41	Nb	Niobium	92.90638	2, 8, 18, 12, 1
77	Ir	Iridium	192.217	2, 8, 18, 32, 15, 2
114	Uuq		(289)	
66	Dy	Dysprosium	162.50	2, 8, 18, 28, 8, 2
96	Cm	Curium	(247)	2, 8, 18, 32, 25, 9, 2
48	Cd	Cadmium	112.411	2, 8, 18, 18, 2
8	O	Oxygen	15.9994	2, 6
2	He	Helium	4.002602	2
3	Li	Lithium	6.941	2, 1
21	Sc	Scandium	44.95591	2, 8, 9, 2
42	Mo	Molybdenum	95.94	2, 8, 18, 13, 1
78	Pt	Platinum	195.078	2, 8, 18, 32, 17, 1
116	Uuh		(289)	
67	Ho	Holmium	164.93032	2, 8, 18, 29, 8, 2
97	Bk	Berkelium	(247)	2, 8, 18, 32, 26, 9, 2
49	In	Indium	114.818	2, 8, 18, 18, 3
9	F	Fluorine	18.9984032	2, 7
10	Ne	Neon	20.1797	2, 8
11	Na	Sodium	22.989768	2, 8, 1
22	Ti	Titanium	47.867	2, 8, 10, 2
43	Tc	Technetium	(98)	2, 8, 18, 13, 2
79	Au	Gold	196.96654	2, 8, 18, 32, 18, 1
57	La	Lanthanum	138.9055	2, 8, 18, 18, 9, 2
68	Er	Erbium	167.26	2, 8, 18, 30, 8, 2
98	Cf	Californium	(251)	2, 8, 18, 32, 28, 8, 2
50	Sn	Tin	118.710	2, 8, 18, 18, 4
14	Si	Silicon	28.0855	2, 8, 4
18	Ar	Argon	39.948	2, 8, 8
19	K	Potassium	39.0983	2, 8, 8, 1
23	V	Vanadium	50.9415	2, 8, 11, 2
44	Ru	Ruthenium	101.07	2, 8, 18, 15, 1
104	Rf	Rutherfordium	(261)	2, 8, 18, 32, 32, 10, 2
89	Ac	Actinium	(227)	2, 8, 18, 32, 18, 9, 2
69	Tm	Thulium	168.93421	2, 8, 18, 31, 8, 2
99	Es	Einsteinium	(252)	2, 8, 18, 32, 29, 8, 2
51	Sb	Antimony	121.76	2, 8, 18, 18, 5
15	P	Phosphorus	30.973762	2, 8, 5
36	Kr	Krypton	83.80	2, 8, 18, 8
37	Rb	Rubidium	85.4678	2, 8, 18, 8, 1
24	Cr	Chromium	51.9961	2, 8, 13, 1
45	Rh	Rhodium	102.9055	2, 8, 18, 16, 1
105	Db	Dubnium	(262)	2, 8, 18, 32, 32, 11, 2
58	Ce	Cerium	140.116	2, 8, 18, 20, 8, 2
70	Yb	Ytterbium	173.04	2, 8, 18, 32, 8, 2
100	Fm	Fermium	(257)	2, 8, 18, 32, 30, 8, 2
80	Hg	Mercury	200.59	2, 8, 18, 32, 18, 2
16	S	Sulfur	32.066	2, 8, 6
54	Xe	Xenon	131.29	2, 8, 18, 18, 8
55	Cs	Cesium	132.90543	2, 8, 18, 18, 8, 1
25	Mn	Manganese	54.93805	2, 8, 13, 2
46	Pd	Palladium	106.42	2, 8, 18, 18, 0
106	Sg	Seaborgium	(266)	2, 8, 18, 32, 32, 12, 2
59	Pr	Praseodymium	140.90765	2, 8, 18, 21, 8, 2
71	Lu	Lutetium	174.967	2, 8, 18, 32, 9, 2
101	Md	Mendelevium	(258)	2, 8, 18, 32, 31, 8, 2
81	Tl	Thallium	204.3833	2, 8, 18, 32, 18, 3
17	Cl	Chlorine	35.4527	2, 8, 7
86	Rn	Radon	(222)	2, 8, 18, 32, 18, 8
87	Fr	Francium	(223)	2, 8, 18, 32, 18, 8, 1
26	Fe	Iron	55.845	2, 8, 14, 2
47	Ag	Silver	107.8682	2, 8, 18, 18, 1
107	Bh	Bohrium	(262)	2, 8, 18, 32, 32, 13, 2
60	Nd	Neodymium	144.24	2, 8, 18, 22, 8, 2
90	Th	Thorium	232.0381	2, 8, 18, 32, 18, 10, 2
102	No	Nobelium	(259)	2, 8, 18, 32, 32, 8, 2
82	Pb	Lead	207.2	2, 8, 18, 32, 18, 4
33	As	Arsenic	74.92159	2, 8, 18, 5
113	Uut			
4	Be	Beryllium	9.012182	2, 2
27	Co	Cobalt	58.9332	2, 8, 15, 2
72	Hf	Hafnium	178.49	2, 8, 18, 32, 10, 2
108	Hs	Hassium	(263)	2, 8, 18, 32, 32, 14, 2
61	Pm	Promethium	(145)	2, 8, 18, 23, 8, 2
91	Pa	Protactinium	231.03588	2, 8, 18, 32, 20, 9, 2
103	Lr	Lawrencium	(262)	2, 8, 18, 32, 32, 9, 2
83	Bi	Bismuth	208.98037	2, 8, 18, 32, 18, 5
34	Se	Selenium	78.96	2, 8, 18, 6
115	Uup			
12	Mg	Magnesium	24.305	2, 8, 2
28	Ni	Nickel	58.6934	2, 8, 16, 2
73	Ta	Tantalum	180.9479	2, 8, 18, 32, 11, 2
109	Mt	Meitnerium	(268)	2, 8, 18, 32, 32, 15, 2
62	Sm	Samarium	150.36	2, 8, 18, 24, 8, 2
92	U	Uranium	238.0289	2, 8, 18, 32, 21, 9, 2
13	Al	Aluminum	26.981539	2, 8, 3
84	Po	Polonium	(209)	2, 8, 18, 32, 18, 6
35	Br	Bromine	79.904	2, 8, 18, 7
117	Uus			
20	Ca	Calcium	40.078	2, 8, 8, 2
29	Cu	Copper	63.546	2, 8, 18, 1
74	W	Tungsten	183.84	2, 8, 18, 32, 12, 2
110	Ds	Darmstadtium	(271)	2, 8, 18, 32, 32, 17
63	Eu	Europium	151.964	2, 8, 18, 25, 8, 2
93	Np	Neptunium	(237)	2, 8, 18, 32, 22, 9, 2
30	Zn	Zinc	65.39	2, 8, 18, 2
5	B	Boron	10.811	2, 3
52	Te	Tellurium	127.60	2, 8, 18, 18, 6
38	Sr	Strontium	87.62	2, 8, 18, 8, 2
39	Y	Yttrium	88.90585	2, 8, 18, 9, 2
75	Re	Rhenium	186.207	2, 8, 18, 32, 13, 2
111	Rg	Roentgenium	(272)	2, 8, 18, 32, 32, 17, 1
64	Gd	Gadolinium	157.25	2, 8, 18, 25, 9, 2
94	Pu	Plutonium	(244)	2, 8, 18, 32, 24, 8, 2
31	Ga	Gallium	69.723	2, 8, 18, 3
6	C	Carbon	12.0107	2, 4
53	I	Iodine	126.90447	2, 8, 18, 18, 7
56	Ba	Barium	137.327	2, 8, 18, 18, 8, 2
40	Zr	Zirconium	91.224	2, 8, 18, 10, 2
76	Os	Osmium	190.23	2, 8, 18, 32, 14, 2
112	Uub		(277)	2, 8, 18, 32, 32, 18, 2
65	Tb	Terbium	158.92534	2, 8, 18, 27, 8, 2
95	Am	Americium	(243)	2, 8, 18, 32, 25, 8, 2
32	Ge	Germanium	72.61	2, 8, 18, 4
7	N	Nitrogen	14.00674	2, 5
85	At	Astatine	(210)	2, 8, 18, 32, 18, 7

Name _____

Organisms are either producers or consumers, depending on the source of their energy. Consumers are either herbivores, carnivores, or omnivores.

Directions: Label the producers, omnivores, herbivores, and carnivores in each food chain.

1.   a. _____   b. _____   c. _____

2.   a. _____   b. _____   c. _____

3.   a. _____   b. _____   c. _____

Food Chains and Webs/Nutrition

Eating Out in the Habitat

Choose a specific habitat and do some research into the plant and animal life in that area.

Directions: Design a food web that includes at least one producer, one consumer, and one decomposer.

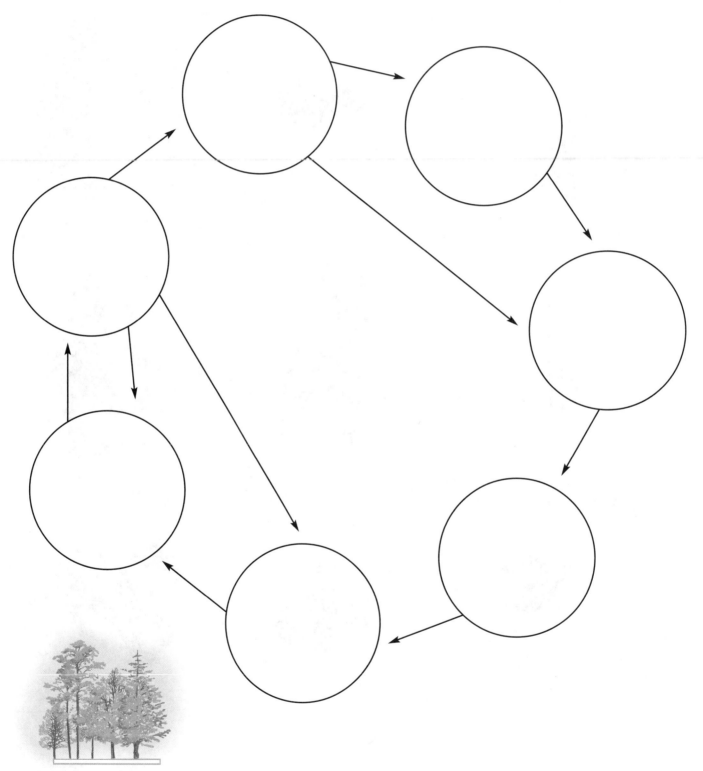

Eating would be boring if we ate only one kind of food. Imagine eating only pizza for breakfast, lunch, and dinner, 365 days a year, for the rest of your life. Most animals, like humans, eat more than one type of food. This means that most animals are members of more than one food chain. Separate food chains that interlock are called food webs.

Directions: Form a food web by drawing arrows from each prey to its predator. Remember that most prey have more than one predator. Use a different color crayon for each food chain.

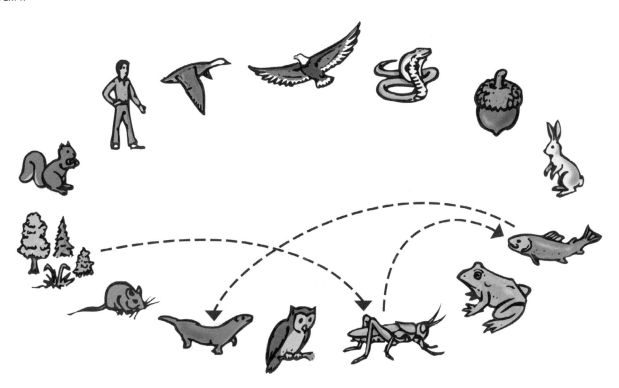

One food chain that you may have found in the web is this one:

plant ⟶ **grasshopper** ⟶ **fish** ⟶ **otter**

Directions: Now, write one more food chain you can find.

_____

_____

_____

What We Need

Just like plants and animals need the proper food and nutrients in their diet each day, so do people. The school lunchroom staff makes sure that the students eating there will receive a balance of the types of foods they need.

The **food pyramid** is a model that shows how many servings of certain foods students should eat each day. If students eat the proper amount of each food group they are sure to develop strong minds and bodies.

Directions: Look at the food pyramid. Write the number of each food item in the list in the correct section of the pyramid.

 WORD BANK

1. orange
2. yogurt
3. cookie
4. carrot
5. chicken leg
6. pancake

7. breakfast cereal
8. milk
9. potato
10. roast beef
11. cupcake
12. cheese

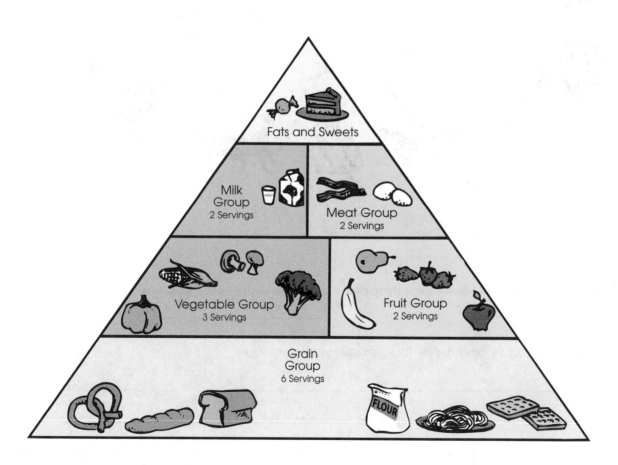

Name That Vegetable

You should be aware of the variety of good healthy things there are to eat. Vegetables are one of the best things to eat. They are low in fat and have many minerals, vitamins, and other nutrients we need.

Directions: Choose a vegetable to research. Find the following information, summarize it, and put on the garden marker below. Then, draw and color a picture of the vegetable.

1. Where is this vegetable grown?
2. How is it grown?
3. What part of the plant is edible?
4. How is it most often prepared?
5. What are the nutritional elements that we get when we eat this vegetable?

Now, cut out the marker, glue onto a tongue depressor, and display with a sample of the vegetable.

Food Chains and Webs/Nutrition

Where's the Energy?

Your garage might be full of tools. Tools need energy to work. Your body does work like the tools in your garage. This means that your body also needs energy to work. You get the energy your body needs from the foods you eat.

Foods contain nutrients that have stored energy. This stored energy is changed into fuel for your body as it is digested. The amount of energy released is measured in calories. A calorie is how much energy proteins, carbohydrates, and fats supply your body. Every gram of protein and carbohydrate provides four calories of energy. Fats provide nine calories of energy.

NUTRIENT	WHAT IT DOES	FOODS WE GET IT FROM
Proteins	Supplies energy and helps build and repair cells to form tissues for proper growth and development	Meat, fish, chicken, eggs, nuts yogurt, cheese, milk, oats, spinach, and beans
Carbohydrates	Supplies energy and helps maintain body warmth	Fruits, vegetables, bread, rice, pasta, potatoes, oatmeal, pretzels, and sugars
Fats	Serves as a source of stored energy, helps your body use vitamins, and insulates your body	Avocados, butter, meat, cheese, eggs, whole milk, nuts, and oils

The number of calories you need every day for your body to perform basic processes, such as blinking your eyes, is ten times your body weight. Most of the calories you consume should come from proteins and carbohydrates. Fats won't hurt you, but you should eat them only in moderation. The key to keeping your body healthy is to find out how many calories your body needs and to eat only as many calories as your body will use.

Directions: Use the information to answer the following questions.

1. What is a calorie? _____

2. Which nutrients supply our energy needs? _____

3. Which nutrients should you eat the most of? _____

   Why? _____

   _____

4. What happens if you consume more calories than you use?

   _____

   _____

What's Your Output?

QUESTION How many calories does my body need?

MATERIALS
- a calculator
- a pencil
- a scale

PROCEDURE

1. Estimate how many minutes each day you spend on the activities below. Skip an activity if you don't do it.

2. Multiply your time spent by the number of calories needed per minute to find the total calories needed for the activity.

ACTIVITY	MINUTES PER DAY	CALORIES NEEDED PER MINUTE	TOTAL CALORIES NEEDED FOR ACTIVITY
Swimming		x 3.2	
Running		x 9.0	
Riding a bike		x 7.0	
Walking		x 2.5	
Playing outside		x 3.5	
Playing soccer		x 4.5	
Playing the piano		x 1.8	
Watching T.V.		x 0.5	
Playing softball or baseball		x 3.4	
Playing basketball		x 4.0	
Playing video games		x 1.1	
In-line skating		x 4.6	
Jumping rope		x 6.6	
Climbing stairs		x 6.0	
Playing football		x 5.3	

Total calories needed for activities: _____

Find the total calories your body needs to perform basic functions:

_____ x 10 = _____
Body weight   Base calories

Add your base calories to your total calories needed for activities to get an estimate of how many calories you need each day:

_____ + _____ = _____
Base calories   Activity calories   Total calories needed

Nutrition Facts About Crackers

Some foods are better for you than others. In this activity, you will examine the labels of three different brands of saltine, cheese, or graham crackers for nutritional data.

Directions: Complete the chart below to determine which of the crackers is the most healthy for you.

	BRAND A	BRAND B	BRAND C
Brand name of product			
Number of crackers/serving			
Calories/serving			
Total fat/serving			
Saturated fat/serving			
Cholesterol/serving			
Sodium/serving			
Total carbohydrate/serving			
Dietary fiber/serving			
Sugars/serving			
Protein/serving			
Vitamin A/serving			
Vitamin C/serving			
Calcium/serving			
Iron/serving			

Nutrition Facts About Cereals

Some cereals have more vitamins in them than others. In this activity, you will examine the labels of three different brands of cereal to compare the nutritional data.

Directions: Complete the chart below for cereal without milk to determine which of the cereals is the most healthy for you.

	BRAND A	BRAND B	BRAND C
Brand name of cereal			
Serving size			
Calories			
Total fat			
Saturated fat			
Cholesterol			
Sodium			
Potassium			
Total carbohydrate			
Dietary fiber			
Sugars			
Protein			
Vitamin A			
Vitamin C			
Calcium			
Iron			
Vitamin D			
Thiamin			
Riboflavin			
Niacin			
Phosphorus			
Magnesium			
Zinc			

You Are What You Eat

Looking closely at the information on a cereal box, you can learn many interesting things about the product.

Directions: Carefully read the information on the illustration of the cereal box. Answer the questions. Compare these answers with the information found on a box of cereal you might eat for breakfast.

	CORN BALLS	YOUR CEREAL
What kind of grain(s) is used?		
Is sugar used?		
What position is sugar on the list of ingredients?		
List other sweeteners.		
How many calories per serving without milk?		
How many calories per serving when eaten with 1/2 cup of skim milk?		
How much protein per serving?		
How many vitamins and minerals does the cereal contain?		
How much cholesterol is in one serving?		
How much fat is in one serving?		
How much carbohydrate is in one serving?		

NUTRITION INFORMATION

SERVING SIZE: 1 OZ. (28.4 g, ABOUT 1 CUP) CORN BALLS ALONE OR WITH 1/2 CUP VITAMINS A AND D SKIM MILK.

SERVINGS PER PACKAGE: 15

	CEREAL	WITH 1/2 CUP VITAMINS A & D SKIM MILK
CALORIES	110	150*
PROTEIN	1 g	5 g
CARBOHYDRATE	26 g	32 g
FAT	0 g	0 g*
CHOLESTEROL	0 mg	0 mg*
SODIUM	90 mg	150 mg
POTASSIUM	20 mg	220 mg

PERCENTAGE OF U.S. RECOMMENDED DAILY ALLOWANCES (U.S. RDA)

PROTEIN	2	10
VITAMIN A	15	20
VITAMIN C	25	25
THIAMIN	25	30
RIBOFLAVIN	25	35
NIACIN	25	25
CALCIUM	**	15
IRON	10	10
VITAMIN D	10	25
VITAMIN B6	25	25
ZINC	10	15

* WHOLE MILK SUPPLIES AN ADDITIONAL 30 CALORIES. 4g. FAT, AND 15mg CHOLESTEROL.
* * CONTAINS LESS THAN 2% OF THE U.S. RDA OF THIS NUTRIENT.

INGREDIENTS: CORN, SUGAR, CORN SYRUP, MOLASSES, SALT, ANNATTO COLOR,

VITAMINS AND MINERALS: VITAMIN C (SODIUM ASCORBATE AND ASCORBIC ACID), NIACINAMIDE, ZINC (OXIDE), IRON, VITAMIN B6 (PYRIDOXINE HYDROCHLORIDE), VITAMIN B2 (RIBOFLAVIN), VITAMIN A (PALMITATE; PROTECTED WITH BHT), VITAMIN B1 (THIAMIN HYDROCHLORIDE), FOLIC ACID, AND VITAMIN D.

Burning Calories to Stay Healthy

Regular exercise makes your heart strong, and it also helps you burn calories so you maintain a healthy weight.

Directions: The activities named below list the number of calories burned by a 150-pound person when he or she engages in an activity for 30 minutes. Circle the 10 activities below that help you burn the most calories.

ACTIVITY	CALORIES BURNED IN 30 MINUTES	ACTIVITY	CALORIES BURNED IN 30 MINUTES
Cross country skiing	210	Homework	55
Running (7 mph)	275	Racquetball	365
Shuffleboard	90	Baseball	60
Bicycling (stationary)	150	Soccer	360
Aerobic dancing	200	Swimming	265
Watching TV	45	Tennis	225
Walking (5.5 mph)	280	Basketball	345

Directions: Complete the chart below to keep a record of the exercise you do for one week.

DAY	TYPE OF EXERCISE	LENGTH OF TIME (MINUTES)	APPROXIMATE CALORIES BURNED
Sunday			
Monday			
Tuesday			
Wednesday			
Thursday			
Friday			
Saturday			

Reading the Label

The labels on medicine containers give us important information. Labels should always be read carefully.

Directions: Read the information on the cough medicine labels below. Answer the questions on the lines provided.

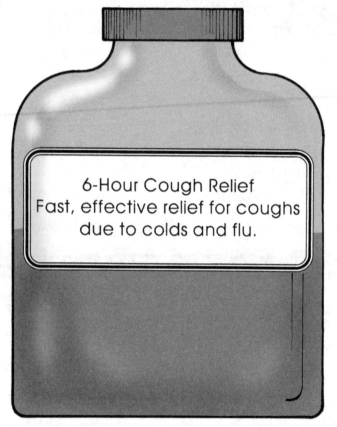

6-Hour Cough Relief
Fast, effective relief for coughs due to colds and flu.

Recommended Dosage:

Children (5 - 12 years): 1 teaspoon every 6 hours.

Adults: 2 teaspoons every 6 hours.

Caution: *Do not administer to children under 5. No more than 4 dosages per day. This product may cause drowsiness; use caution if operating machinery or driving a vehicle. Should not be taken if you are pregnant or nursing a child.*

If cough or fever persists, consult a physician.

Exp. Date: 8/2006

1. What is the adult dosage? _____

2. What is a child's dosage? _____

3. What is a side effect of this medicine? _____

4. Who should not take this medicine? _____

5. How many dosages per day can be taken safely? _____

6. What is the expiration date of this medicine? _____

7. What action should be taken if the medicine does not relieve your cough?

    _____

8. For what symptoms should this medicine be taken? _____

Caution: Poison!

Children are always very curious. They love to touch things and pick them up. Very young children like to put things into their mouths. What action do you take if a child swallows a poisonous material?

Directions: Read the following safety procedures.

**CALL YOUR POISON CONTROL CENTER, HOSPITAL, PHYSICIAN,
OR EMERGENCY PHONE NUMBER IMMEDIATELY!!**

If you cannot obtain emergency advice, follow these procedures.

- If the poison is **corrosive**: paint remover, household cleaners, gasoline, drain opener, ammonia or lye, **DO NOT** make the patient vomit. Give the patient water or milk to dilute the poison.

- If the poison is **not corrosive**: insect spray, aspirin, pesticides or medicine, **make the patient vomit**, or use a poison control kit. To force the patient to vomit touch the back of his or her throat.

Directions: Write a bold **V** on each picture that shows poison that should be vomited if swallowed. Circle each poison that should not be vomited if swallowed.

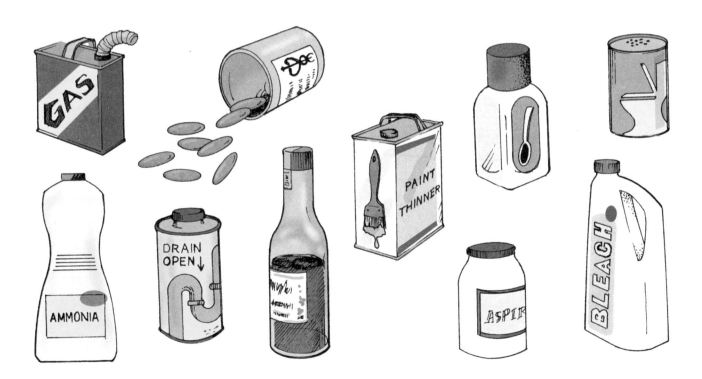

Name _____

An **environment** includes all living and nonliving things with which an organism interacts. These living and nonliving things are **interdependent**; that is, they depend on one another. The living things in an environment (plants, animals) are called **biotic factors**, and the nonliving things (soil, light, temperature) are called **abiotic factors**. **Ecology** is the study of the relationships and interactions of living things with one another and their environment.

Living things inhabit many different environments. A group of organisms living and interacting with each other in their nonliving environment is called an **ecosystem**. The different organisms that live together in an ecosystem are called a **community**. Within a community, each kind of living thing (i.e., frogs) makes up a **population**.

Directions: Study the picture. Follow the directions.

1. Label two biotic factors and two abiotic factors in the picture.

2. Explain the relationships among the living things in the pictured environment. _____

_____

3. Name the type of ecosystem pictured. _____

4. Circle all the members of the community.

5. Explain how the organisms in this environment are dependent upon one another. _____

_____

6. List the different kinds of populations that live in the environment. _____

_____

It's a Small World

Most of the living things in your neighborhood can be classified into one of two main groups—plants and animals. Plants and animals are classified, or compared to something else, based on their physical structure and behavior. Each different kind of plant and animal is known as a **species**. A group of the same species is called a **population**.

Populations of living things live in an **ecosystem**, an area in which living things interact with each other and their environment. Like neighborhoods, ecosystems can be very small or extremely large. Within each ecosystem, there may be many different habitats. A **habitat** is the place where a population normally lives in an ecosystem. The habitat must supply the needs of organisms, such as food, water, temperature, oxygen, and minerals. If the population's needs are not met, it will either move to a better habitat or die out.

Different populations need different habitats. A population of fish needs a body of water. A population of monkeys needs a jungle. Habitats can be shared. When several populations share a habitat, it is called a **community**. All of the populations living in the community work together to meet their needs.

If something in the community changes, such as the population of fish in a lake increasing, then another population, such as the insects, may become endangered. If conditions do not change or the habitat vanishes, then all of the members of the population may die and the species may become extinct.

Directions: Use the information to answer the following questions.

1. What are the two main groups of living things? _____

2. How are they classified? _____

3. How are an ecosystem, a habitat, and a community alike? _____

   _____

   How are they different? _____

4. What needs of a living thing does a habitat supply? _____

   _____

   _____

5. What happens if a habitat cannot supply the needs named in question 4?

   _____

   _____

Environment

What's in Your Neighborhood?

Name

QUESTION What living and nonliving things are in different habitats in my neighborhood?

MATERIALS
- a large trash bag
- 8 tongue depressors
- a hand lens
- string

PROCEDURE

1. Find a place in your neighborhood where a lot of people walk.

2. Lay the trash bag on the ground and use the tongue depressors and string to outline this area. Fold the trash bag and put it to the side.

3. Use the hand lens and your eyes to observe all of the things in the area. Write your observations in the table. Count or estimate the number of each population and then write it in your table.

Observations and Sketches	Number Observed
Plants	
Animals	
Nonliving things	

Find a place where very few people walk and repeat steps 2–3.

Observations and Sketches	Number Observed
Plants	
Animals	
Nonliving things	

Directions: Answer the questions.

1. Which habitat had more species of plants and animals? _____

   Why do you think this is? _____

2. Which habitat had more nonliving things? _____

   Why do you think this is? _____

Incredible Ecosystems

On your way to school, did you walk or drive through a neighborhood? Did you see houses or businesses? Did you see people, animals, trees, and grass? These are all part of that one neighborhood. An ecosystem is similar to a neighborhood. It is the whole community of living and nonliving things. All of these things exist together and interact with one another.

Ecosystems can be on land or water. They are all different from one another for many reasons. Those reasons include the amount of water in an area, the type of soil, and the kinds of plants and animals that live there.

Directions: Look at the two ecosystems. Compare the two. Name three differences.

_____

_____

_____

_____

_____

_____

_____

_____

Environment

Make a Difference

Remember that any change in an ecosystem causes a chain reaction of more changes. Do this activity with a partner or at home. Record the results of your experiment.

Materials
- outdoor study site with loose earth
- shade
- corrugated cardboard
- potato slices
- water
- string, sticks

Directions:

1. Locate a small study site and mark with the string and sticks. Write a brief description of the site, including plant and animal life.

2. Place raw potato slices on top of the soil in your study site.

3. Get small pieces of cardboard completely wet. Place the pieces over the potato slices. Use rocks to keep the cardboard In place.

4. Do not disturb for several days.

5. Remove the cardboard pieces. Observe and record any small organisms that are now in the site.

6. Read the first description of the study site. Compare that to the way the site is now. What is different? What is the same? What caused the changes?

_____

_____

_____

_____

Name _____

Different types of organisms adapt to different types of habitats. Microhabitats are the smaller living environments within larger habitats, such as ants living in a piece of dead wood.

Directions: For this activity, locate two microhabitats. For each habitat, make observations and notes about the plants, animals, and other living things you find.

SUNNY, DRY AREA	SHADY, MOIST AREA

Compare the two habitats. What differences and similarities did you discover?

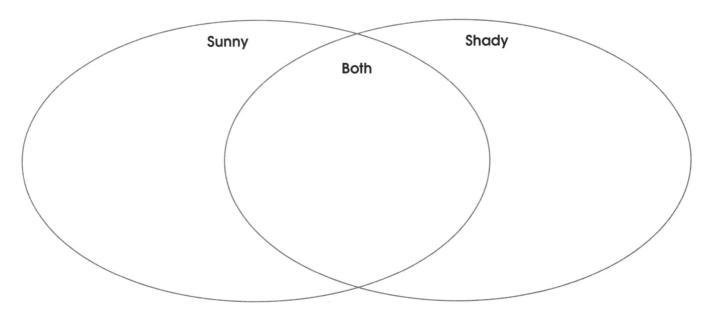

Environment

Habitat in a Jar

Directions: For this activity, you will construct a habitat in a terrarium.

1. Go to a field or forest to collect plant specimens. Dig out the entire plant, including roots and surrounding soil.
2. On the bottom of a glass aquarium, spread small rocks and charcoal.
3. Cover the rocks and charcoal with a soil mixture about 2 inches deep.
4. Add plants to the terrarium and sprinkle with water.
5. You may add insects or snails to the terrarium, but be sure you have plants that provide the appropriate food for them.
6. Cover tightly with plastic wrap, and place the terrarium near a window but not in direct sunlight.
7. To check whether you have enough water, you should see water droplets on the plastic wrap. Add water if necessary.

Materials
- a glass aquarium
- plant specimens
- small stones
- crushed charcoal
- soil
- water
- an insect (optional)

Describe the environment that you created in your terrarium. List the types of plants and animals that you placed in the habitat.

_____

_____

Observe your terrarium over a period of time to see how the different plants and animals grow and survive.

WEEK 1	WEEK 2	WEEK 3	WEEK 4

After one month, decide whether you need to make any changes to the terrarium. If so, what is the problem in the habitat and what can you do to address the issue?

_____

_____

_____

_____

Habitat Happenings

Directions: Pick a habitat such as a desert, grassland, savanna, or tundra. Research plants and animals that are found in the environment. Write a paragraph describing the habitat with its wildlife and plant life.

_____

_____

_____

_____

_____

_____

Sketch a picture of that specific environment.

Environment

Name _____

Directions: Imagine you will be visiting a natural habitat. Develop a checklist of what clothes and other supplies you will need in that habitat. Also, write a list of "must see" plants and animals.

CLOTHES AND MATERIALS	"MUST SEE" PLANTS AND ANIMALS

Definition

Physical Characteristics of the Habitat

Habitat

_____

Specific Examples of Animal Life

Specific Examples of Plant Life

Name _____

Directions: Circle the correct answers.

1. A habitat is a(n)

   a. action we do everyday.

   b. location where specific animals and plants live and interact.

   c. specific weather pattern.

2. Living organisms are one of three things that help maintain the balance in an ecosystem. They can be

   a. producers, consumers, or decomposers.

   b. plants, trees, or grass.

   c. animals, plants, or rocks.

3. Succession is the process of change in the plants and animals of a community over a period of time.

   true or false

4. Ecology is the study of

   a. living things and what they eat.

   b. animals that live and grow.

   c. living things and their environment.

5. A group of _____ and _____ things interacting with each other is considered an ecosystem.

   a. living, nonliving

   b. moving, growing

   c. habitat, plant

Directions: Use complete sentences to answer the following question.

Think about the impact of humans on natural habitats. Write a position statement about your opinion on this issue. Your position could be against the destruction of habitats or for development that can lead to destruction of habitats.

_____

_____

_____

_____

_____

_____

Investigating a Pond

PURPOSE Inspect living plants and animals, as well as non-living materials from a pond in order to do a biological survey. Measure the physical parameters of the pond including temperature and size.

MATERIALS
- pencils
- thermometer
- scoop nets
- yard stick
- magnifying glass
- clear plastic tub (shoe box size)
- string ball
- wash bottle
- field guides

INTRODUCTION A pond is a good topic for study since it is large enough to house a variety of life-forms and yet small enough to be measured by conventional means. In this activity, students will be measuring the physical characteristics of the pond and looking for common macroinvertebrates. Using a field guide, living things can be identified. Encourage the students to use magnifying glasses to inspect the muds and algae collected and observe microscopic forms of life. It may be possible to classify the condition of the water on the basis of the kinds of life-forms that can be found in the pond.

PROCEDURE To measure the pond, work with a partner and stretch a string across the selected part of the pond. When finished, measure the string length and record the measurement. Use a yard stick to measure the string as your partner rolls it back into a ball.

IDENTIFY THE SHAPE OF THE POND AND FIND THE AREA

Circular-Shaped Pond
1. Measure the diameter of the pond by stretching the string from one side to the other, going through the pond's center.
2. Divide the diameter by 2 to find the radius.
3. To find the area of the pond, multiply the radius times itself. Then, multiply that times the value *pi* (*mathematical constant with an approximate value of 3.14*).

Data on Circular-Shaped Pond

Diameter: _____ feet

Radius: _____ feet

Area: _____ square feet

Rectangular-Shaped Pond
1. Measure the width of the pond by stretching the string from one side of the pond to the other.
2. Using the string, find the length of the pond.
3. Find the area of the pond by multiplying width times the length.

Data on Rectangular-Shaped Pond

Width: _____ feet

Length: _____ feet

Area: _____ square feet

Irregular-Shaped Pond
1. Using the string, take several width measurement of the pond.
2. When finished, add the widths and divide your answer by the number of measurements taken to find the average width.
3. Measure the length of the pond using the string.
4. Multiply the width times the length to find the area.

Data on Irregular-Shaped Pond

Average Width: _____ feet

Average Length: _____ feet

Area: _____ square feet

MEASURING THE POND TEMPERATURE

1. Using a thermometer, take the temperature of the water in at least four places around a circular pond or on each side of a rectangular pond. Record the temperatures.
2. When finished, add the measurements together and then divide by the number of measurements taken to find the average temperature.

Temperature #1 = _____° F

Temperature #2 = _____° F

Temperature #3 = _____° F

Temperature #4 = _____° F

(Total) _____ ÷ 4 = _____° F (Average)

IDENTIFYING POND RESIDENTS

1. Using the scoop net, scrape the bottom of the pond and bring up the mud, rock, algae, plant material, and animals collected in the net.
2. Quickly put the material into the plastic tub.
3. Use the wash bottle to squirt water onto the material, washing it from the bottom of the rocks into the tub.
4. Carefully inspect the material in the tub for macroinvertebrates, or animals that you can see without the aid of a microscope.
5. Using a reference book, try to identify the specimens.
6. Using a magnifying lens, look at the plants and animals that you have collected. Draw them on the back of this page and label them appropriately.
7. Put some of the mud from the bottom of the pond under the hand lens and draw anything that you recognize as plant or animal material.

Directions: Answer the questions.

1. How many indicators of good water did you find? How many indicating poor water?

_____

_____

_____

2. Given the materials you were able to find in the pond, is the water in the pond in good or in poor health?

_____

Environment

Life on a Rotting Log

The forest community is not limited to animals and plants that live in or near living trees. As the succession of the forest continues, many trees will die and fall to the ground. The actions of plants, animals, bacteria, lichens, and weather help break the dead log down and return its components to the forest soil.

Directions: Answer the following questions.

1. List the different kinds of plant life that are found on the rotting log. _____

   _____

2. How do the small plants help the log decay? _____

   _____

3. How do the plants benefit from the log? _____

   _____

4. What kinds of small animals are found in or on the rotting log? _____

   _____

5. How do these animals help the log decay? _____

   _____

The lichen found on the rotting log is an interesting type of plant. It is actually made up of two organisms living together in symbiosis. What two organisms form a lichen? What does each of these organisms need to live? How do the organisms help each other?

_____

_____

_____

_____

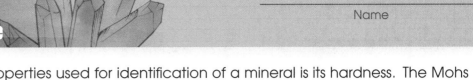

Mohs Hardness Scale

One of the most useful properties used for identification of a mineral is its hardness. The Mohs hardness scale measures a mineral's hardness by means of a simple scratch test.

Directions: Name the mineral that belongs in each step of the Mohs Hardness Scale chart.

WORD BANK
talc   diamond   gypsum   corundum
calcite   topaz   fluorite   quartz
apatite   feldspar/orthoclase

MOHS HARDNESS SCALE		
HARDNESS	**MINERAL**	**COMMON TESTS**
1		Fingernail will scratch it.
2		
3		Fingernail will not scratch it; a copper penny will.
4		Knife blade or window glass will scratch it.
5		
6		Will scratch a steel knife or window glass.
7		
8		
9		
10		Will scratch all common materials.

Name That Mineral

Name

One can identify many minerals by carefully observing their physical characteristics. Some of these characteristics are:

Hardness—This is determined with a scratch test.

Color—Color depends on the substances that make up the crystals. Varies greatly.

Luster—This refers to how light reflects off the mineral.

Directions: Enough information has been given to you here to help you find the unknown minerals and fill in the chart.

MOHS HARDNESS SCALE		
HARDNESS	MINERAL	COMMON TESTS
1	Talc	Fingernail will scratch it.
2	Gypsum/Kaolinite	
3	Mica/Calcite	Copper penny will scratch it.
4	Fluorite	Knife blade or window glass will scratch it.
5	Apatite/Hornblende	
6	Feldspar	Will scratch a steel knife or window glass.
7	Quartz	
8	Topaz	
9	Corundum	
10	Diamond	Will scratch all common materials.

COLOR	MINERAL
White	Quartz, Feldspar, Calcite, Kaolinite, Talc
Yellow	Quartz, Kaolinite
Black	Hornblende, Mica
Gray	Feldspar, Gypsum
Colorless	Quartz, Calcite, Gysum

LUSTER	MINERAL
Glassy	Quartz, Feldspar, Hornblende
Pearly	Mica, Gypsum, Talc
Dull	Kaolinite

The Unknown Minerals

HARDNESS	COLOR	LUSTER	MINERAL
Will scratch a steel knife or window glass.	yellow	glassy	
Will scratch a steel knife or window glass.	gray	glassy	
A copper penny will scratch it.	black	pearly	
Fingernail will scratch it.	white	pearly	
Knife blade or window glass will scratch it.	black	glassy	

Classy Rocks

There are three main groups of rock: **igneous** rock, **metamorphic** rock, and **sedimentary** rock. Each of the rocks pictured on this page belongs to one of these groups.

Directions: Fill in the definitions. Then, in the space below each picture, tell which group each rock belongs to.

 WORD BANK   layers of loose material which solidified
cooled magma
rock that has been changed into a new rock

KIND OF ROCK	DEFINITION
Igneous	
Metamorphic	
Sedimentary	

granite

gneiss

limestone

sandstone

_____

marble

shale

basalt

_____

slate

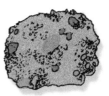

obsidian

conglomerate

_____

Mineral Identifications

Minerals are the most common solid materials found on the earth. Minerals may vary in the way they feel and look. Some identifying characteristics of minerals are listed below.

Directions: Use your text and reference materials to complete the mineral chart.

MINERAL	HARDNESS	SPECIFIC GRAVITY	STREAK COLOR	LUSTER
Siderite	3.5–4		white	
Gypsum		2.32		vitreous
Kaolinite			white	dull
Halite	2.5		white	
Fluorite		3–3.3		glassy
Calcite	3	2.7		
Barite		4.3–4.6	white	
Pyrite	6–6.5		green-black	
Galena		7.4–7.6		metallic
Magnetite			black	
Topaz			colorless	glassy

The hardness of a mineral is measured by its ability to be scratched. Some identification tests can be made using common items.

Hardness

0–2.5	Mineral can be scratched by one's fingernail.
3	Mineral can be scratched by a copper penny.
5.5	Mineral can be scratched with a knife but not a penny.
5.5–6.5	Mineral will scratch glass.
6.5	Mineral can be scratched slightly with a file.
above 6.5	Mineral cannot be scratched with a file.

1. Which of the minerals above can be scratched by one's fingernail? _____

_____

2. Which of the minerals above can be scratched by a copper penny?

_____

3. Which of the minerals above will scratch glass? _____

_____

4. Which of the minerals above cannot be scratched by a file? _____

_____

Directions: Use what you have learned about rocks and minerals to complete this puzzle.

WORD BANK

hardness	crystal	streak
gem	cleavage	texture
fracture	luster	mineral

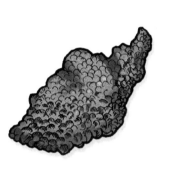

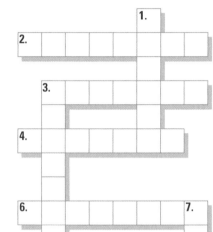

ACROSS

2. An uneven break
3. Substance with 3-dimensional plane faces
4. Feel of a surface when rubbed
6. Measured with Mohs Scale
8. Quartz is an example of a _____.

DOWN

1. Light reflected from a mineral's surface
3. Smooth break in a mineral
5. Large mineral crystal with brilliant color
7. A _____ test shows the color of a mineral when it is rubbed into a fine powder.

Rock Crystals

PURPOSE How are crystals formed in the earth?

MATERIALS

- hot, salty water
- nail
- empty jar
- pencil
- 12 inches of string

INFORMATION

Salt is a natural mineral that is found in the ground and in the ocean. Salt dissolves in water. If you heat water, it can be forced to dissolve more salt than it usually can. This is called *supersaturation*. If you then let the water cool, the salt will reappear as crystals. In this activity, you will grow those crystals on the nail and string over a period of about 10 days.

PREDICTION On your record sheet, predict how long you think it will take to grow crystals using salt water, a nail, and a glass jar.

PROCEDURE

1. Have an adult help you pour the hot, salty water into the jar.
2. Tie the nail onto the string. Tie the other end of the string onto the pencil.
3. Lay the pencil across the mouth of the jar so that the nail is suspended in the middle of the water.
4. Leave the jar undisturbed for 10 days.

RESULTS After 10 days, observe the contents in the jar. On your record sheet, draw a picture of what is in the jar.

CONCLUSIONS

Answer the following questions on your record sheet: What other crystals can you think of that will dissolve in water?

Can you think of any crystals that are valuable to people? Why are they valuable?

Rock Crystals Record Sheet

Name

QUESTION   How are crystals formed in the earth?

PREDICTION   How long do you think it will
take to grow crystals using salt water, a nail, and a glass jar?

_____

RESULTS   After 10 days, observe the contents in the jar.
In the box below, draw a picture of what is in the jar.

```
[                                                            ]
[                                                            ]
[                                                            ]
[                                                            ]
[                                                            ]
[                                                            ]
[                                                            ]
[                                                            ]
[                                                            ]
```

CONCLUSIONS

What other crystals can you think of that will dissolve in water?_____

_____

Can you think of any crystals that are valuable to people? Why are they valuable?

_____

_____

_____

Erosion by Glaciers

PURPOSE

- Explain how rock particles embedded in moving ice are responsible for most glacial erosion.
- Identify types of evidences that glaciers have been involved in erosion.
- Speculate on factors that can affect the rates of erosion by glacial action.

MATERIALS

- very large tray
- sand and pebble mixture
- large soap bars
- ice cubes

SETUP

To prepare for the activity, have an adult cut the soap into thin slices. Chill the slices to ensure that the soap will be hard, not soft and sticky.

PROCEDURE

1. On the bottom of the tray, arrange the soap slices to cover one end.
2. Cover the rest of the tray with the sand and pebble mixture.
3. While pushing down on an ice cube, move the ice cube across the sand and pebble mixture to and across the soap slices.
4. Observe the bottom side of the ice cube.
5. Observe the top side of the soap slices.

QUESTIONS

1. What changes did you observe in the bottom surface of the ice from the beginning of the demonstration to the end of the demonstration?

   _____

2. What is the shape of the path left by the ice? Are the sides of the path steep like a "U" or shallow like a "V"?

   _____

3. What is the evidence left behind on the surface of the soap that the model of a glacier had passed?

   _____

4. Would the results differ if there was a change to the amount of downward pressure exerted on the ice?

   _____

5. What evidence in real rocks can be found that a glacier had passed? _____

6. How would repeated advances and retreats by glaciers affect the geology of a region?

   _____

Glaciers

Name

Glaciers are thick masses of ice created by the accumulation and crystallization of snow.

Directions: Match the clues about glaciers with the terms below.

1. _____ VALLEY GLACIER

2. _____ CIRQUE

3. _____ CONTINENTAL GLACIER

4. _____ CREVASSE

5. _____ DRUMLIN

6. _____ END MORAINE

7. _____ ESKER

8. _____ FIORD

9. _____ KETTLE

10. _____ PLUCKING

11. _____ ROCK FLOUR

12. _____ SURGE

13. _____ TARN

14. _____ TILL

A. Material deposited directly by a glacier

B. Glacier generally confined to mountain valleys

C. A crack in the glacier caused by movement

D. Rapid movement of a glacier

E. The process whereby a glacier loosens and lifts rocks into the ice

F. Pulverized rock caused by a glacier's abrasion

G. A bowl-shaped depression at the head of a glacial valley

H. A small lake formed after a glacier has melted away

I. A U-shaped depression formed by a glacier below sea level in a river valley that is flooded by the ocean

J. Massive accumulations of ice that cover a large portion of a landmass

K. A hilly ridge of material formed at the end of a valley glacier

L. An oval-shaped hill consisting of rock debris

M. A depression left in part of a glacier formed by the melting of a block of ice

N. Ridges of sand and gravel deposited by flowing rivers of melted ice through a glacier

Fossil Models

A fossil is the remains of plants and animals preserved in rock. Some of these plants and animals lived millions of years ago.

Directions: Try making some models of fossils.

MATERIALS

- assorted shells
- nonhardening clay
- spoon
- two-liter plastic soda bottle with its top cut off
- petroleum jelly
- plaster
- toothpick
- baby powder
- water

PROCEDURE

1. Select a shell. Place a small amount of petroleum jelly on the shell and spread it evenly over the surface.

2. Make a ball of clay slightly bigger than the shell. Push the shell into the clay firmly and then remove it carefully. Set the shell aside. Place a small amount of baby powder in the impression left by the shell. Let an adult know that you are ready for the plaster.

3. After an adult puts the plaster in the impression, tap the clay slightly to remove air bubbles. Let the plaster harden slightly and use the toothpick to write your initials. Let the clay and plaster dry overnight.

4. The next day, carefully remove the plaster from the clay. Compare the shell, clay impression, and the plaster.

Draw a picture of your fossils.

The earth has four layers.

Directions: Color the layers of the earth and the key.

WATER

LAND

CRUST (5 – 20 mi thick)

MANTLE (1,800 mi thick)

OUTER CORE (1,400 mi thick)

INNER CORE (800 mi thick)

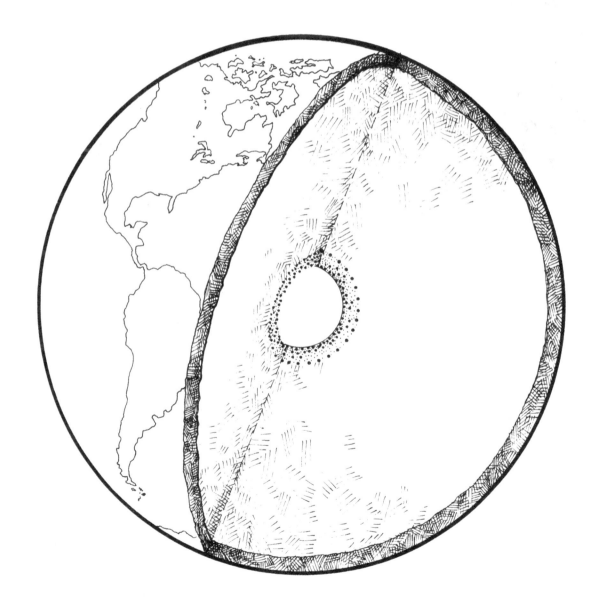

The Layered Look

Name

Do you have an apple at home? Ask an adult to cut it open. What do you see? The apple has layers. The top layer is the peel. It is thin but tough and protects the fruit. The next layer is the fruit. It can be soft or hard and most of the apple is the fruit. The inside layer is the core. It is harder than the rest of the apple and protects the seeds that are in the center.

The earth is very much like the apple. It has four layers. The outer layer is the **crust**. It is solid rock. The rock is from 5 to 20 miles thick, and is thicker underneath the continents. The next layer is called the **mantle**. It is the thickest layer, about 1,800 miles thick and made up of rock. This rock may move because of the high temperatures and great pressure found there. The third layer is the **outer core**. It is liquid, or melted iron. This layer is about 1,400 miles thick. The innermost layer is the **inner core**. It is made of iron and nickel. It is extremely hot, reaching temperatures of more than 9,000°F. This is a solid mass of rock and is about 800 miles thick.

Directions: Label the layers of the earth. Then, answer the questions.

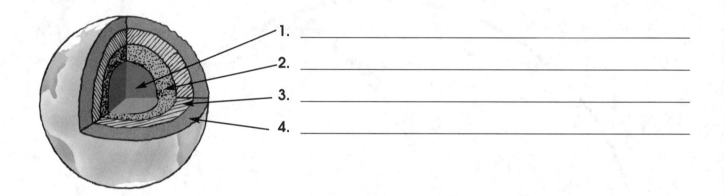

1. _____

2. _____

3. _____

4. _____

5. Which layer of the earth do you think shows the most evidence of an earthquake?

_____

_____

6. How do you think scientists find out about the inner cores of the earth?

_____

_____

Molten Rocks

There are three main classes of rocks. **Sedimentary** and **metamorphic** are two classes. The other class of rocks in the earth's crust formed from cooled lava, or **magma**. The lava came to the surface of earth, and the magma solidified.

Directions: To find out this last class of rocks, correctly fit the rocks listed below into the spaces. The circled letters will spell out the other class of rocks to which all of these rocks belong.

WORD BANK

basalt   diorite
feldspar   granite
obsidian   olivine
quartz

1. ___ ___ (___) ___ ___ ___ ___

2. (___) ___ ___ ___ ___ ___ ___ ___

3. ___ ___ ___ ___ (___) ___ ___

4. ___ (___) ___ ___ ___ ___ ___

5. ___ (___) ___ ___ ___ ___

6. ___ (___) ___ ___ ___

7. ___ (___) ___ ___ ___

8. Class of rocks: ___ ___ ___ ___ ___ ___ ___

9. Use a reference book to identify some of the major uses of these rocks.

_____

_____

_____

10. Where are these rocks found in the world?

_____

_____

_____

Five Types of Mountains

Geologists classify mountains into five basic types: dome, fold, fault-block, volcanic, and erosion.

Directions: Make a sketch of each type below. You may wish to use an atlas to help you.

DOME MOUNTAINS
Black Hills of South Dakota
Weald Mountains in England

FOLD MOUNTAINS
Appalachian Mountains in the eastern U.S.
Alps in Europe, Himalayas of Asia

FAULT-BLOCK MOUNTAINS
Teton Range in Wyoming
Wasatch Range in Utah
Harz Mountains in Germany

VOLCANIC MOUNTAINS
Mount St. Helens in Washington
Mount Fuji in Japan

EROSION MOUNTAINS
Catskill Mountains in New York

Name _____

A volcano is an opening in the earth's surface through which gases, lava, and ash erupt.

Directions: To learn more about volcanoes, complete the crossword puzzle below.

WORD BANK

caldera
cone
crater
dike
dormant
extinct
geyser
lava
magma
Mt. St. Helens
pumice
pyroclastics
ring of fire
shield
strato
tsunami
vent

ACROSS

2. A large crater formed by the collapse of an overlying volcanic cone

5. The range around the Pacific Ocean where volcanoes mainly occur

8. Fluid rock that pours from a volcano

9. A volcano that is not erupting and is not likely to erupt in the future

11. A composite volcano composed of alternating layers of lava and pyroclastic material

12. Type of volcano that has a broad profile, such as Mauna Loa and Mauna Kea

14. The volcano that erupted in the state of Washington in 1980

15. A large seismic sea wave caused by a volcanic eruption or earthquake

16. Groundwater which can be heated by volcanic activity and produces a hot-water fountain that spouts, such as Old Faithful

DOWN

1. An opening in the earth's surface through which gases and lava may escape

3. An inactive volcano which is likely to erupt in the future

4. Depression which can be caused by the collapse of a volcano

6. Various-sized particles ejected by a volcano

7. A body of molten rock injected into a fissure in the earth

10. A cinder _____ volcano is one that has a conical shape and is composed mostly of cinder-sized pyroclastics.

13. A light, glassy rock formed from a frothy lava

14. Molten rock inside the earth

Name

The earth's crust is made of rigid plates that are always moving. The boundaries of some of these plates are along the edges of the continents, while others are in the middle of the ocean. The map on this page shows the major plates near North and South America.

Directions: Using an encyclopedia or some other source, label the eight plates pictured below.

 WORD BANK

Gorda Plate   North American Plate   Cocos Plate
Pacific Plate   South American Plate   Nazca Plate
Antarctic Plate   Caribbean Plate

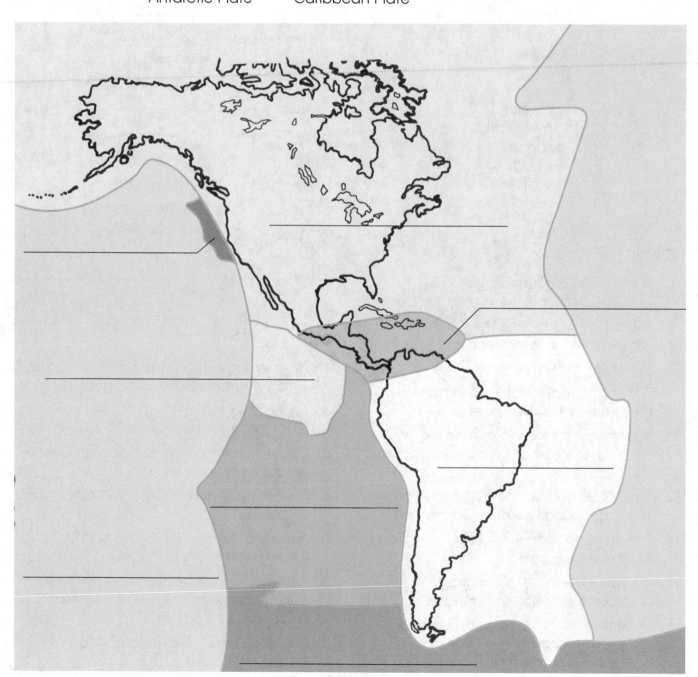

According to the theory of plate tectonics, the earth's crust is broken into about twenty plates. These **plates** are slowly moving. The edges of some of these plates are moving toward each other. A **trench** is formed when one plate bends and dives under another. These diving edges then descends into the earth's hot **mantle** and starts melting into **magma**. The magma can then rise and break through the earth's crust and burst out of a **volcano**. The edge of the above-riding plate crumples, resulting in a mountain range.

Directions: Label the diagram below.

WORD BANK

| volcano | ocean | trench | magma |
| continent | descending plate | above-riding plate | |

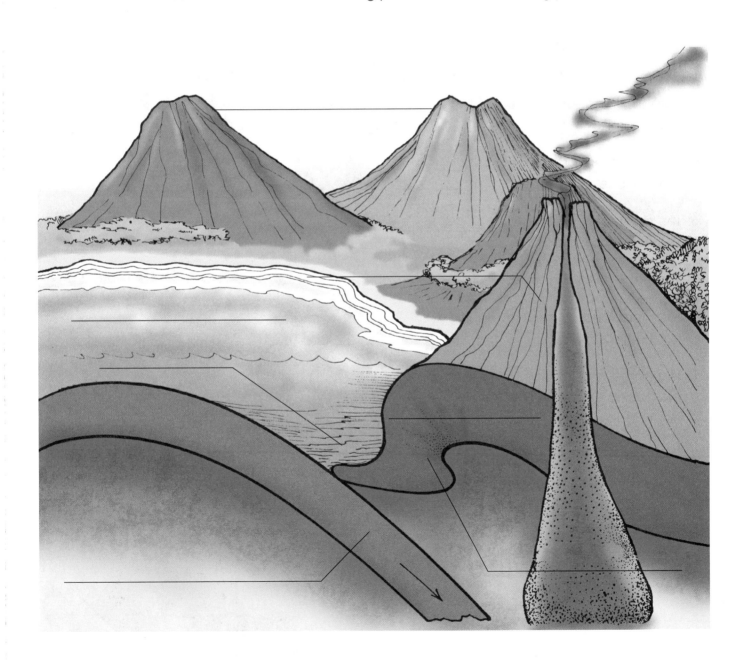

Name _____

An earthquake is a sudden shock of the earth's surface.

Directions: Identify the name of the study of earthquakes by reading the clues below and writing the answers. The circled letters will spell out the name of this science. Print the name at the bottom of the page.

1. Large ocean waves created by an earthquake

 __ ◯ __ __ __ __

2. These waves, created by the earthquake, are the strongest at the epicenter.

 __ ◯ __ __ __ __

3. The area on the surface of the earth directly above the occurrence of the earthquake

 __ __ ◯ __ __ __ __

4. Famous earthquake fault in California

 ◯ __ __ __ __ __ __

5. The instrument used to record earthquake waves

 __ __ __ __ ◯ __ __ __ __

6. The origin of an earthquake under the surface of the earth

 __ ◯ __ __ __

7. A breaking point in layers of the earth

 __ __ __ ◯ __

8. The vibrational tremors sent out from an earthquake

 __ __ ◯ __ __ __ __ __

9. The name given to the area around the Pacific Ocean in which many earthquakes occur

 __ __ __ ◯ __ __ __ __

10. The fastest waves from an earthquake; also called push waves

 __ __ __ __ __ ◯

The science of the study of earthquakes is

__ __ __ __ __ __ __ __ __ __ .

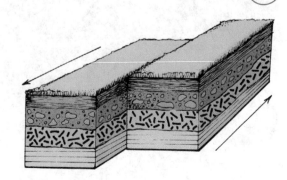

An earthquake is the sudden shaking of the ground that occurs when masses of rock change positions below the earth's surface.

Directions: Learn more about earthquakes by reading the clues below. Locate the term in the magic square that matches each clue. Then, write the number of the clue in the space. By recording all of the correct numbers, you will have produced a magic square. When you add the numbers across, down, or diagonally, you should get the same answer. The four squares in each corner of the big square and the four squares in the center of the big square will also give you the same answer when added together.

fault	San Francisco	strike-slip fault	focus
_____	_____	_____	_____
normal fault	**Richter scale**	**primary waves**	**Buffalo, NY**
_____	_____	_____	_____
secondary waves	**surface waves**	**oil and fossils**	**epicenter**
_____	_____	_____	_____
reverse fault	**San Andreas Fault**	**seismograph**	**seismologist**
_____	_____	_____	_____

1. A fracture within the earth where rock movement occurs
2. An instrument used to measure earthquakes
3. A large fault in California
4. The point in the earth where seismic waves originate
5. The point on the earth's surface directly above the focus
6. A numerical scale used to express the strength of an earthquake
7. Seismic waves from the focus that are compressional
8. Seismic waves from the focus that are perpendicular to this motion
9. Location of the National Center for Earthquake Engineering Research
10. The most powerful shock waves from an earthquake
11. Sometimes located in the earth by seismic waves from explosions
12. Rock above a fault that moves downward
13. Rock above a fault that moves upward
14. Rocks that move in opposite horizontal directions
15. City which had major earthquakes in 1906 and 1989
16. Scientist who studies earthquakes

Name _____

The largest earthquake in the United States occurred in the winter of 1811–1812 in an area along the New Madrid Fault. Use the map of the United States on page 207, a ruler, a thumbtack, a piece of corrugated cardboard, a 15 in. piece of string, and a pencil to locate the New Madrid Fault.

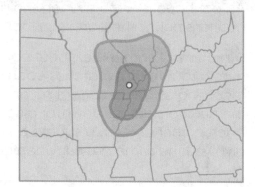

1. Place the map on a piece of corrugated cardboard.

2. Locate the following cities on the map: San Francisco, El Paso, Miami, Chicago, Atlanta, and Denver.

3. Calculate the actual distance in miles for each city below by using the scale, 1 inch=390 miles. The distances between the New Madrid Fault and the cities listed are below.

a. San Francisco	5 inches	_____	miles
b. El Paso	3 inches	_____	miles
c. Miami	$2\frac{1}{2}$ inches	_____	miles
d. Chicago	1 inches	_____	miles
e. Atlanta	1 inches	_____	miles
f. Denver	2 inches	_____	miles

4. Using the ruler, measure 5 inches east from San Francisco. Mark the distance using the pencil. Make a loop in the string, place the pencil in the loop, and hold the tip of the pencil on the mark you have made. Stretch the string to San Francisco and attach the string using the thumbtack. Draw a large arc on the paper using the pencil.

5. Repeat the measurements and sketches with the other five cities. Make sure the arcs you draw are large from top to bottom.

6. The location of the New Madrid Fault is the area where the six arcs seem to cross or intersect.

In what state is the New Madrid Fault located? _____

Which cities in the U.S. would be greatly affected by an earthquake in this region today?

_____

_____

Name _____

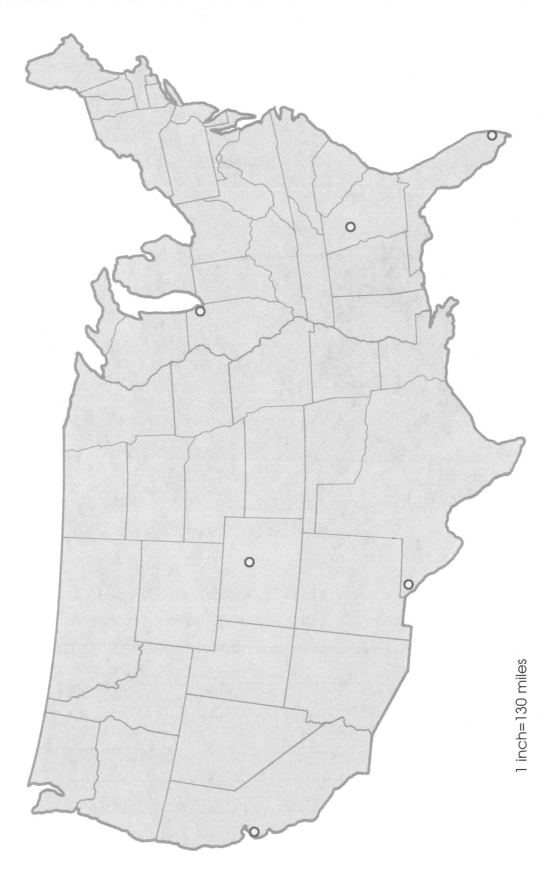

1 inch=130 miles

Geology

U.S. Climate Zones

The word **climate** is used to describe the weather in a particular place over a long period of time. Because the United States covers such a large area, it has a number of different climate zones. Some areas have long, cold winters and short, cool summers, while other areas are warm in both summer and winter.

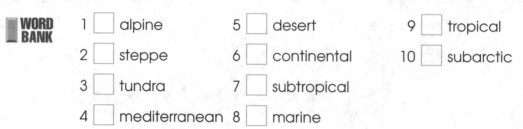

WORD BANK

1 ☐ alpine   5 ☐ desert   9 ☐ tropical

2 ☐ steppe   6 ☐ continental   10 ☐ subarctic

3 ☐ tundra   7 ☐ subtropical

4 ☐ mediterranean   8 ☐ marine

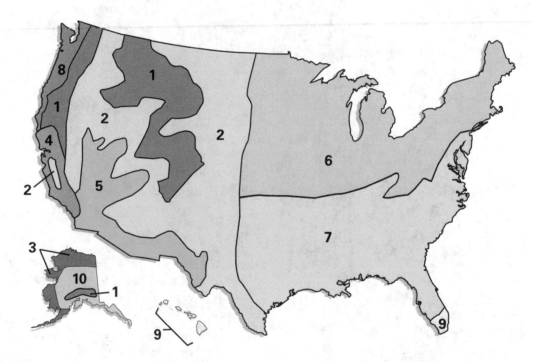

Directions: Choose colors to color-code the Map Key and the climate zone map. Then, determine the . . .

climate zone you live in. _____

climate zone of the Northeast. _____

climate zone of the Rocky Mountains. _____

climate zones found in Alaska. _____

climate zones found in Texas. _____

climate zones of Florida. _____

climate zone of Michigan. _____

Balloon Barometer

Make a barometer to measure air pressure.

MATERIALS

- medium to large balloon
- strong glue
- wide-mouth container such as a coffee can
- broom straw
- heavy rubber band
- sheet of unlined paper

Directions:

1. Inflate and deflate the balloon to stretch it out. Cut out a piece of balloon large enough to cover the mouth of the can. Secure with a rubber band.

2. Attach one end of the straw to the center of the balloon piece with glue so the straw is lying on its side.

3. Fold the paper and stand it upright. Move the can next to the paper with the straw lightly against it. Put a red mark exactly where the straw touches. Record the location of the straw three times a day for five days. Label each mark with a symbol to indicate the time of day.

Directions: Keep a chart of the barometric pressure observations and the weather conditions. Look for relationships.

1. Were there any relationships between the readings and the weather?

   _____

2. Can you think of a way to improve the design of the barometer? Describe.

   _____

	First Reading Time: _____	Second Reading Time: _____	Third Reading Time: _____	Weather Report
BAROMETER READING				
Day 1				
Day 2				
Day 3				
Day 4				
Day 5				

Warm and Cold Front Movement

PURPOSE
• Investigate the effect of temperature on the relative densities of a fluid.
• Apply this knowledge in the construction of a model of two types of weather fronts.
• Define the terms **cold front** and **warm front**.
• Explain the differences between the characteristics of cold and warm fronts.

MATERIALS
• plastic shoe box
• wood block
• ice
• hot plate

• 2-8 oz. beakers
• tongs
• thermometer
• red and blue food coloring

• long neck funnel
• water
• dishpan

PROCEDURE
Note: This investigation can be demonstrated by an adult or by older responsible students with adult supervision. It is important to allow the water to become room temperature.

PROCEDURE
Assemble the plastic shoe box and wood block as shown in the diagram. Fill the plastic shoe box about one-quarter full of water.

1. Record the temperature of the water: _____ °F.

2. Prepare the two beakers:
   • Pour about 6 oz. of water into each beaker.
   • Put several drops of red food coloring into one beaker.
   • Add several drops of blue in the other beaker.

3. Place the red water beaker on a hot plate. Place the blue water beaker into the container of ice.

4. Allow the temperature of the cold water to fall about 15 degrees.

   • Record the final temperature: _____ °F.

5. Pour the cold water into a long neck funnel that extends to the bottom of the shallow end of the plastic shoe box.

6. Describe how the cold water moves:_____

   _____

7. Allow the temperature of the warm water to rise about 15 degrees.

   • Record the final temperature: _____ °F.

8. Using tongs to avoid touching the hot beaker, gently pour the warm water into the long neck funnel placed at the shallow end of the plastic shoe box.

9. Describe how the warm water moves: _____

Directions: Answer the questions based on what you observed in the experiment.

1. Which colored water is more dense than the room temperature water? How do you know?

   _____

   _____

2. Which colored water is less dense than the room temperature water? How do you know?

   _____

   _____

3. Cold fronts are named for the cold air that replaces warmer air. Is the red water or the blue water demonstration more like a cold front?

   _____

   _____

4. Warm fronts are named for the warm air that replaces cooler air. Is the red water or the blue water demonstration more like warm air trying to push cold air out of the way?

   _____

   _____

5. Was the blue water or red water in contact with the bottom of the container more quickly?

   _____

   _____

6. If the water is like air, and the bottom of the container is like the earth's surface, which kind of air, warm or cold, affects the surface of the earth more quickly?

   _____

   _____

7. Would cold fronts or warm fronts affect the weather more quickly?

   _____

   _____

8. Can you explain the differences between a cold front and a warm front in terms of density and rate of weather changes?

   _____

   _____

Predicting the Weather With Wind and Air Pressure

WIND DIR.	BAROMETER READING	GENERAL WEATHER FORECAST
SW to NW	30.10 and above—steady	Fair, with little temperature change.
SW to NW	30.10 to 30.20—rising rapidly	Fair, followed within 2 days by rain.
SW to NW	30.20 and above—falling slowly	Fair and slowly rising temperature for 2 days.
S to SE	30.10 to 30.20—falling slowly	Rain within 24 hours.
S to SE	30.10 to 30.20—falling rapidly	Increasing wind; rain in 12-24 hours.
SE to NE	30.10 to 30.20—falling slowly	Increasing wind; rain in 12-18 hours.
SE to NE	30.10 to 30.20—falling rapidly	Increasing wind; rain within 12 hours.
E to NE	30.10 and above—falling slowly	Summer: rain in 2 to 4 days. Winter: rain or snow within 24 hours.
E to NE	30.10 and above—falling rapidly	Summer: rain in 12-24 hours. Winter: rain or snow, with increasing winds, within 24 hours.
SE to NE	30.00 or below—falling slowly	Rain will continue for 1 to 2 days.
SE to NE	30.00 or below—falling rapidly	Rain (or snow) with high wind; then clearing (and colder in winter) within 36 hours.
S to SW	30.00 or below—rising slowly	Clearing within a few hours.
S to E	29.80 or below—falling rapidly	Severe storm within a few hours, followed within 24 hours by colder weather.
E to N	29.80 or below—falling rapidly	Severe NE gale with heavy precipitation. In winter, heavy snow followed by cold wave.
Going to W	29.80 or below—rising rapidly	End of storm—clearing and colder.

NOTE: A rapid rise or fall is 0.05 to 0.09 inches or more in 3 hours; a slow rise or fall is less than 0.05 inches in 3 hours.

Name _____

Directions: To answer the following questions, refer to the chart "Predicting the Weather With Wind and Air Pressure" on page 212.

1. The wind is S to SE. The barometer is at 30.10 and has been falling slowly. What's your prediction?

   _____

2. The wind is SE to NE. _____ The barometer is at 30.10 and has been falling slowly. What's your prediction?

   _____

3. The wind is SE to NE. _____ The barometer is at 30.00 and is falling rapidly. What would you predict if this happened in June? _____
   What would you predict if this happened in December?

   _____

4. The wind is S to SW. The barometer is at 29.80 and has been rising rapidly. What's your prediction?

   _____

5. It is stormy. Now the wind is shifting to the west. The barometer is at 29.80 and is rising rapidly. What's your prediction?

   _____

6. In general, barometer readings of 30.10 and above that are steady or rising mean (circle the correct answer)

       fair weather   it's raining   severe storms

7. In general, barometer readings of 30.10 and above that are falling mean (circle the correct answer)

       rain may be on the way   it's raining   severe storms

8. In general, barometer readings between 30.00 and 29.80 that are falling mean (circle the correct answer)

       fair weather   it's raining   severe storms

9. In general, barometer readings of 29.80 and below that are falling mean (circle the correct answer)

       fair weather   it's raining   severe storms

10. When the barometer registers 30.10 at 10:00 A.M. and 30.02 at 1:00 P.M., the pressure is (circle the correct answer)

        falling slowly   rising rapidly   falling rapidly

Water, Water Everywhere

Directions: Make a shallow puddle of water in each plate. Trace each puddle with the same color to indicate its size. Number the plates and place them in three different areas: direct sun, complete dark, and in the center of the room.

Predict what will happen to the water in each plate:

Sun _____

Dark _____

Partly sunny _____

Check the puddles after one hour. Trace each puddle with the second color marker. Describe how the puddles have changed.

_____

_____

Check the puddles the next day. Trace each puddle with the third color marker. Draw pictures of your plates using the colors to show what happened.

SUN	DARK	PARTLY SUNNY

Which puddles shrank? _____

What do you think happened to the water? _____

_____

Why do you think the puddles shrank at different rates? _____

_____

What is the process called?   E __ __ __ O __ __ T __ __ __

What is it called when the air is full of water?   S__ __ __ __ __ __ __ D

In what three states does water exist? _____   _____   _____

Rain Maker

How is rain made?

MATERIALS   • jar of hot water   • ice cubes

PREDICTION   What do you think will happen when ice cubes are put on top of a jar of hot water?

_____

Draw two pictures of the jar of hot water—one as soon as the ice is placed on top and one after 5 minutes. Write your observations below.

OBSERVATIONS

1 minute _____

2 minutes _____

3 minutes_____

4 minutes_____

5 minutes_____

Why do you think the hot water and ice reacted the way they did? _____

_____

List some elements of the water cycle._____

_____

Explain the process of the water cycle. _____

_____

Cloud Words

The names of clouds come from Latin words that describe their appearance. Here are five words that are used alone or in combination to name the basic cloud types.

Cirrus   feathery (from Latin *cirrus*, meaning "curl, filament, tuft")

Cumulus   piled up (from Latin *cumulus*, meaning "heap, mass")

Stratus   sheet (from Latin *stratus*, meaning "stretched out, extended")

Nimbus   rain (from Latin *nimbus*, meaning "heavy rain; rain cloud")

Alto   high (from Latin *altus*, meaning "high")

The names of the ten basic cloud types use these words alone or in combination.

Directions: See if you can figure out what each of these clouds looks like from its name.

1. Cirrus clouds are _____

2. Cirrocumulus clouds are _____

3. Cirrostratus clouds are _____

4. Altocumulus clouds are _____

5. Altostratus clouds are _____

6. Nimbostratus clouds are _____

7. Stratus clouds are _____

8. Stratocumulus clouds are _____

9. Cumulus clouds are _____

10. Cumulonimbus clouds are _____

Name That Cloud

Directions: Using what you have learned about cloud shapes and altitudes, label the clouds in the chart below.

 WORD BANK

Altocumulus (Ac)	Cirrocumulus (Cc)	Cirrus (Ci)
Cumulus (Cu)	Stratocumulus (Sc)	Altostratus (As)
Cirrostratus (Cs)	Cumulonimbus (Cb)	Nimbostratus (Ns)
Stratus (St)		

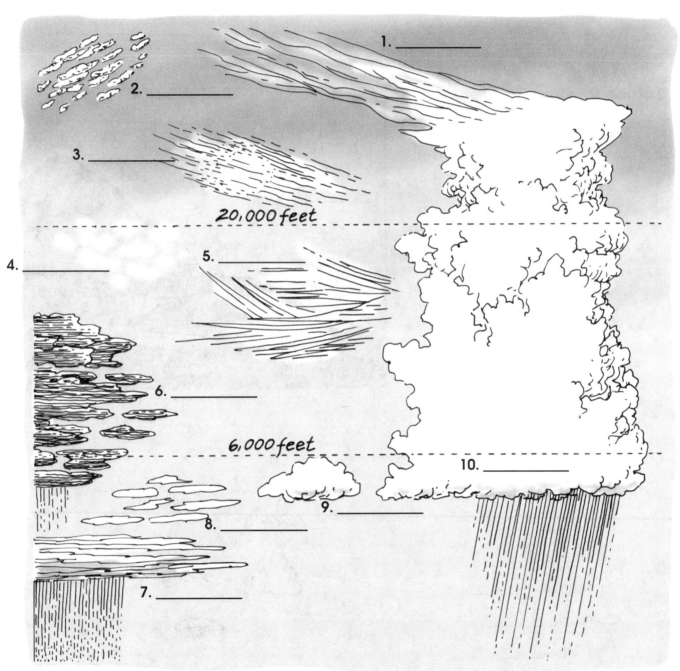

1. _____

2. _____

3. _____

20,000 feet

4. _____

5. _____

6. _____

6,000 feet

10. _____

9. _____

8. _____

7. _____

1. Draw a line between each type of cloud and the type of weather it will produce.

   Nimbus   Fair weather

   Cirrus   Thundershowers

   Cumulus   Rain

   Cumulonimbus   Fair, with rain possible within two days

2. Label the following parts of the water cycle model:

   Prevailing winds

   Clouds

   Rain

   Source of water vapor

3. In each blank below, write the level at which the cloud is found: high, middle, or low.

   Stratus_____

   Cirrus_____

   Cirrocumulus _____

   Cumulus _____

   Altostratus _____

Temperature Highs and Lows Around the World

Directions: Refer to a map of the world to answer the following questions.

1. Find Libya (which holds the world's high temperature record) on the map.
   Find Antarctica (which holds the world's low temperature record) on the map.

   Which one is closer to the equator? _____

2. What is the record high temperature in Alaska? _____

   What is the record low temperature in Alaska? _____

   What is the range of temperature—from record high to record low—in Alaska?

   _____

3. What is the record high temperature in Hawaii? _____

   What is the record low temperature in Hawaii? _____

   What is the range of temperature—from record high to record low—in Hawaii?

   _____

4. Does Hawaii or Alaska have a greater temperature range? _____

   Give two reasons why Hawaii and Alaska have different temperature ranges. _____

   _____

   _____

   _____

   _____

Precipitation Highs and Lows Around the World

RECORD RAINFALLS

Location	Amount (inches)	Record for	Date
1. Cherrapunji, India (25° N 91° E)	1,042	1 year (world)	Aug. 1860 – Aug. 1861
2. Mt. Waialeale, Kauai, Hawaii (22° N 159° W)	460	Annual average	Annual average
3. Cherrapunji, India (25° N 91° E)	366	1 month (world)	July 1861
4. Belouve, Reunion Island	53	12 hours (world)	Feb. 28, 1964
5. Alvin, Texas (29° N 95° W)	43	24 hours (U.S.)	July 25, 1979
6. Holt, Missouri (30° N 30° W)	12	42 minutes (world)	June 22, 1947
7. Unionville, Maryland (15° N 30° W)	1.2	1 minute (world)	July 4, 1956

RECORD SNOWFALLS

Location	Amount (inches)	Record for	Date
8. Paradise Ranger Station, Mt. Ranier, Washington (47° N 121° W)	1,122	1 year (U.S.)	1971- 1972
9. Tamarack, California (38° N 119° W)	390	1 month (world)	January 1911
10. Mt. Shasta Ski Bowl, California (41° N 122° W)	189	1 snowstorm (world)	Feb. 13 -19, 1959
11. Silverlake, Boulder Co., Colorado (40°N 105°W)	76	24 hours (world)	April 14 – 15, 1921

RECORD DRY SPOTS

Location	Amount (inches)	Record for	Date
12. Arica, Chile (18° N 70° W)	0.03	Lowest annual average rainfall (world)	Annual average
13. Bagdad, California (35° N 116° W)	0.0	Longest period without measurable precipitation (U.S.)	Aug. 1909 – May 1912 (933 days)

Name _____

Directions: Refer to a world map for help in answering the following questions.

1. Give two reasons why Hawaii and Reunion Island are the locations of rainfall records.

   _____

   _____

2. In what area of the United States have the record snowfalls occurred? _____

   _____

   Give two reasons for heavy snows in this area. _____

   _____

3. Locate the Sahara Desert. Give two reasons why there is so little precipitation there.

   _____

   _____

4. Look up *monsoon* in a dictionary or encyclopedia. Then, explain why Cherrapunji, India, holds world records for rainfall.

   _____

   _____

   _____

   _____

   _____

   _____

   _____

Name _____

Below are words relating to weather.

Directions: Write the number of the word which fits a clue in a box on the grid. If you have matched the correct numbers in all 16 squares, the sums of the rows, columns, and diagonals will be the same. This is called a *magic square*.

1. atmosphere
2. troposphere
3. ionosphere
4. ozone

5. jet streams
6. stratosphere
7. mesosphere
8. exosphere

9. wind
10. greenhouse effect
11. convection
12. sea breeze

13. land breeze
14. doldrums
15. trade winds
16. front

mass of air that surrounds earth _____	air that rushes in from the north and south to warm the air along the equator _____	calm areas of earth where there is little wind _____	a gas in the upper part of earth's atmosphere _____
cold air from the ocean that moves into the warmer land _____	the zone of the atmosphere above the troposphere _____	the zone of the atmosphere above the stratosphere _____	a movement of air close to earth's surface _____
the outer zone of earth's atmosphere _____	air above earth that is warmed by the reflection of the sun's rays and is prevented from easily passing back into space _____	transfer of heat by currents of air or water _____	strong, steady winds high in the atmosphere; used by pilots _____
cold air from land that moves out to warmer air over oceans _____	zone of the atmosphere which affects the transmission of radio waves _____	the zone of the atmosphere which is closest to the surface of earth _____	the line along which air masses meet _____

What is the magic number for this puzzle? _____

Can you discover other number combinations in the puzzle which give you the same answer?

_____

_____

Symbol Sense

Forecasters use symbols to show others their weather predictions. These symbols are often used in television and newspaper forecasts. How well do you know these symbols?

Directions: The boxes below contain 12 standard weather symbols plus four "fake" symbols. At the bottom of the page are descriptions of the symbols, but there are two extra symbols. First, cross out the fake symbols. Then, match the real symbols with their correct labels by writing the number of each in a blank by its label. Finally, cross out the two extra symbols.

1.	2.	3.	4.
5.	6.	7.	8.
9.	10.	11.	12.
13.	14.	15.	16.

_____ A. thunderstorm

_____ B. fog

_____ C. calm

_____ D. missing data

_____ E. wind direction and speed

_____ F. drizzle

_____ G. warm front

_____ H. cold front

_____ I. 1/2 cloud

_____ J. snow

_____ K. no cloud

_____ L. rain shower

_____ M. mist

_____ N. high pressure system

Weather Instruments

Directions: Weather conditions are measured using standard instruments. Find out what some of these instruments are by using the clues below to unscramble the letters of each weather instrument. The circled letters will then spell the source of all weather conditions on earth.

1. an instrument carried aloft by a weather balloon to measure upper-level pressure, temperature, humidity, and winds

   O R I S E D N O D A   __ __ __ __ ◯ __ __ __ __

2. a type of radar that continuously measures the wind, moisture, and temperature of the upper atmosphere

   P L E D R O P   __ ◯ __ __ __ __ __

3. measures the ceiling or base height of cloud layers

   M O L I C E R E E T   __ __ __ ◯ __ __ __ __ __ __

4. measures precipitation in inches

   N A I R   A G G E U   __ ◯ __ __ __ __ __ __ __

5. measures the intensity of rainfall or snowfall

   A R D A R   __ __ __ __ ◯

6. measures surface wind speeds

   E M O N E R T A M E   __ __ __ __ __ __ ◯ __ __ __

7. measures wind direction

   E V A N   __ __ ◯ __

8. measures air pressure

   R O B E T E R A M   __ __ __ __ __ ◯ __ __

9. measures temperature

   T R O M E M T H E E R   __ __ __ ◯ __ __ __ __ __ __ __

10. a special thermometer that measures temperature continuously

    G E R M A P T H O R H   __ __ __ __ __ ◯ __ __ __ __

11. measures relative humidity, vapor pressure, and dew point

    G R O T R Y E M E H   __ ◯ __ __ __ __ __ __ __

Answer: __ __ __ __ __   __ __ __ __ __ __ __

Atmospheric Circulation

Directions: There are five zones of atmospheric circulation on earth. To find out what they are, begin with the letter D on the spiral and skip every other letter to spell out these five zones. Write the names of the zones in the spaces at the bottom of the page.

START ▶

D R O W L A D M R E U C M B S U T X R C A D S E T F E J R M L O I N
S A C I E L O I T N U G W E C A D S E T F E U S T E W Z E P D N A
P U R P E R V S H P O P N R G S W E U S T E Y L I A M R I N
R E Y E F V G A L I N L O I R S S V T E Y L I B A E S D
E L G I J E L S N H P O S R T S V T A E Y L B A E F C N
R U P Y R E I G J E L T G T L U M D E A F C S G S R
I S E D S N R I A W Z E P D O I N L M R A E T Y I
P U R Y E L G I J E R C E A T Y I L B A E S
S R E N S D S R I A W Z E P D O I N L M R

The five zones are: __ __ __ __ __ __ __ __

__ __ __ __ __   __ __ __ __ __

__ __ __ __ __ __ __ __ __ __   __ __ __ __ __ __ __ __ __ __

__ __ __ __ __ __ __ __ __ __ __

__ __ __ __ __ __ __ __

Stormy Weather

Directions: Below is a list of stormy weather words. Locate and circle these words in the grid. The words may be written up, down, forward, backward, or diagonally. Then, look for a hidden word that is a type of storm. Draw a box around this word.

WORD BANK

blizzard	cyclone	hail	hurricane
ice	lightning	monsoon	sandstorm
sleet	snow	squall	thunder
tornado	twister	waterspout	wind

```
D  N  A  S  M  Q  S  M  O  L  T  E  A  R  E
B  A  C  M  R  O  A  T  L  E  S  L  E  E  T
C  L  E  G  I  D  N  H  B  F  O  N  J  L  O
V  L  I  A  H  P  D  U  D  S  U  W  Y  Q  R
A  H  E  Z  T  L  S  N  O  C  F  G  I  H  N
D  J  L  G  Z  L  T  D  Q  S  U  N  P  N  A
N  Y  Z  W  K  A  O  E  A  R  W  I  X  V  D
I  E  G  C  H  U  R  R  I  C  A  N  E  B  O
W  J  L  P  N  Q  M  D  O  K  T  T  Q  E  R
H  N  R  I  U  S  X  V  W  S  E  H  W  N  T
M  O  Y  E  D  A  E  O  G  D  R  G  C  O  B
P  O  Z  F  T  H  N  I  K  M  S  I  N  L  J
R  S  V  Q  O  S  H  E  A  R  P  L  T  C  U
Z  N  X  A  D  W  I  Z  C  G  O  B  F  Y  E
J  O  L  I  N  P  R  W  K  M  U  H  E  C  I
Y  M  T  S  U  D  O  Z  T  A  T  Y  W  U  S
```

Write about an experience you have had in one of these storms.

_____

_____

_____

_____

_____

There is a lot to learn about weather. See how much you already know.

Directions: Place a **T** before each true statement below and on page 228 about weather. Place an **F** before each false statement about weather.

1. _____ Fog is a cloud at ground level.

2. _____ A barometer is used to measure wind speed.

3. _____ Storms in the Pacific Ocean are called *hurricanes*.

4. _____ Hail is frozen rain.

5. _____ A barometer reading usually rises sharply before a storm.

6. _____ The greatest amount of gas in the air is oxygen.

7. _____ The troposphere is the area of the atmosphere closest to earth.

8. _____ Hurricanes form over land.

9. _____ Hurricanes are named for men and women.

10. _____ Warm air can hold more water vapor than cold air.

11. _____ Sleet can be a mixture of rain and ice pellets.

12. _____ Acid rain forms when certain gases in the air mix with rain.

13. _____ Much of North America was covered with ice during the Ice Age.

14. _____ Dew is water vapor dropping from thunderstorms.

15. _____ Thunder is heard before the flash of lightning is seen.

16. _____ Lightning never hits tall trees.

17. _____ All life on earth exists in the ionosphere.

18. _____ The amount of water in the air is called *condensation*.

19. _____ Evaporation occurs when liquid water changes to water vapor.

20. _____ A scientist who specializes in weather is called an *archaeologist*.

21. _____ Jet streams are high-altitude belts of high-speed winds.

22. _____ Winds blow clockwise in high pressure areas north of the equator.

23. _____ Condensation is the changing of ice into snow.

24. _____ Tornadoes usually form over land.

25. _____ Weather conditions are caused by the sun, earth, water, and air.

26. _____ Weather usually moves from east to west in the United States.

27. _____ A wind vane measures the speed of the wind.

28. _____ A rapidly falling barometer indicates the approach of a storm.

29. _____ In an open field during lightning, always seek shelter under a tree.

30. _____ The hygrometer measures the amount of dust in the air.

31. _____ The highest layer of the atmosphere is called the *exosphere*.

32. _____ Water heats up and cools down faster than land.

33. _____ The boundary between air masses is called a *front*.

34. _____ The layer directly above the troposphere is called the *ionosphere*.

35. _____ Weather balloons carry instruments high into the atmosphere.

36. _____ The word RADAR stands for RAdio Detection And Range.

37. _____ A rain gauge measures the amount of rainfall.

38. _____ The National Meteorological Service is located in Miami, Florida.

39. _____ NOAA stands for National Oceanic and Atmospheric Administration.

40. _____ Weather predictions, such as "red sky at night," are called folklore.

41. _____ Computers are extremely helpful today in weather forecasting.

42. _____ GOES satellites send weather pictures that are shown on television.

43. _____ Radar signals will pick up precipitation but not clouds.

44. _____ A psychrometer measures the amount of snowfall in 24 hours.

What Do You Know About Tornadoes?

Tornadoes are the most violent of all storms. Test your knowledge about tornadoes.

Directions: Place a **T** before each true statement and an **F** before each false statement.

1. _____ Tornadoes occur only in the United States.

2. _____ Tornadoes are also called *cyclones*.

3. _____ In a tornado, the air spirals mostly vertically.

4. _____ The funnel cloud can be seen when it contains dust or debris.

5. _____ Tornadoes are very predictable.

6. _____ The central plains states experience the most tornadoes.

7. _____ If you are in a car during an approaching tornado, you should always try to outrun it.

8. _____ If you are in an open field during an approaching tornado, you should always seek a low-lying area and lie flat.

9. _____ You should take time to open all windows and doors during a tornado.

10. _____ Flying glass is a great danger in the home.

11. _____ Heavy rain and lightning often occur before and during a tornado.

12. _____ Most tornadoes last only a few seconds or minutes.

13. _____ A basement, utility room, or inside hallway are good places to seek shelter during a tornado.

14. _____ Intense cold fronts and squall lines create tornado conditions.

15. _____ A late afternoon calmness and a yellow sky are good warning signs that a tornado could occur.

16. _____ Tornadoes can skip or bounce from one site to another.

17. _____ Tornadoes can produce roaring sounds.

18. _____ Tornadoes over water are called *waterspouts*.

19. _____ The dark base cloud of tornado conditions is called the *wall cloud*.

20. _____ Most tornadoes hit small outlying cities rather than big cities.

21. _____ Fallen electric lines are an extreme danger after a tornado.

22. _____ A car is a very safe place during a tornado.

23. _____ The funnel of a tornado always touches the ground.

24. _____ Tornadoes always occur during the spring and summer.

Name _____

PURPOSE
Observe the vortex of a homemade tornado.

MATERIALS
- two clear two-liter soda bottles (from which labels have been removed)
- duct tape (or hot glue)
- water
- food coloring
- graduated cylinder

PROCEDURE

1. Pour 6 cups of water in one of the two-liter bottles.

2. Add three drops of blue food coloring to the bottle. Shake the bottle to mix the food coloring with the water.

3. Place the empty bottle upside down on top of the bottle with water and food coloring. Place the openings of the two bottles so that they are lined up evenly with each other. Use duct tape to secure the two bottles together. Make certain the seal is very tight. An alternative to taping is to hot glue the bottles together (see Figure 1).

4. Once the bottles are securely attached, hold the taped area with your left hand and place your right hand under the bottom of the bottle containing the liquid.

5. Invert the two bottles so that the bottle with water is now upside down on top of the empty bottle. Place the bottle system on the table.

6. You will see water begin to enter the empty bottle on the table. Move the top bottle around and around in a circular motion so that the water is making a swirling motion. Now hold the bottles steady. Notice what occurs.

7. Repeat step 6 two more times. Notice what occurs each time.

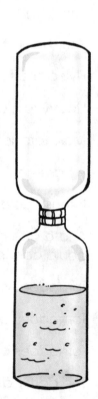

Figure 1: The empty bottle secured on top of the bottle with food coloring

Directions: Answer the following questions.

CONCLUSIONS

1. In a whirlpool, water moves in a pattern called a *vortex*. A vortex is created when water or air moves rapidly through a small opening. Explain the relationship between a tornado and a vortex.

   _____

   _____

   _____

2. In the atmosphere low pressure may get trapped beneath an area of high pressure. The low pressure then will find a weak spot and move up through the high pressure area. As it moves upward, the air takes on a violent, swirling vortex action. This is a tornado. Explain how this is different from what actually happened in lab today with your water in the bottle.

   _____

   _____

3. Explain how water draining from a bathtub simulates a vortex. _____

   _____

   _____

   _____

4. What types of weather patterns might cause the formation of a vortex? _____

   _____

   _____

   _____

5. Explain why you think tornadoes are called *funnel clouds*. _____

   _____

   _____

   _____

What's in a Name?

Read the brief history of the naming of hurricanes below. Then, place the hurricanes that follow in their proper time frame.

THE HISTORY OF NAMING HURRICANES IN AMERICA

Hurricanes that strike the Atlantic Basin are given names to expedite communication about their paths and development, but this was not always the case. Storms in early America were identified only by their latitude and longitude. The general names they were assigned which made reference to related events, places, or persons were created only after the storms had passed, so historians talk of the Charleston Hurricane of 1811 or the Benjamin Franklin Eclipse Hurricane, but those who lived through the storms knew them only by their locations.

Identifying a hurricane by its longitude and latitude became cumbersome and prone to error when radio communications and forecasting methods made it possible to warn residents of an approaching storm. So, air force and navy meteorologists began identifying storms with female names during World War II. Meteorologist Clement Wragge had already begun this tradition in Australia 50 years earlier, and author George R. Steward had, too, in his 1941 novel called *Storm*.

Still the United States weather services did not start naming storms until 1950, when they experimented with assigning names according to the phonetic alphabet (Able, Baker, Charlie, etc.). In 1953 they abandoned that failed experiment for the less confusing use of female names to identify hurricanes in America. In 1978 they added male names to the array.

Today, scientists have devised a six-year rotation of hurricane names. The first storm of a season takes on the name that begins with *A* for that year, the second storm takes on the name that begins with *B*, etc. Since the names cycle through a six-year rotation, the first four storms of the year 2000, for example, were called Alberto, Beryl, Chris, and Debby, just as the first four of 1994 were named. Once a hurricane has caused enormous damage, its name is retired and a new one takes its place.

Directions: Identify the proper time period for each of the following storms according to the name it claims. The first one has been done for you.

WORD BANK

Hurricane Easy	1860—Hurricane I	Hurricane Audrey
The Great Hurricane of 1780	Hurricane King	Hurricane George
Hurricane Hugo	Hurricane Able	Hurricane Mitch
The Late Gale at St. Joseph	Hurricane Hazel	Hurricane Eloise

BEFORE 1950	1950 – 1952	1952 – 1978	1978 – PRESENT
1860 – Hurricane I			

Directions: Use the words from the WORD BANK and the clues provided to complete the crossword puzzle of earthquake terminology. There is no space between two-word answers in the puzzle.

WORD BANK

tsunami
seismologist
aftershock
body wave
crust
epicenter
hypocenter
plate
seismic
fault
focus
foreshock
liquefaction
magnitude
scale
intensity

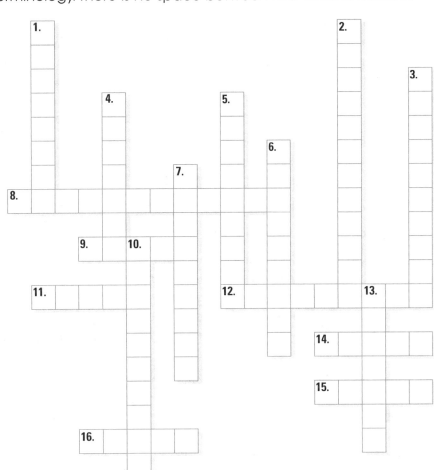

ACROSS

8. Scientist who studies earthquakes
9. The Richter _____ measures the magnitude of an earthquake.
11. The earth's outer layer
12. The point on the earth's surface directly above the hypocenter
14. A fracture in the earth's crust
15. A _____ boundary is where two or more tectonic plates meet.
16. Point where the quake originated

DOWN

1. A wave that travels through the interior of the earth
2. Soil acting like a liquid
3. Calculated location of the focus
4. A _____ belt is also known as an earthquake zone.
5. A measure of energy released from an earthquake
6. Measure of a quake's effects on humans and structures
7. Small tremor that precedes larger quake
10. A minor vibration that follows a larger quake
13. A huge sea wave

Defining Droughts

Directions: Drought is a relative term, and scientists do not agree on a single definition for the word. Read some of the drought definitions below and then answer the questions that follow.

DROUGHT DEFINITIONS

#1: Wayne Palmer of the National Weather Service devised a drought index that compares precipitation and stored soil moisture with evaporation and a region's requirements for moisture. According to a formula, the drought index defines a water balance between -2 and +2 as normal, a balance between -2 and -3 as a moderate drought, a balance between -3 and -4 as a severe drought, and a balance of 4 or below as an extreme drought.

#2: Scientists in Great Britain define an absolute drought as a period of 15 consecutive days in which each day received less than .01 inches of rain. They consider 29 consecutive days with a mean daily average rainfall less than .01 a partial drought.

#3: In India a drought is declared when the annual rainfall is 75% less than average.

#4: Libya does not declare a drought until it has experienced no rain for two years.

#5: The Swedish hydrologist Malin Falkenmark created the following definition of dry climates:
Aridity—permanently dry climate
Drought—irregularly dry climate
Desiccation—dry soils due to overgrazing and deforestation
Water Stress—water shortages due to a growing population relying on a fixed supply of run-off water

#6: One operational definition of drought categorizes a dry spell into its effects, defining a meteorological drought according to degree and duration of dryness, an agricultural drought as one that affects agriculture, a hydrological drought as one that affects the hydrologic system, and a socioeconomic drought as one that affects supply and demand of commodities necessary to human life.

_____ Which two definitions would be most helpful in directing national policy on agriculture and population growth?

_____ Which definition would be most helpful to scientists who wish to quantify drought seasons for comparative purposes?

_____ Which definition would probably be most simply explained to everyday citizens?

_____ Which definition considers dry conditions a drought only if those conditions are abnormal to a region?

_____ Which definition associates a specific quantity of rainfall with the term *drought*?

_____ Which definition considers how much rainfall an area needs in determining the existence of a drought?

_____ Which three definitions consider the length of a dry spell in their definitions of drought?

_____ Which definition considers the causes of a region's dry spells and water shortages?

Every three to seven years, the sea surface of the southeastern tropical Pacific warms to an unusually high temperature. Since ocean temperatures substantially affect the earth's weather, man and nature feel the effects of these El Niños. Historians suggest, in fact, that many flooding episodes and other weather events throughout history have been caused by El Niño's warming of ocean waters. What do you know about El Niños?

Directions: Place a **T** before each true statement and an **F** before each false statement.

_____1. A Peruvian fisherman named the El Niño effect after the Christ Child because El Niños affect weather patterns from around Christmas until near Easter time.

_____2. During the 1997-1998 El Niño, coastal flooding increased in California, Oregon, and Washington.

_____3. El Niños increase easterly winds blowing across the tropical Pacific.

_____4. El Niños commonly increase hurricane activity in the North Atlantic.

_____5. The abnormal ocean temperature warming of an El Niño typically occurs during the months of December through March.

_____6. During the 1997-1998 El Niño, southern Alaska experienced warmer and wetter conditions than normal.

_____7. During a 1982–1983 El Niño, the French Polynesia suffered six major typhoons.

_____8. The 1982-1983 hurricane season in the Atlantic experienced only two storms—the fewest it had experienced in a single season in 50 years.

_____9. Weaker than normal trade winds alert meteorologists to a possible El Niño season.

_____10. A 1972-1973 El Niño ruined fishing in Peru by turning the normally deep, cold, nutrient-rich waters of the western Pacific into warm, shallow waters that did not support anchovy life.

_____11. Because expected monsoon rains fell before they reached the continent, the 1972-1973 El Niño caused a severe drought in India.

_____12. Because the earth's weather patterns are not significantly tied together, El Niños do not affect the entire globe.

_____13. During 1982 and 1983, eastern Australia, southern Africa, and Indonesia suffered severe droughts due to the effects of an El Niño.

_____14. Fish that live in cold waters and birds that eat them usually survive the warm waters of an El Niño.

_____15. The continent that suffers the most economic hardships from El Niño is South America.

_____16. The most severe El Niño of the twentieth century occurred in 1997-1998.

Weather Wisdom

Name

Directions: The following are sayings about weather. Write **T**, for true, if you think the saying has some basis in science. Write **F**, for false, if you think it has no basis in scientific fact. Be prepared to explain your choices.

_____ 1. An old timer says, "I can tell it's going to rain. My feet hurt."

_____ 2. When an old cat acts like a kitten, a storm is on the way.

_____ 3. Kill a snake and turn it on its belly for rain.

_____ 4. Frogs croak before a rain, but in the sun they stay quiet.

_____ 5. When bees stay close to the hive, rain is close by.

_____ 6. Red sky at night, sailor's delight—Red sky in morning, sailors take warning.

_____ 7. A tough apple means a hard winter is coming.

_____ 8. When the night has a fever, it cries in the morning.

Directions: Think about how weather affects you and complete the following.

Why do you think people want to predict the weather? _____

_____

_____

Give an example of when the weather might affect what you do. _____

_____

_____

When might the weather affect how you feel? _____

_____

_____

When do you talk about the weather? _____

_____

_____

Fill in the vowels **e** and **o** to spell the word for the science of weather.

M ___ T ___ ___ R ___ L ___ G Y

Meteorology

236

Natural Weather Forecasters

Human beings are not the only ones who can predict a rainstorm like the one that broke the South Fork Dam. Plants and animals sense atmospheric changes, too.

Directions: Match the following weather sayings with the reasons they often hold true. The first one has been done for you.

___B__ 1. Birds flying low, expect rain and a blow.

_____ 2. If garden spiders forsake their webs, it indicates rain.

_____ 3. Bees never get caught in the rain.

_____ 4. If ants their walls do frequent build, Rain will from the clouds be spilled.

_____ 5. The gnats bite and I scratch in vain Because they know it is going to rain.

_____ 6. When leaves show their undersides Be very sure that rain betides.

_____ 7. Seaweed dry, sunny sky. Seaweed wet, rain you'll get.

_____ 8. Flowers smell best just before a rain.

_____ 9. Knots get tighter before a rain.

_____ 10. When the milkweed closes its pod, expect rain.

_____ 11. Frogs croaking in the lagoon Means that rain will come real soon.

_____ 12. Mushrooms and toadstools are plentiful before rain.

A. Ice crystals in clouds destroy the polarization of sunlight, making it difficult for bees to navigate, so they stay close to the hive in wet weather.

B. Low barometric pressure, which indicates precipitation, makes flying low in the sky easier than flying higher for birds.

C. Leaves curl and turn over on their branches before a rain.

D. Mushroom growth requires high humidity.

E. Insects fly lower and bite more in lowering pressure and rising humidity.

F. Plants sense moisture in the air and either close for protection or open to gather more rain water.

G. Water molecules help aromatic molecules bind better to the moisture in your nose.

H. When spider web threads absorb moisture, they break.

I. Ants reinforce their nests and cover their entrances before a rain.

J. Cold-blooded, aquatic animals require warm, moist conditions to be active.

K. Rope made of plant fibers expands when moisture fills its cellulose fibers.

L. Seaweed and moss absorb moisture.

Directions: Answer the questions.

1. How cold does it feel when the wind speed is 30 mph and the temperature is 30°?

   _____

2. How cold does it feel when the wind speed is 40 mph and the temperature is 50°?

   _____

3. How cold does it feel when the wind speed is 5 mph and the temperature is 40°?

   _____

4. What are the actual temperature and the wind speed when it feels like -116°?

   _____

5. What is the actual temperature right now? _____

   What is the wind speed right now? _____

   How cold does it feel? _____

WIND CHILL FACTOR

Wind Speed (mph)	Thermometer Readings (° F)									
	50	40	30	20	10	0	−10	−20	−30	−40
	Equivalent Temperatures (° F)									
Calm	50	40	30	20	10	0	-10	-20	-30	-40
5	48	37	27	16	6	-5	-15	-26	-36	-47
10	40	28	16	4	-9	-21	-33	-46	-58	-70
15	36	22	9	-5	-18	-36	-45	-58	-72	-85
20	32	18	4	-10	-25	-39	-53	-67	-82	-96
25	30	16	0	-15	-29	-44	-59	-74	-88	-104
30	28	13	-2	-18	-33	-48	-63	-79	-94	-109
35	27	11	-4	-20	-35	-49	-67	-82	-98	-113
40	26	10	-6	-21	-37	-53	-69	-85	-100	-116
	little danger				increasing danger			great danger		

Did your teacher suggest you wear your jacket on the playground? Are you wishing you had shorts on? Are the slides too hot to slide down? The answers to these questions often can be answered by thinking about the **weather**. Weather is the condition of the air surrounding us. Scientists talk about four properties of air when they speak about the weather. They are air temperature, air pressure, wind, and humidity.

Air temperature is determined by the sun. The sun's energy heats up the earth and the surface warms the air above it. Air temperature is measured using a thermometer.

Air pressure is the amount of force that air is pushing on something. Warm air is lighter and gives less pressure. The air particles are farther apart than in cool air. Air pressure is measured using a barometer.

Wind is air in motion. It is caused when the surface of the earth heats unevenly. The air will move from high pressure to low pressure. This results in the movement of air, or wind. Scientists measure wind using an anemometer.

Humidity is how much water vapor is in the air. The presence of water vapor depends on location. If you are near a large body of water you may experience more humid air. The humidity is measured with a hygrometer.

Directions: Answer the following questions using the information above.

1. What are the four properties of air used to describe weather?

   _____

   _____

2. Describe what you might wear on the playground if it was hot and humid.

   _____

   _____

3. What are a barometer and an anemometer used to measure?

   _____

   _____

4. Describe what the weather is like on your playground today and what is was like yesterday.

   _____

   _____

   _____

Earth and Moon

As you travel to school, look up. What do you see? Perhaps it is a clear blue sky. Maybe it is cloudy and rainy. It might even still be early enough for you to see the moon. The moon is the earth's nearest neighbor in space. Have you ever thought about the moon? What is it like? Is it important to us?

Look at the chart below. It has some information comparing the earth and moon.

EARTH	MOON
1. Atmosphere is a combination of gases, such as water vapor and oxygen	1. Little or no atmosphere
2. Surface has liquid water and life	2. Dusty and lifeless on surface
3. Gravity is six times stronger than moon	3. Weak gravitational pull
4. Earth revolves around the sun in 365 days	4. Moon revolves around the earth in about 28 days
5. Many landforms including mountains, rivers, and plains	5. Landforms include mountains, plains, and craters
6. Diameter of 7,926 mi.	6. Diameter of 2,160 mi.
7. 5th largest planet, 3rd from the sun	7. Natural satellite orbiting the earth

Directions: Use the chart to answer the following questions.

1. Which is larger, the earth or moon? How do you know? _____
_____

2. Describe what you think the surface of the earth is like compared to the moon's surface.
_____
_____

3. What four events occur as a result of the earth's revolving around the sun every 365 days?
_____
_____

Changing Faces

As the moon revolves around the earth, we can see different amounts of the moon's lighted part.

Directions: Study the drawing of the moon's different phases and each phase as it would be seen from the earth. Label each phase.

WORD BANK

new moon	waxing crescent	first quarter
waxing gibbous	full moon	waning gibbous
last quarter	waning crescent	

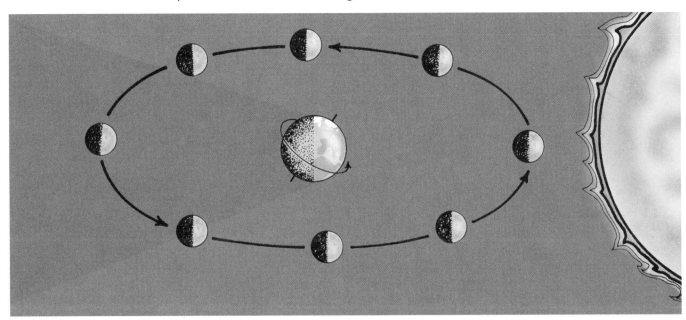

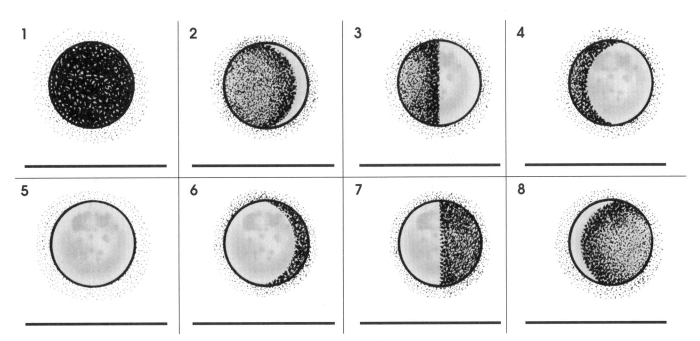

1

2

3

4

5

6

7

8

Solar System

Name _____

The ocean tides are caused mostly by the moon's gravity. When the sun, moon, and earth line up, the gravitational pull is greatest causing the highest tides, the spring tides. The lowest tides, neap tides, occur when the sun, earth, and moon form right angles.

Directions: Label the neap tides, spring tides, sun, earth, and moon.

WORD BANK   neap tides   spring tides   sun
                moon   earth

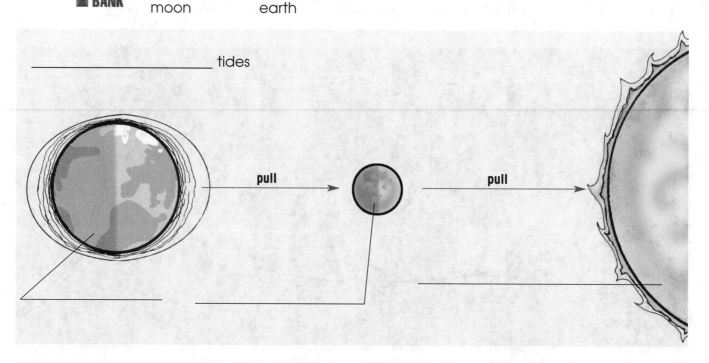

_____ tides

pull   pull

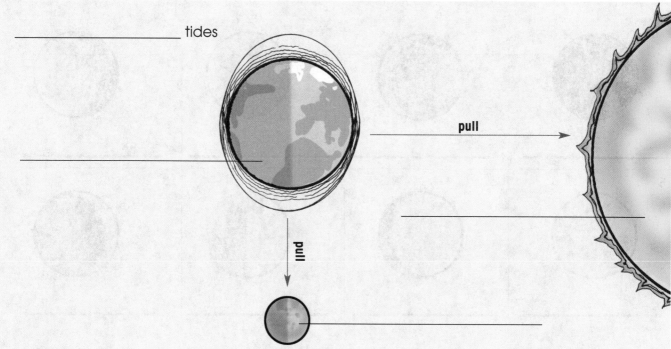

_____ tides

pull

pull

A Sunny Star

Looking out of the bus or car window, or looking around you as you walk to school, you can see the effects of the sun. It lights your way to school. It heats up the air around you. It helps plants grow and its energy even provides people with some needed vitamins.

The sun is a star. A star is really a ball of hot, glowing gases with no ground to stand on like the earth. Hydrogen is the main gas in the sun. It is the hydrogen that provides the energy the sun needs to make the light and heat for the earth, which is millions of miles away.

The sun is the star in the center of the solar system. All planets revolve around the sun. It is average in size for a star, with a diameter of about 863,710 mi. The sun is almost half way through its life, which is about 9 billion years long.

Directions: Answer the following questions using the information above.

1. What is a star?

   _____

   _____

2. What is the diameter of the sun? How does it compare to the size of other stars?

   _____

   _____

3. We know the earth revolves around the sun. What happens on the earth as a result of that revolving?

   _____

   _____

4. What might it be like on the earth if the sun were to burn out?

   _____

   _____

   _____

Our Closest Star—the Sun

Directions: The sun is the closest star to the earth. Use the WORD BANK to label the different layers and features of the sun.

 WORD BANK

core	radiative zone	sunspot
photosphere	chromosphere	flare
prominence		

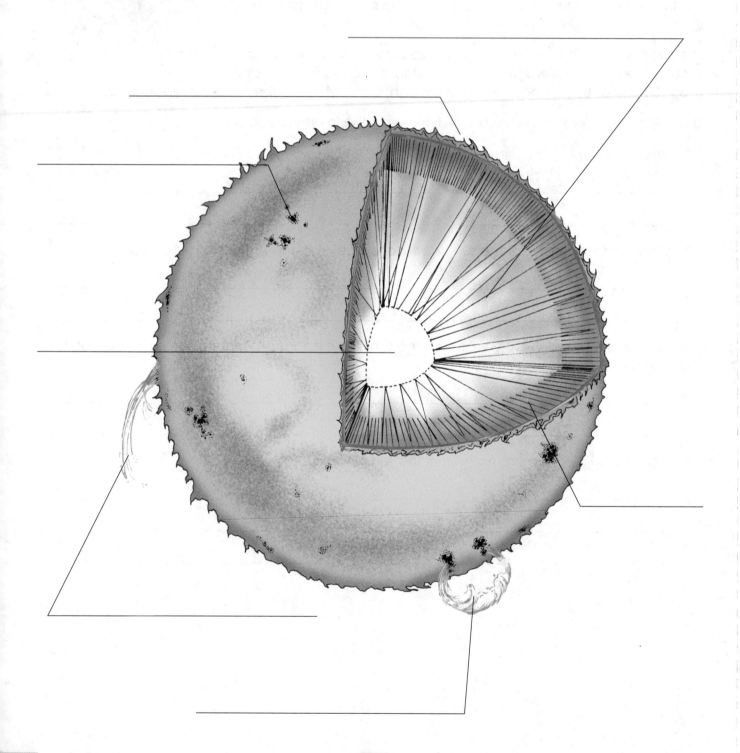

The diagram below shows the earth's position in its orbit on four different dates.

Directions: On the solid line label the equinox dates. On the dotted lines name the season for the Northern Hemisphere.

 WORD BANK

| March 21 | December 22 | spring | fall |
| September 22 | June 21 | winter | summer |

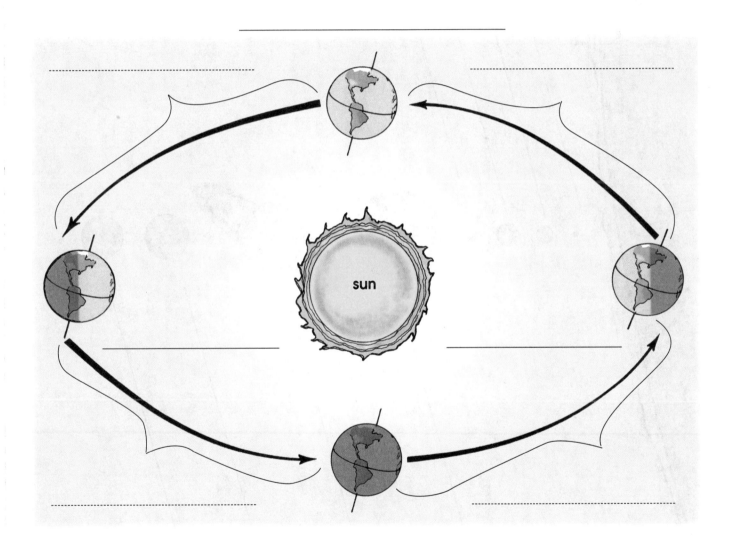

Directions: All of the planets of the solar system travel around the sun. Label the planets.

WORD BANK

Mercury	Venus	Earth
Mars	Jupiter	Saturn
Uranus	Neptune	

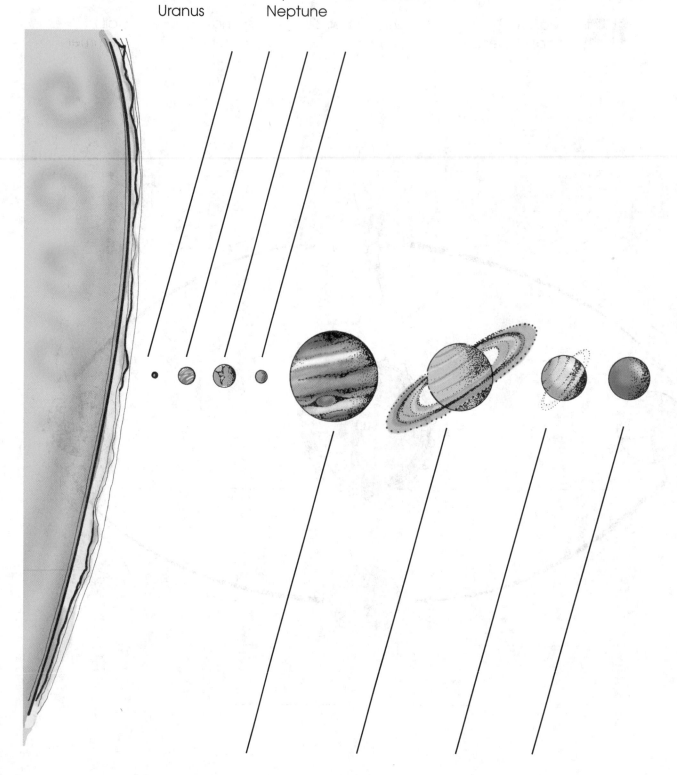

Puzzling Planets

Directions: Use what you have learned about the planets of our solar system to complete the puzzle. You may need to refer to your science book or an encyclopedia

WORD BANK

Mercury	Venus	Earth
Mars	Jupiter	Saturn
Uranus	Neptune	Pluto

ACROSS

3. I am the closest in size to Earth.
4. I am a dwarf planet.
5. I have the greatest number of natural satellites.
6. I am the only planet known to support life.
7. I am called the "red planet."
8. I am the most distant planet that can be seen without a telescope.

DOWN

1. I am usually the 8th planet from the sun, but every 248 years I move inside Pluto's orbit for 20 years.
2. I am a large planet known for my "great red spot."
5. I am the closest planet to the sun.

Solar System

Physical Characteristics of the Planets

How far around the sun can you walk in one minute in each planet's orbit? Compare the distances.

	Mercury	Venus	Earth	Mars	Jupiter	Saturn	Uranus	Neptune
Average Distance to Sun (Millions of Miles)	36	67	93	142	484	885	1,781	2,788
Scale Distance (Feet)	1.80	3.34	4.66	7.12	24.17	44.31	89.54	139.76
Your Scale Distance								

Directions: Answer the questions.

1. What did you notice about the distances of the inner planets from the sun compared to the outer planets' distances from the sun?

   _____

   _____

2. Describe what happened to the distance you traveled around the sun on each planet's orbit as you got further away from the sun.

   _____

   _____

3. Why do you think it takes a longer period of time for Neptune to travel around the sun than it does for Mercury?

   _____

   _____

4. If it takes longer for the outer planets to travel around the sun, what happened to the length of each planet's year? Explain your answer.

   _____

   _____

   _____

The North Star

Because the earth rotates, all the stars in the sky appear to move from east to west. Because Polaris is directly above the North Pole it does not move, and so it is also called the North Star. Polaris is found in the constellation Ursa Minor, also called the Little Dipper. The Big Dipper is found in the constellation Ursa Major, also called the Great Bear.

Directions: Trace the Big Dipper and Little Dipper. Label Polaris.

WORD BANK   Big Dipper   Little Dipper   Polaris

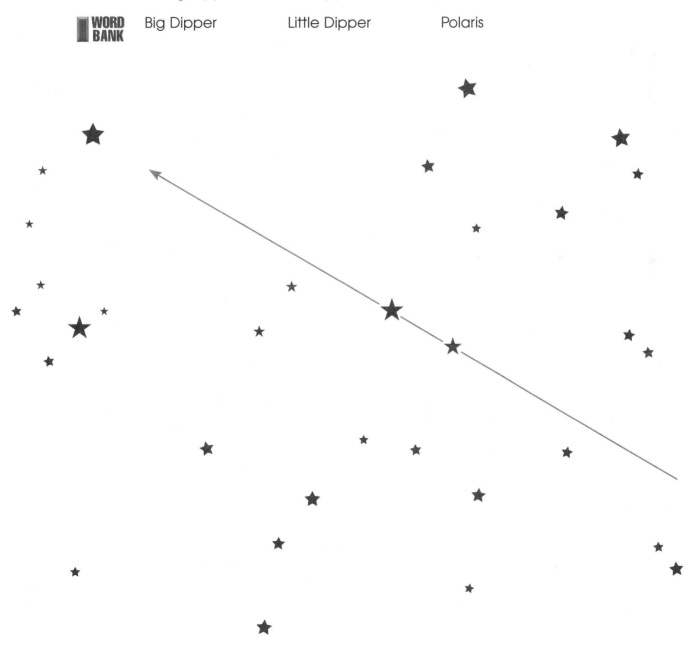

Solar System

Name _____

Astronomers have divided the sky into 88 constellations. The letters in the blocks below will spell out the names of 12 constellations found in the sky. The beginning letter of each constellation is in the star.

Directions: Draw straight lines between the letters to find the name of each constellation. No lines will cross. Write the name of each constellation at the bottom of the page.

1. T T A U R I S S G I A	**2.** U A Q R U I A S	**3.** E G M I N N I
4. C I C A O P R U N S	**5.** O R C O S I P	**6.** E C P S I S
7. S A T U U R	**8.** C E C N R A	**9.** O I V G R
10. L I B A R	**11.** A R E S I	**12.** L E O

1. _____   7. _____

2. _____   8. _____

3. _____   9. _____

4. _____   10. _____

5. _____   11. _____

6. _____   12. _____

Hello Out There!

Our earth and sun belong to a vast number of stars called the Milky Way Galaxy. The word galaxy comes from a Greek word meaning "milk."

Directions: Use the code below to design a message you would send to outer space to tell any possible life forms in the Milky Way about earth.

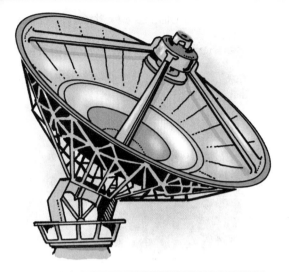

The code chart (a six-dot braille-style grid) gives the letters:

A B C D E F G H I J K L M

N O P Q R S T U V W X Y Z

1. Decode the message.

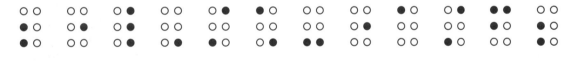

___ ___ ___ ___ ___ ___ ___ ___ ___ ___ ___ ___

2. Design your own message to send. Exchange it with a friend to decode.

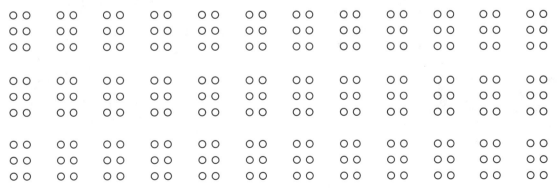

Galaxies

Beyond our galaxy lie billions of other galaxies.

Directions: Use the WORD BANK to label the shapes of some of these galaxies.

 WORD BANK   elliptical   spiral   barred spiral   irregular

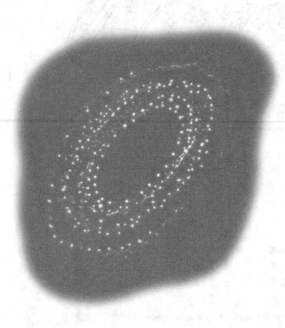

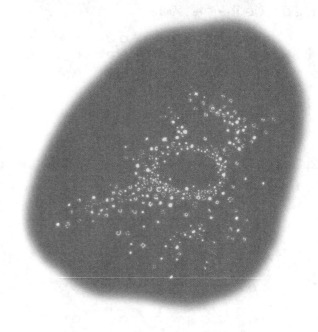

Astronomical Alterations

Several astronomical definitions appear below. The terms for each also appear below, but each has been altered.

Directions: Your job is to properly change each term and match it to the correct definition. To do this, change just one letter in each word and then rearrange the letters. The first one has been solved as an example.

	New Word	Definition

1. heard   _____   __K__   A. Any body that revolves around the sun

2. square   _____   _____   B. A planet's natural satellite

3. slurps   _____   _____   C. A "shooting star"

4. riots   _____   _____   D. An extremely bright, compact object far beyond our galaxy

5. mask   _____   _____   E. The star nearest earth

6. pleats   _____   _____   F. Collapsed neutron star that emits pulsing radio waves

7. loom   _____   _____   G. A heavenly body with a star-like head and often with a long, luminous tail

8. ants   _____   _____   H. The path of a heavenly body revolving around another

9. bus   _____   _____   I. The imaginary line around which a body rotates

10. metro   _____   _____   J. A sphere of matter held together by its own gravitational field and generating nuclear fusion reactions in its interior

11. taxi   _____   _____   K. The third planet from the sun

12. remove   _____   _____   L. Nicknamed the "red planet"

Our Solar System

There is so much to know about our solar system. To learn a little about it, solve the crossword puzzle below.

Directions: Use the terms in the box and the clues under the box to help you.

WORD BANK

asteroids	emit
Lowell	moon
Saturn	Triton
Ceres	Halley's
Mars	Neptune
spot	Uranus
comet	Io
Mercury	Pluto
sun	Venus
Earth	Jupiter
meteors	rings
tail	way

Across

1. Rocky particles which orbit the sun mainly between Mars and Jupiter
4. Another name for a satellite of a planet
8. The center of our solar system
9. The seventh planet from the sun
11. Planets do not ____ light energy of their own.
13. One of the moons of Neptune
14. Sometimes called "the red planet"
15. Consists of a head and tail
18. A comet that appears every 76 years
20. Known as Earth's twin
21. Saturn is probably best known for its ____.
22. Our solar system is in the galaxy called "The Milky ____."
23. A dwarf planet

Down

2. The sixth planet from the sun
3. One of the moons of Jupiter
5. The planet discovered in 1846
6. Planet covered with dark and light bands
7. Planet whose atmosphere is mostly oxygen and nitrogen
10. The Great Red ____ is a prominent feature of Jupiter.
12. Often called "falling stars" or "shooting stars"; results when a meteoroid enters Earth's atmosphere from space
15. The largest asteroid
16. Planet closest to the sun
17. The ____ of a comet may be over 100 million miles long.
19. American astronomer who began the search for Pluto in 1905

On July 20, 1969, the first person stepped onto the surface of the moon. He said, " . . . one small step for a man, one giant leap for mankind."

Directions: Identify this person by solving the clues and writing the words in the spaces. The circled letters will then spell out the person's name.

1. Latin word for "moon"
　　__ __ Ⓞ __

2. Our moon is a _____ of earth.
　　__ __ __ Ⓞ __ __ __ __

3. During a lunar _____, the moon becomes dark when it passes through the shadow of earth.
　　__ __ __ Ⓞ __ __ __

4. The space mission to the moon was called _____.
　　__ __ __ Ⓞ __ __

5. Letters that stand for the organization that conducts research into problems of flight within and beyond earth's atmosphere
　　__ Ⓞ __ __

6. American space scientists and explorers are called _____.
　　__ __ __ Ⓞ __ __ __ __ __

7. The moon's average distance from earth is about 240,000 _____.
　　Ⓞ __ __ __ Ⓞ

8. The moon's surface is pitted with _____.
　　__ __ __ Ⓞ __ __

9. The circling of the spacecraft around the moon is called its _____.
　　__ Ⓞ __ __ __

10. During a _____ eclipse, the moon comes between the sun and earth.
　　__ Ⓞ __ __

11. A _____ rocket carried the first astronauts to the moon.
　　__ __ __ __ __ Ⓞ

12. The moon's _____ is about one-sixth that of earth's.
　　Ⓞ __ __ __ __ __ __

The first person to step upon the moon was

__ __ __ __　__ __ __ __ __ __ __ __ __ .

In Your Own Words

Directions: Imagine that you are one of the very first astronauts, encountering many unusual and difficult circumstances. First, do some reading on living conditions in space, such as dealing with weightlessness, living in tight quarters, and so on. Then, write a first-person account of your own fictional experience on any two of the following topics. Write three or four paragraphs for each one.

1. Leaving the launchpad

2. Eating your first meal in outer space

3. Moving about inside the space capsule

4. Communicating with other crew members

5. Taking a shower

6. Changing your clothes

7. Writing a letter

8. Seeing the earth from space

9. Catching your first close-up glimpse of the moon

10. Walking outside the spacecraft

11. Exploring the moon in a moon rover

12. Docking with a foreign space vessel

13. Performing scientific experiments in space

14. Landing back on earth

15. Deciding whether or not to make another space flight

Directions: The periodic table can give you a lot of information about each of the elements. Use the WORD BANK to label the type of information that the symbols, names, and letters represent for each of the elements.

WORD BANK

atomic number   element's symbol   electrons in outer shell
atomic mass   element's name

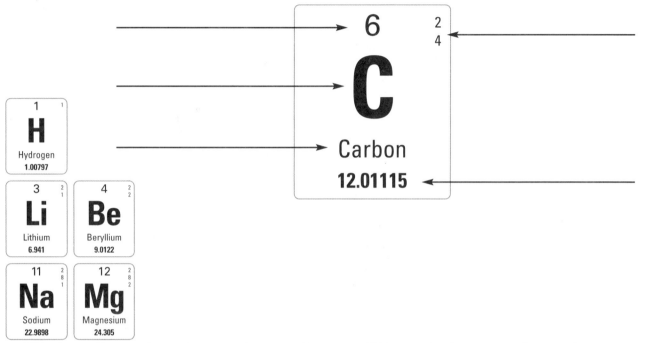

1	1
H	
Hydrogen	
1.00797	

6	2 4
C	
Carbon	
12.01115	

3	2 1
Li	
Lithium	
6.941	

4	2 2
Be	
Beryllium	
9.0122	

11	2 8 1
Na	
Sodium	
22.9898	

12	2 8 2
Mg	
Magnesium	
24.305	

19	2 8 8 1	20	2 8 8 2	21	2 8 9 2	22	2 8 10 2	23	2 8 11 2	24	2 8 13 1	25	2 8 13 2	26	2 8 14 2	27	2 8 15 2	28	2 8 16 2
K		**Ca**		**Sc**		**Ti**		**V**		**Cr**		**Mn**		**Fe**		**Co**		**Ni**	
Potassium		Calcium		Scandium		Titanium		Vanadium		Chromium		Manganese		Iron		Cobalt		Nickel	
39.0983		40.08		44.956		47.88		50.942		51.996		54.9380		55.847		58.9332		58.69	

37	2 8 18 8 1	38	2 8 18 8 2	39	2 8 18 9 2	40	2 8 18 10 ?	41	2 8 18 12 1	42	2 8 18 13 1	43	2 8 18 13 2	44	2 8 18 15 1	45	2 8 18 16 1	46	2 8 18 18 0
Rb		**Sr**		**Y**		**Zr**		**Nb**		**Mo**		**Tc**		**Ru**		**Rh**		**Pd**	
Rubidium		Strontium		Yttrium		Zirconium		Niobium		Molybdenum		Technetium		Ruthenium		Rhodium		Palladium	
85.4678		87.62		88.905		91.22		92.906		95.94		(98)		101.07		102.905		106.4	

55	2 8 18 18 8 1	56	2 8 18 18 8 2	57–71	72	2 8 18 32 10 2	73	2 8 18 32 11 2	74	2 8 18 32 12 2	75	2 8 18 32 13 2	76	2 8 18 32 14 2	77	2 8 18 32 15 2	78	2 8 18 32 17 1
Cs		**Ba**		Rare Earth Elements	**Hf**		**Ta**		**W**		**Re**		**Os**		**Ir**		**Pt**	
Cesium		Barium			Hafnium		Tantalum		Tungsten		Rhenium		Osmium		Iridium		Platinum	
132.905		137.33			178.49		180.948		183.85		186.2		190.2		192.2		195.09	

87	2 8 18 32 18 8	88	2 8 18 32 18 8 2	87–103	104	2 8 18 32 32 10 2	105	2 8 18 32 32 11 2	106	2 8 18 32 32 12 2	107	2 8 18 32 32 13 2	108	2 8 18 32 32 14 2	109	2 8 18 32 32 15 2	110	2 8 18 32 32 17 1
Fr		**Ra**		Actinide Series	**Rf**		**Db**		**Sg**		**Bh**		**Hs**		**Mt**		**Uun**	
Francium		Radium			Rutherfordium		dubnium		Seaborigium		Bohrium		Hassium		Meitnerium		Ununnilium	
(223)		(226.0254)			(261)		(262)		(263)		(262)		(265)		(266)		(269)	

Name _____

Directions: Label the parts of the helium atom pictured below.

 WORD BANK
proton   nucleus   neutron
orbit (shell)   electron

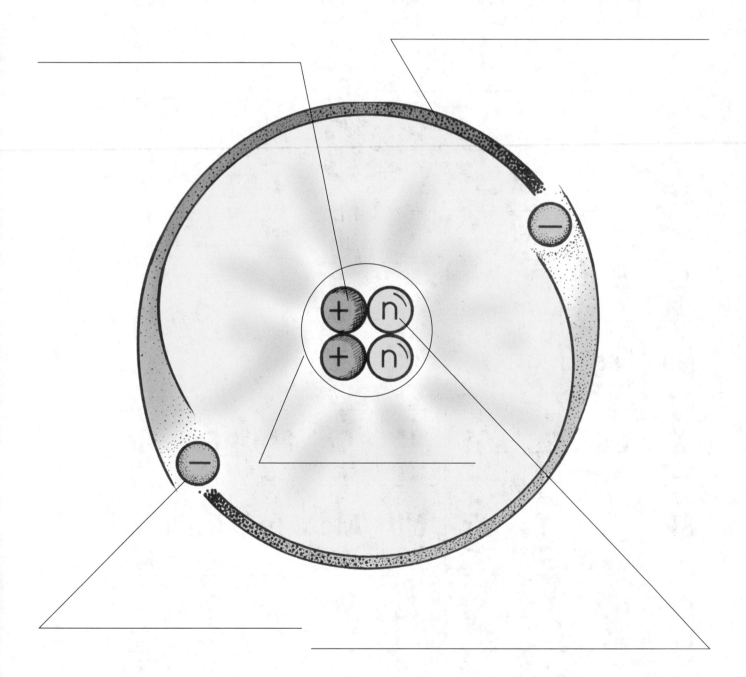

Name That Molecule!

Directions: Write the chemical formula for each molecule pictured below.

H₂O   CH₄   H₂S   Fe₂O₃

C₂H₅OH   CO₂   NH₃

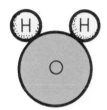

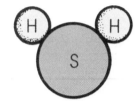

_____   _____   _____

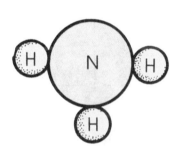

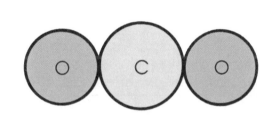

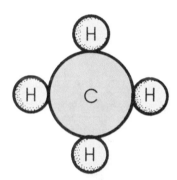

_____   _____   _____

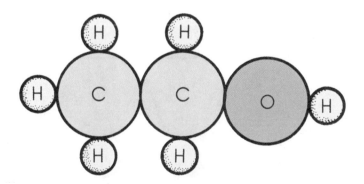

_____

Elements, Compounds, and Mixtures

Chemical Magic Square

Use the Periodic Table on page 257 to help you complete this activity.

Directions: Read the clues concerning the elements in the boxes below. Write the correct atomic number in the box. Add the numbers across, down, and diagonally to produce a magic square.

What is your answer? _____

This element is located directly above lithium. _____	This element is located to the left of sulfur. _____	This element is located directly below carbon. _____	This element is located directly above magnesium. _____	_____
This element is located to the right of sodium. _____	This element is located to the left of nitrogen. _____	This element is located directly above phosphorus. _____	This element is located directly above chlorine. _____	_____
This element is located to the left of fluorine. _____	This element is located below helium. _____	This element is located directly above potassium. _____	This element is located directly above aluminum. _____	_____
This element is located to the left of silicon. _____	This element is located directly below hydrogen. _____	This element is located directly above neon. _____	This element is located to the left of chlorine. _____	_____
_____	_____	_____	_____	

Chemical and Physical Changes

Substances can exist in three different states of matter: solids, liquids, or gases. A substance can change from one state of matter to another. Changes in matter can occur as a result of temperature or pressure changes. Changes in matter can be classified as either **physical changes** or **chemical changes**.

PHYSICAL CHANGES

Physical changes are changes that do not involve changes in the basic elements or compounds that make up a substance. A physical change is a change in size, shape, or state of matter. We can see a physical change when ice melts to water and again when the water freezes to ice. Physical changes are changes in the appearance of the material. Physical changes do not involve the creation of something new.

CHEMICAL CHANGES

A chemical change completely changes the object from one material to another material. There is a change to the chemical makeup. The initial elements or compounds are not the same. After a chemical change has occurred, it usually cannot be reversed.

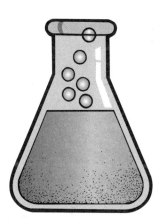

LAW OF CONSERVATION OF MASS

Matter cannot be created or destroyed during a chemical change. This is called the **law of conservation of mass**. (Mass is the amount of matter a substance contains.) Energy can cause changes in matter. For example, heat energy can change ice into water into steam.

EXOTHERMIC AND ENDOTHERMIC REACTIONS

During a chemical reaction, the bonds between the atoms (of substances) are broken. The atoms rearrange themselves and form bonds with new partners. During a chemical reaction, energy is always either taken in or given out. Breaking bonds requires energy and creating new bonds releases energy. A reaction that produces heat is called **exothermic reaction**. If heat is taken in it is considered an **endothermic reaction**.

Name _____

COMPARISON OF CHEMICAL AND PHYSICAL CHANGES

Chemical changes usually cannot be reversed. Chemical reactions involve changing the materials into new materials. For example, when matter undergoes a physical change, the change can usually be reversed because you have not created something totally different. The materials have not changed in their basic composition, such as the physical change of a liquid becoming a solid.

ACIDS AND BASES

Chemicals can be grouped according to their qualities. **Acids** are one group of chemicals. Acids will react in a certain way with other substances. Foods that taste sour, like lemon juice, are usually acids. They contain hydrogen. **Bases** are the opposite of acids. Bases contain a hydroxide ion, and often feel slippery or soapy. In food, bases don't have a strong taste. Baking soda is an example of a base. Acids can neutralize bases. Most liquids are either an acid or a base. Scientist use a pH scale to measure the acidity or base of liquids. The pH scale goes from 0 to 14. Acids measure between 0 and 7 on the scale, and bases are from 7 to 14 on the scale.

Chemical and physical changes can occur with different materials. A physical change is a change in size, shape, or state of matter. A chemical change completely changes the object. A major difference between chemical and physical changes is that in chemical changes there is actually a change in the composition of the materials, or a change in what basic elements are present.

Acids and Bases

Acids and bases are chemical compounds. Some of these compounds are strong and abrasive. Many are used as cleaning agents. Litmus paper is an indicator. Indicators are affected when acid or base is present in a substance. Blue litmus paper turns red when dipped in an acid. Red litmus paper turns blue when dipped in a base.

Directions: Use blue and red litmus paper to test each one of the substances on the chart. Record the results by writing the color the paper turns when dipped and whether the substance is an acid or a base. The first one is done for you.

SUBSTANCE	BLUE LITMUS	RED LITMUS	ACID, BASE, OR NEITHER
Lemon juice	red	red	acid
Vinegar			
Ammonia			
Orange juice			
Tea			
Milk			
Baking soda and water			
Cleanser and water			
Water			
Vinegar and salt			
Grapefruit juice			
Antacid pills and water			
Cola			

Matter is anything that has mass and takes up space. Everything is matter. We can classify all of the matter in the world into one of three groups: elements, compounds, and mixtures.

An **element** is matter that is made up of only one ingredient. Oxygen, hydrogen, and carbon are elements. We can find the names of the different elements that make up our world on a special table known as the Periodic Table. Most of the elements on this table are made by nature. The other elements are made by scientists. Elements are just one type of matter, but without them, compounds and mixtures could not exist.

A **compound** is matter that is made up of two or more ingredients that are joined together. The ingredients cannot be taken apart easily. Water, sugar, a piece of cake, a fork, and the wood on a cabinet drawer are compounds. Most of the matter in our world exists as a compound.

A **mixture** is matter that is made up of two or more ingredients that are mixed together. The ingredients in a mixture are easy to take apart. Cereal in milk, trail mix, and Italian salad dressing are mixtures.

Matter has observable properties. A property is a characteristic we can use to identify something. We make observations using our senses and measurements. Observable properties include color, texture, size, weight, taste, smell, and sound. The color and texture of a chocolate chip cookie allow us to identify it from a sugar cookie.

Directions: Answer the questions using the information in the reading.

1. What is matter? _____

2. What are the three different types of matter? _____

   _____

3. How are the three types of matter alike? _____

   _____

4. How are the three types of matter different? _____

   _____

5. What is a property? _____

   _____

6. Name at least four different properties that can be used to identify you.

   _____

Its Own Space

Matter has observable properties—matter takes up space.

QUESTION

Can two bits of matter occupy the same space?

MATERIALS

- clear plastic glass
- marker
- 8–10 marbles
- spoon

PROCEDURE

1. Fill the glass half full of water.

2. Mark the water level on the glass with a marker.

3. Ask students to predict what will happen when you put the marbles into the water. Have them record their predictions on a separate sheet of paper.

4. Slowly place the marbles into the water and mark the new water level.

5. Now ask students to predict what will happen when the marbles are removed from the water. Have them record their predictions.

6. Remove the marbles with the spoon and recheck the water level.

CONCLUSIONS

Why is the water level higher with the marbles in?

_____

_____

_____

_____

_____

_____

Milk Shake Mixture

Substances interact with other substances—making a mixture.

QUESTION What is a mixture?

MATERIALS

- blender
- vanilla ice cream
- milk
- large spoon
- paper cups
- bananas, strawberries, or other fruits
- knife
- lab sheet

PROCEDURE

1. You will be making a mixture of several different substances.

2. Fill the blender half full with ice cream.

3. Cut the fruit into small chunks and put them into the blender.

4. Pour milk into the blender until it is about two inches from the top.

5. Blend. Pour into cups and enjoy.

CONCLUSIONS

Is there still ice cream, fruit, and milk in the milk shakes? _____

The ingredients are mixed together, but each one still has the same chemical properties as before. This is called a *mixture*.

Fill out the lab sheet on the next page.

Milk Shake Mixture Record Sheet

What were the different parts that went into the milk shake mixers?

_____   _____   _____

What other foods or beverages can you think of that are mixtures? _____

_____

What are the separate parts? _____

_____

FOOD/BEVERAGE	PARTS

Elements, Compounds, and Mixtures

Make It Mix

Substances interact with other substances—making an **emulsion**.

QUESTION

How can you force oil and water to mix?

MATERIALS

- water
- oil
- jar with a lid
- liquid detergent
- lab sheet

PROCEDURE

1. Fill the jar half full of water and half full of oil.

2. Put on the lid and shake the jar. Observe for several minutes.

3. Ask: What happens to the water and the oil?

4. Now add about 10 drops of liquid detergent.

5. Shake again and observe.

6. Ask: What happened this time?

CONCLUSIONS

The detergent coats the oil droplets so that they cannot stick back together. Then, they float (are suspended) throughout the water. This type of substance is called an emulsion.

Make It Mix Record Sheet

Directions: Draw and write what happened in each step of the activity.

It looked like this color:

When I poured oil and water in the jar, _____

_____

_____

_____

When I shook it, _____

_____

_____

_____

_____

When I added detergent and shook it, _____

_____

_____

_____

_____

I learned that an emulsifier does this: _____

_____

_____

Elements, Compounds, and Mixtures

Salt and Ice

Adding solute to a liquid creates a **solution**. This solution will be denser than the liquid water by itself. The denser a solution is, the more slowly molecules in it will move. Imagine trying to swim in a swimming pool full of pudding, which is much denser than water. It would be harder for you to move quickly in the denser medium, just as it is more difficult for molecules. The denser a solution is, the colder it has to be before the solution will freeze.

PART 1

Fill a bowl or a glass with water almost to the top, and float an ice cube in it. Set an unlighted wooden match across the top of the ice cube. Make sure that some of the match hangs off the edge of the ice cube. Sprinkle salt lightly over it. Wait approximately 2 minutes. Then, try to lift the match upward.

What happened? _____

_____

Why do you think this happened? _____

_____

PART 2

Fill three glasses half-full with water, each having the same temperature. Put a little piece of masking tape on each one and label them #1, #2, and #3. Leave #1 as plain tap water. Add 1 teaspoon of salt to #2 and stir. Add 1 tablespoon of salt to #3 and stir. Next, place an ice cube in each glass. Add the cubes to the three glasses at the exact same time, and do not stir. Time how long it takes for the ice cube in each glass to melt. Record your data on the chart below.

SAMPLE	TIME TO MELT (SECONDS)
#1	
#2	
#3	

Crystal Pictures

Substances interact with other substances—removing a solute from a solution.

QUESTION

How can you remove a solute from a solution?

MATERIALS

- water
- baking soda
- table salt
- epsom salt
- sugar
- spoons
- paper cups
- clean paintbrushes
- black construction paper
- lab sheet

PROCEDURE

1. Fill one cup about one-third full of water.

2. Make a saturated solution of baking soda and water by adding baking soda to the water and stirring until no more will dissolve and some falls to the bottom.

3. Swish the paintbrush through the solution and use it to draw a picture or design on a sheet of black construction paper. Swish the brush again as necessary.

4. Set the picture aside to dry.

5. After about 20 minutes, see what it looks like.

CONCLUSION

The baking soda is dissolved in the water that you painted with. When the water evaporates, the soda stays behind, leaving a visible picture made of soda crystals.

Directions: Now make additional saturated solutions of table salt, epsom salt, and sugar. Fold a sheet of black construction paper into four parts and paint a large letter with each substance into one of the squares. Be sure to rinse your brush well between solutions. Let your crystal pictures dry and rank them as first, second, third, and fourth clearest.

Record what you predict will happen on the chart and then what really does happen.

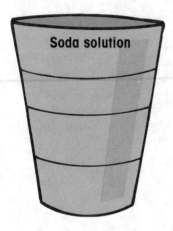

Soda solution

Prediction: _____

Actual result: _____

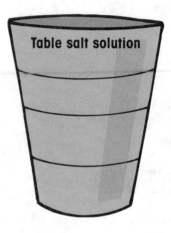

Table salt solution

Prediction: _____

Actual result: _____

Epsom salt solution

Prediction: _____

Actual result: _____

Sugar solution

Prediction: _____

Actual result: _____

Name _____

Directions: Anything that contains space is considered to be matter. Matter can be a solid, a liquid, or a gas. Read the definitions below. Use the words in the box to fill in the blanks after each definition. Then, write the circled letters in order to spell out the names of a person who studies the changes in the states of matter.

WORD BANK

boiling	freezing	solidification
condensation	liquefaction	sublimation
evaporation	melting	vaporization

1. Molten lava changes into solid rock.   ◯ __ __ __ __ __ __ __ __ __ __ __ __ __

2. Dew forms on the grass.   ◯ __ __ __ __ __ __ __ __ __ __ __

3. Hot lava flows into the ocean and quickly changes water into water vapor.   __ __ __ __ ◯ __ __ __ __ __

4. Solid ice changes to a liquid.   __ ◯ __ __ __ __ __

5. Water reaches 212 degrees Fahrenheit.   __ __ __ __ ◯ __

6. Water in a vase changes to water vapor.   __ __ __ __ __ __ ◯ __ __ __

7. Water reaches 32 degrees Fahrenheit.   __ __ __ __ ◯ __ __

8. Dry ice changes from a solid to a gas.   ◯ __ __ __ __ __ __ __ __ __

9. Oxygen in the air is cooled until it becomes a liquid.   __ __ __ __ __ __ ◯ __ __ __

Person: __ __ __ __ __ __ __ __ .

Name _____

Objects undergo many kinds of changes. Place a **P** in front of each physical change below and a **C** in front of each chemical change.

_____ 1. Rusting of iron

_____ 2. Breaking of a tree limb

_____ 3. Cutting paper

_____ 4. Action of yeast in breadmaking

_____ 5. Souring of milk

_____ 6. Wadding up a sheet of paper

_____ 7. Erasing a pencil mark

_____ 8. Freezing of water

_____ 9. Boiling water

_____ 10. Salting the ice on a sidewalk

_____ 11. Action of baking powder in cooking a cake

_____ 12. Bending a metal wire

_____ 13. Etching glass with acid

_____ 14. Formation of stalagmites in a cave

_____ 15. Fertilizing a lawn

_____ 16. Crushing ice in a blender

_____ 17. Evaporation of water in a lake

_____ 18. Eating foods

_____ 19. Burning gasoline in a car engine

_____ 20. Burning logs in a fireplace

_____ 21. Toasting marshmallows over a campfire

_____ 22. Adding bleach to a washer of clothes

_____ 23. Slicing a block of cheese

Matter is anything that occupies space. All things consist of matter.

Directions: Match the terms below to the definitions. Then, solve the crossword puzzle about matter.

 WORD BANK

boiling point
crystals
freezing point
liquid
melting point
condensation
evaporation
gas
matter
solid

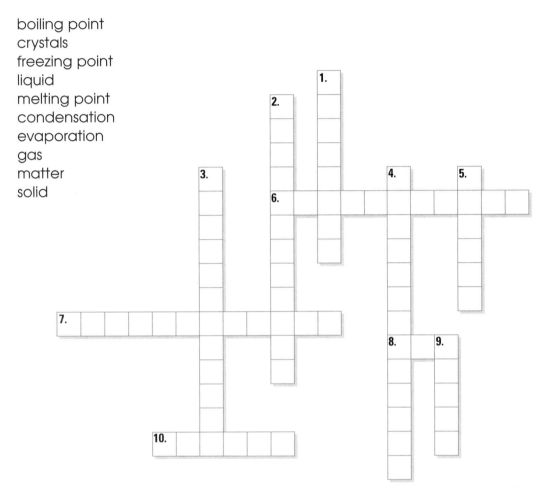

ACROSS

6. The change of a liquid to a gas
7. The temperature at which a liquid has gained enough heat energy to change to a gas
8. A state of matter that has no fixed shape
10. A gas, liquid, or solid that has mass and takes up space

DOWN

1. Patterns of particles packed together in a repeating order
2. The change of a gas to a liquid when heat energy is lost
3. Temperature at which a solid becomes a liquid
4. Temperature at which a liquid becomes a solid
5. State of matter that has a fixed volume but no shape of its own
9. State of matter that has a fixed volume and shape

Melt Down

Materials have observable properties—observing changes created by heat.

QUESTION

What will happen to chocolate in various degrees of heat?

MATERIALS

- chocolate pieces
- paper plates
- aluminum foil
- lab sheet

PROCEDURE

1. Discuss what kinds of physical changes might be made to chocolate. This experiment will show how varying degrees of heat change chocolate.

2. Use several pieces of chocolate for this experiment. (They need to be the same size—chocolate chips, chocolate Kisses™, squares from a chocolate bar, etc.)

3. Prepare the chocolate pieces as indicated on page 277.

4. Record how fast the chocolate melts.

CONCLUSIONS

Did the same physical change occur to all the chocolate pieces? Why or why not? Why did some melt faster than others?

NOTE:

This activity works best with fairly small bits of chocolate. If the sun is not strong enough to melt the chocolate, you can use a magnifying glass to concentrate the rays onto the chocolate.

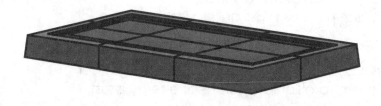

A. Put one piece of chocolate on a plate in the sun.

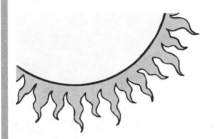

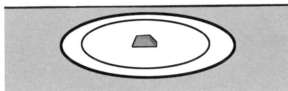

B. Put one piece of chocolate on a plate out of the sun.

C. Put one piece of chocolate on a piece of aluminum foil in the sun.

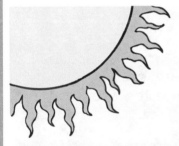

D. Put one piece of chocolate in your mouth.

In which order did the pieces melt?

1st	2nd	3rd	4th

Freezing Hot Water

Some people say that hot water freezes faster than cold water. What do you think? Could this be possible? Doesn't water have to get colder before it can freeze? If so, it would make more sense to start with very cold water when you want to make ice. But did you know that between the periods of a hockey game the ice is resurfaced with hot water? Could it be that hot water does freeze faster than cold water under certain conditions? Let's find out!

STATE THE PROBLEM:

Write a question that asks what you want to find out from your investigation.

FORM A HYPOTHESIS:

What do you think your scientific investigation will prove? Make a smart guess. Write a sentence that states what you think the answer to your question will be.

PLAN THE PROCEDURE:

1. Before a scientist begins experimenting, he or she usually does some research on the topic to find what other scientists have learned. This information is used to plan the procedure for the experiment. Finding the answer to the following questions will help you understand water and how it "behaves":

    a. What is a water molecule?

    b. What are the three forms (states) of water?

    c. At what temperature does each form of water change into a new form?

2. Here is an example of how you could do the experiment. Take two identical ice cube trays and fill them to the same level with water, one with hot, the other with cold. Use a thermometer to record the water temperature. Place the trays in the freezer and check them at 5-minute intervals. Note which one has ice crystals forming first.

When designing a test for your hypothesis, it is very important that you control all the variables. For example, use the same kind of container for each trial and put the container in the same spot in the freezer each time.

3. Write a step-by-step description of your experiment.

4. Make a detailed list of materials.

A Chemical Change

One way that matter changes is chemically. A chemical change, also called a **chemical reaction**, actually changes the matter from the original form to something else. This type of change involves giving off or taking in energy. The energy that helps the change happen may be in several different forms, such as electricity or heat. Sometimes the change occurs so slowly, we hardly notice.

One example of chemical change that we can observe in the lunchroom is fresh baked cookies resulting from the heating of cookie dough. Another is old, brown apple slices on a dish.

Directions: On the line write **Chemical** if it is a chemical change or **Physical** if it is a physical change.

_____ **1.** Tarnish on silver

_____ **2.** Bread baking in the oven

_____ **3.** Cutting paper hearts from red paper

_____ **4.** Mixing sugar into water

_____ **5.** Burning toast in the toaster

_____ **6.** Rust forming on a tin can

Name _____

Conduct the following two experiments. Make observations. Decide why these changes are considered chemical changes rather than physical changes.

ACTIVITY ONE: DISAPPEARING INK

Use the fresh lemon juice and a cotton swab to write a secret message on your paper. Let the paper dry completely. Take the paper and move it slowly over the light.

Draw your observations below.

Materials
- lemon juice
- cottton swabs
- plain white paper
- a lamp or flashlight

Directions: What did you observe? Why is it an example of a chemical change?

_____

_____

_____

_____

_____

Chemical Changes, cont.

ACTIVITY TWO: VINEGAR AND STEEL

Use a piece of steel wool and put it in a glass jar. Pour the vinegar over the steel wool. Wait.

Draw your observations below.

Materials
• steel wool
• glass jar
• vinegar

Directions: What did you observe? Why is it an example of a chemical change?

_____

_____

_____

_____

_____

Name _____

Light energy is also called radiant energy. This kind of energy includes infrared rays, radio waves, ultraviolet rays, and X-rays.

Directions: Place a **T** before each true statement and an **F** before each false statement about light energy.

_____ **1.** People can see the ultraviolet rays of the electromagnetic spectrum.

_____ **2.** Radar is an instrument that uses radio waves to detect objects.

_____ **3.** The longest wavelength of visible light is violet.

_____ **4.** Infrared lamps are used to keep food warm in a restaurant.

_____ **5.** Laser beams have one wavelength and travel in one direction.

_____ **6.** Ultraviolet rays help people produce vitamin D.

_____ **7.** X-rays are used to examine luggage at an airport.

_____ **8.** Microwaves are used to fast-cook foods.

_____ **9.** The number of waves passing one point in a second is called a *crest*.

_____ **10.** Radio waves have the shortest wavelength.

_____ **11.** Radio waves are used to broadcast television programs.

_____ **12.** Cameras can record the infrared waves from people and animals.

_____ **13.** The shortest wavelength of visible light is violet.

_____ **14.** Gamma rays have the shortest wavelength and the highest energy.

_____ **15.** Visible light is made up of a spectrum of colors.

_____ **16.** Red-orange-yellow-green-blue-indigo-violet is the correct order of colors in the spectrum of visible light.

_____ **17.** The distance from one wave crest to the next is called the *trough*.

_____ **18.** A high-frequency wave has short wavelengths.

_____ **19.** Microwaves can be seen by people.

_____ **20.** Laser beams are often used at outdoor light shows.

_____ **21.** Gamma rays are emitted by radioactive elements.

_____ **22.** X-rays are used in medicine to locate broken bones.

Light Waves

Materials
- a flashlight
- a protractor
- a mirror
- black construction paper
- a sheet of white paper

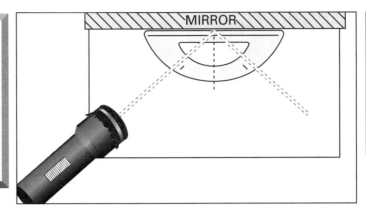

Angle of Incidence ($\angle i$)	Angle of Reflection ($\angle r$)
15°	
40°	
55°	

OBSERVING REFLECTION

Set up your materials as shown above. Once the protractor is in place, mark two points on either side of the 90° mark and connect that line all the way to the base of the mirror. Replace the protractor so that the 90° mark sits on this line. This will make it easier to judge the angles of the light.

Cut a 1/4 in. slit in the black paper and tape it over the front of the flashlight. Shine the flashlight in at the angles listed in the chart above and find the degree readings for the angle of the light reflected. (This is called the angle of incidence.) Subtract that number from 90° to determine the angle of reflection.

OBSERVING DIFFRACTION

Take two index cards and hold them very close together in front of a window. Look carefully at the edges of the cards that are close together. What do you notice about them?

_____

_____

_____

MAKING A HYPOTHESIS

What generalization can you make about the angles of incidence and reflection when a wave strikes a smooth surface?

_____

_____

What happens to waves when they travel through narrow slits? _____

_____

Name _____

Directions: Use the terms in the WORD BANK to complete the statements relating to the behavior of light in the acrostic puzzle below.

WORD BANK

bent	flat	index	mirror	reflected
concave	focal	lens	photon	retina
convex	image	light	real image	virtual

1. When light travels from one medium to another, it is refracted, or ____ .

2. When rays of light strike and bounce off a mirror, the rays are ____ .

3. ____ is electromagnetic radiation and includes infrared, visible, and ultraviolet.

4. A ____ ____ can be projected on a screen.

5. A ____ image cannot be projected on a screen.

6. A ____ is a reflecting surface.

7. A ____ lens is thinner in the center than at the edges.

8. The back of the eye that receives an image is called the ____ .

9. A ____ lens is thicker in the center than at the edges.

10. The ____ point is the point at which light beams converge.

11. A ____ is a piece of glass or other transparent material which refracts light.

12. The ____ of refraction is the ratio of the speed of light in a vacuum to its speed in another medium.

13. A visual impression of an object in a mirror or through a lens is an ____ .

14. A ____ is a tiny package of electromagnetic energy.

15. A plane mirror is a ____ mirror.

1.   B __ __ __

2.   __ __ __ __ E __ __ __ __ __

3.   __ __ __ H __

4.   __ __ __ __ __ __ A __ __

5.   V __ __ __ __ __ __

6.   __ I __ __ __ __

7.   __ O __ __ __ __ __

8.   R __ __ __ __ __

9.   __ O __ __ __ __

10.   F __ __ __ __

11.   L __ __ __

12.   I __ __ __ __

13.   __ __ __ G __

14.   __ H __ __ __ __

15.   __ __ __ T

Making Rainbows

Make a miniature rainbow.

PURPOSE Light can be refracted by a lens and split into its component colors.

MATERIALS

- tall drinking glasses made of glass, one for each team
- water
- sunny day
- lab sheet

PROCEDURE

1. Fill each glass about 3⁄4 full of water. Take the glasses and lab sheets to a sunny part of the room.

2. Hold the glass above the paper, and sunlight will pass through it and form patterns of light on the page. Some parts of the pattern will be white light and other parts will have color. Try holding the glass at different heights, tilting it, and turning it.

3. What colors do you see? Are they always in the same order?

CONCLUSIONS

Each wavelength of light produces a different color. When blended together, as in daylight, the light looks colorless to us. A glass of water acts as a lens that refracts, or bends, the light waves. At certain angles, different wavelengths bend different amounts. They then separate into distinct bands as in a rainbow, and we can see the different colors.

Making Rainbows, cont.

Directions: Draw one of the miniature rainbows made by your glass of water. Show the bands of different colors. What shape were they? How broad were they?

Let the Sun Shine In

What color is light?

Directions: Recreate the model below and observe the light shining through water. Describe and draw what you see on the paper.

Observations: _____

_____

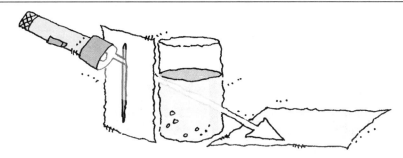

Light is made up of waves of energy that you cannot see. Different colors have waves of different lengths. What does this diagram tell you about blue light and red light?

_____

_____

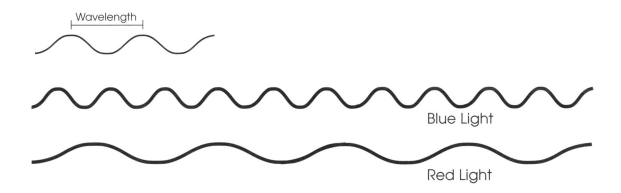

Puzzle: Use the hints below to put the seven colors of visible light in order from the longest wavelength to the shortest.

red _____ _____ _____ _____ _____ violet

longest   **shortest**

Yellow is shorter than orange but longer than green.
Indigo looks so much like violet, they blend together.
Green lies between yellow and blue.

What Is Electricity?

Electricity is a very important form of energy. It produces light and heat, and provides power for household appliances and industrial machinery among many other things.

Directions: Rearrange the letters below to spell out words related to electricity.

1. T A B E T R Y   _ _ _ _ E _ _ _

2. B L U B   _ _ L _

3. E S I T R S R O   _ E _ _ _ _ _ _

4. H E G C A R   C _ _ _ _ _

5. D E L E T E C R O   _ _ _ _ T _ _ _ _ _

6. T I U R I C C   _ _ R _ _ _ _

7. S U T I L R O N A   _ _ _ _ _ _ _ O _

8. N U C C O D R O T   _ _ N _ _ _ _ _ _

9. W I H C T S   S _ _ _ _ _ _

10. S O T E I V I P   _ O _ _ _ _ _ _

11. G A N I V E T E   N _ _ _ _ _ _ _

12. T W T A   _ _ T _

13. M O H   _ H _

14. S E U F   _ _ _ E

15. E M E R A P   _ M _ _ _ _

16. N E T R O G E R A   _ _ _ _ _ _ O _

17. T O V L   V _ _ _

18. R U T N I B E   _ _ _ _ _ _ E

Charge It

What makes your missing sock stick to the back of a shirt? What causes the shock and spark you get when you walk across the carpet and touch a doorknob? **Static electricity** is a form of electrical energy that is found freely in nature. Static electricity cannot run a television or turn on a light. But it can produce great bolts of lightning that light up the sky.

Matter is made of tiny particles called **atoms**. These particles are so small that we can't even see them with a regular microscope. Even though they're very small, atoms are made of even smaller particles. Some of these particles have a positive charge, and some have a negative charge. For atoms, opposites attract. Negative charges are attracted, or pulled, toward positive charges. The same charges (positive to positive and negative to negative) repel, or push away from each other. Positive and negative charges make your hair stand up when you take off a wool hat. The wool hat rubs against your hair. When you remove the hat, it takes some of the negatively charged particles that were in your hair. Your hair is left with a positive charge. Your hair stands up as its positive charges push away from one another.

Static electricity is an imbalance of positive and negative charges caused by **friction**, a force between two objects that are rubbing against one another. You might notice that your feet get warmer as you drag them across a carpeted floor. This is due to friction between your feet and the carpet. What you won't notice as you do this is that friction is causing negative particles to jump from the carpet to your socks. Touch a doorknob (a conductor) and ZAP! The negative charges from the carpet move through the doorknob to give you a shock.

Directions: Use the information above to answer the questions.

1. Where are positive and negative charges found? _____

2. Positive and negative charges _____ each other.

3. Two positive charges _____ each other.

4. What is static electricity? _____

5. What causes static electricity? _____

Do I Detect a Charge?

QUESTION How can I make and use a device to measure the strength of static electricity?

MATERIALS
- tape
- a balloon
- a piece of corrugated cardboard
- a large metal paper clip
- a piece of wool
- a needle
- an aluminum pie pan
- a foam plate
- a plastic bottle
- a piece of silk thread
- a glass jar
- 2 foam peanuts

PROCEDURE

1. Unfold the paper clip so the bottom is a hook.
2. Tape the paper clip to the cardboard so the hook hangs below the cardboard.
3. Use the needle to thread the 2 foam peanuts together, about 2 inches apart.
4. Hang the foam peanuts over the hook.
6. Blow up the balloon and tie it off.
7. Holding the edges of the cardboard, bring the foam peanuts close to the balloon, but not touching. Write your observations in the table.
8. Rub the balloon with the wool for 30 seconds.
9. Repeat step 7. Write your observations in the table.
10. Repeat steps 7–9 with the other materials. Answer the questions.

OBJECT	BEFORE CHARGE	AFTER CHARGE
balloon		
aluminum pie pan		
foam plate		
plastic bottle		
glass jar		

1. What happened to the object when you rubbed it with wool? _____

_____

2. How did the device you made detect static electricity? _____

_____

3. The same charges cause objects to push away from each other. Based on this, which objects do you think had the same charge as the foam peanuts?

_____

4. Opposite charges cause objects to pull toward each other. Based on this, which objects do you think had the opposite charge as the foam peanuts?

_____

Series Circuit

Electricity in circuits can produce light.

QUESTION

What happens when an electrical circuit runs through more than one lightbulb?

MATERIALS

- six-volt battery for each team
- two 6- or 12-volt light bulbs in sockets for each team
- insulated wire with the ends stripped, one 2-foot piece for each team
- insulated wire with the ends stripped, two 1-foot pieces for each team
- lab sheet

PROCEDURE

1. Have each team build a circuit that includes the battery and one lightbulb in a socket, as shown in the top sketch on the activity sheet. When both battery terminals are hooked up, what happens?

2. Have the teams disconnect the long wire at both ends and attach one end of it to the second socket. Then use a short wire to connect the other screw of the second socket to the empty screw of the first socket. *When they touch the free end of the long wire to the free battery terminal, what happens?*

3. Leave all the wires connected as in step #2, but unscrew one of the bulbs. *What happens?* Screw the bulb back in. *What happens?*

CONCLUSIONS

In a series circuit, current runs through two or more appliances (the bulbs) before returning to the battery. Removing a bulb, like a switch being turned off, breaks the circuit.

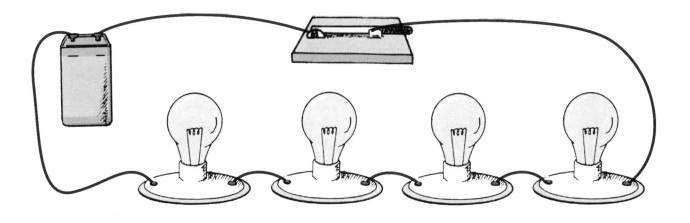

Electricity and Sound

Name _____

Directions: Draw colored lines to show the current.

What happens?

_____

_____

_____

_____

_____

What happens?

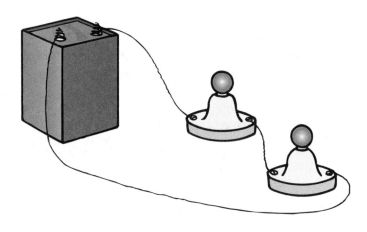

_____

_____

_____

_____

_____

What happens?

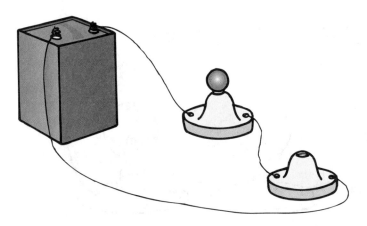

_____

_____

_____

_____

_____

Parallel Circuit

QUESTION What happens when a circuit runs in loops through more than one light bulb? Electricity in circuits can produce light.

MATERIALS

- batteries, wires, bulbs, and sockets as in "Series Circuit," on page 291
- one more 1-foot length of wire, ends stripped, for each team
- lab sheet

PROCEDURE

1. Have each team build a circuit that includes both bulbs as in the sketch on the lab sheet. *When both battery terminals are hooked up, what happens?*

2. Leaving all the wires connected as in step #1, unscrew one bulb. *What happens?*

CONCLUSIONS

In a parallel circuit like this, current runs to two or more appliances (bulbs) in separate loops. Removing one bulb does not interrupt the circuit, so current continues to flow to the other bulb.

Note:

Standard diagrams of series and parallel circuits look like this:

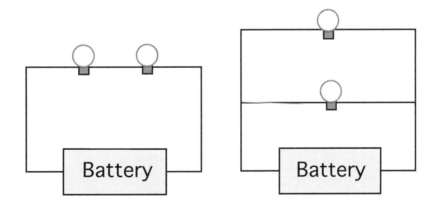

Directions: Use two different colored lines to show the current to the two bulbs.

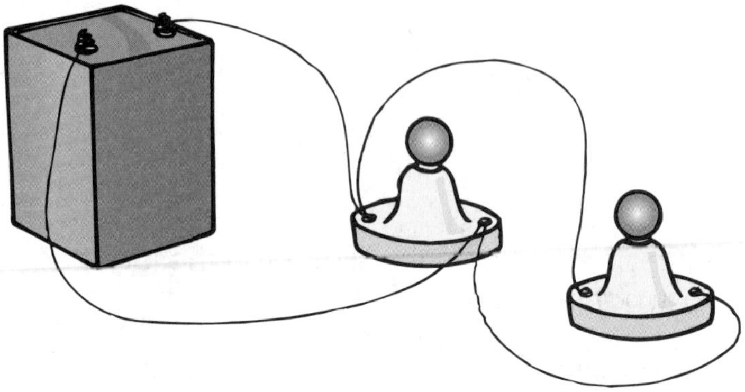

What happens?

_____

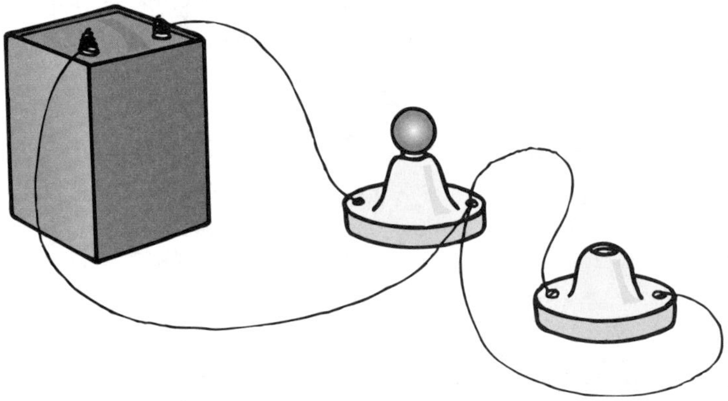

_____

_____

_____

_____

_____

What happens?

_____

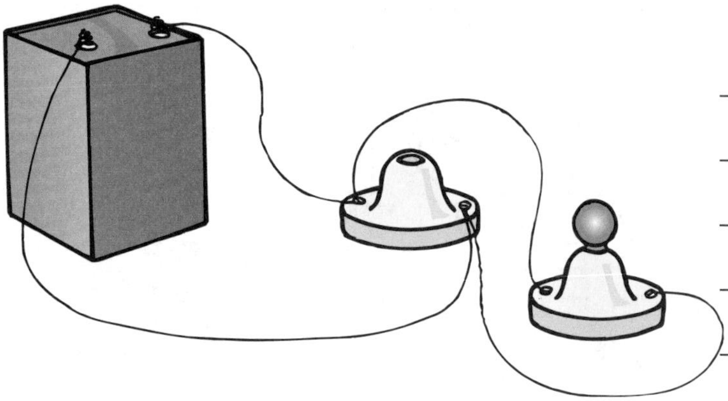

_____

_____

_____

_____

_____

What happens?

_____

_____

_____

_____

_____

_____

Dry Cells

The **dry cell** is a source of portable power used in flashlights, toys, and radios. There are three basic kinds of dry cells that are commonly used—carbon-zinc, alkaline, and mercury.

Directions: Label the parts of this carbon-zinc dry cell illustration.

WORD BANK

positive terminal   zinc container   chemical paste
negative terminal   carbon rod

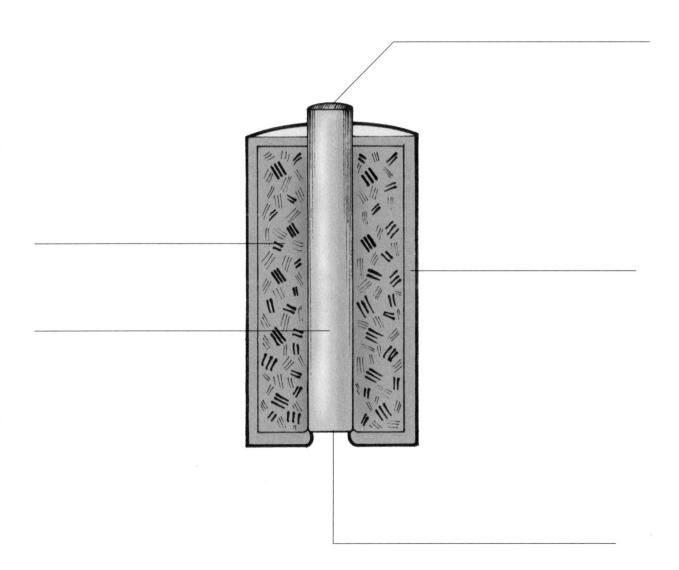

How Many Volts?

Voltage is a measure of the force that pushes current through a conductor. It is expressed in volts. Circle the word **VOLT** in the grid. It may be written forward, backward, up, down, or diagonally.

How many volts can you find? _____

V	L	B	T	L	O	V	L	O	T	L	O	V
O	T	I	B	M	J	F	R	C	L	I	A	O
L	A	V	E	H	V	L	U	W	O	P	N	L
T	L	O	V	G	V	A	D	I	V	J	B	T
D	S	L	X	O	O	T	K	O	Z	M	L	O
Y	F	T	R	E	L	G	L	S	V	O	U	C
N	L	P	W	Y	T	T	L	O	V	X	Z	K
V	T	L	O	V	B	E	L	F	T	O	G	A
O	C	H	K	M	I	T	O	L	P	J	L	Q
R	V	O	L	T	S	V	Y	T	V	O	L	T
D	O	V	Z	W	V	O	C	N	E	A	U	L
V	L	F	J	H	O	L	M	B	T	R	D	O
O	T	N	V	X	L	T	P	L	G	L	Q	V
L	T	L	O	V	T	K	L	V	T	W	O	S
T	I	O	L	U	A	E	X	O	I	P	B	V
Y	C	F	T	H	K	T	L	O	V	R	O	D
V	O	L	T	Z	G	J	S	W	L	L	Q	O
T	N	Y	U	M	A	C	V	B	T	L	O	V

Name

QUESTIONS
What do you know about the flow of electricity in a circuit? Can you think of anything that would stop, or interrupt, the flow of electricity? Use a piece of tape to attach a wire to the bottom of a D-cell battery. Attach the other end to the side of a lightbulb. Put your finger on top of the battery between the bulb and the battery. Describe what happened and explain why.

MATERIALS
- one D-cell battery
- tape
- 8 in. of insulated wire with the ends stripped
- one flashlight bulb
- potential conductors and insulators:
  - eraser
  - paper
  - aluminum foil
  - steel wool
  - Popsicle™ stick
  - cardboard
  - metal key
  - paper clip
  - sponge
  - plastic lid
  - metal washer
  - pencil
  - penny
  - metal lid

INFORMATION
An item that stops electrons from flowing freely is called an **insulator**. An item that allows electric current to flow freely is called a **conductor**.

PROCEDURE
You will test the given items to determine whether they are conductors or insulators. You should look for similarities in the items that are insulators. Make predictions before testing the items. To set up the circuit, tape the stripped end of the wire to the bottom of the battery and tape the other end to the side of the metal base of the lightbulb. Or, use the recycled battery holder from a previous lesson.

CONCLUSIONS
Discuss what the conductors have in common. Discuss what the insulators have in common. Can you make up a rule that would help identify which items are conductors and which are insulators? Discuss what this list has in common with the items that are magnetic.

PREDICTION
Think of ten additional items and predict whether they are conductors or insulators. Test each one.

Real-World Applications

Discuss how electrical wires are coated with plastic, which acts as an insulator.

Conductors and Insulators, cont.

QUESTION Which items are conductors and which are insulators?

1. Tape the stripped end of the wire to the bottom of the battery. Tape the other end to the side of the metal base of the lightbulb.
2. Predict whether each item is a conductor or an insulator.
3. Test each item by placing the item between the battery and the contact point of the lightbulb. If the lightbulb lights, the item you are testing is a conductor. An insulator will interrupt the circuit and the bulb will not light.
4. Record the results on the data table.

ITEM	YOUR PREDICTION	IS IT A CONDUCTOR OR AN INSULATOR?

What do all of the conductors have in common?

____

What do all of the insulators have in common?

____

What rule can you come up with to help identify items that are conductors and which are insulators?

____

Understanding Insulation

QUESTION How does what a cup is made of affect its insulation?

MATERIALS

- measuring cup
- glass jar
- styrene foam cup
- insulated plastic mug
- ceramic mug
- water
- thermometer(s)
- timer/clock

PROCEDURE

Pour hot tap water into the measuring cup. Take the temperature of the water. By adding cold or hot water, adjust the water so that the temperature is 120° F. Pour 4 oz. of the water into the jar. Set the jar on a flat surface where it will not be touched, such as a desktop or table. Start the timer. The temperature at zero minutes is 120° F, as shown on the data chart. After five minutes, take the temperature of the water. Record the result. Take another temperature reading after 10 minutes and again after 15 minutes.

Measure another 4 oz. of hot water. Take the temperature and adjust it until the thermometer reads 120° F. Pour the water into the ceramic mug. Set the mug in the same area as the jar, though not in the exact same spot. This spot may still be warm from the jar. The temperature at zero minutes is 120° F. After 5 minutes, take a temperature reading and record. Repeat at 10-and 15-minute intervals.

Repeat the procedure for the insulated plastic mug and the styrene foam cup. If more than one thermometer is available, two or more mugs may be tested at the same time. Record all temperature readings. Make a graph of the results and complete the lab sheet.

The control group is the glass jar because jars are not thought of as having any insulation value. The jar represents a mug with no insulation. The variables being controlled are the starting temperature of the water, the amount of water, the room temperature, and where the mugs are placed.

Data for cup material affecting insulation:

MINUTES	JAR	CERAMIC MUG	PLASTIC MUG	FOAM MUG
Water temperature At 0 min.				
Water temperature At 5 min.				
Water temperature At 10 min.				
Water temperature At 15 min.				

What's That Sound?

A sound is made when an object **vibrates** (moves quickly back and forth). This makes the air around the object vibrate. When the vibrating air reaches our ears, we hear sound. Even though all sound is made this way, there are countless different sounds. Each sound has special qualities. They have different pitches and travel in different ways, too.

You can do the following experiment. You will listen and then practice telling the difference between many sounds. You can also describe the sounds you hear.

MATERIALS

- six small plastic containers with lids
  (all the same size)
- items such as pebbles, coins, nails, marbles, rice, and sand

PROCEDURE

Put a different object in each of the containers, making sure no one sees you setting up the project. Number the containers. Make a chart that shows the container number, the item, and columns to keep a tally of correct guesses.

Now ask at least ten people to listen as you shake each container. Have them guess what is inside. Keep a tally of the correct guesses. Ask the listeners to describe what the shaking sounded like. Take notes on the comments. Then, answer the following questions.

CONCLUSIONS

1. How many people made all of their guesses correctly? _____

   _____

2. Which items do you think made the loudest sounds? _____

   _____

3. Were there any sounds that were very similar? Which ones? Why? _____

   _____

   _____

Electricity and Sound

Bottle Flutes

QUESTION

How can you change the sound made by blowing into a bottle? The pitch of a sound can be varied by changing the rate of vibration.

MATERIALS

- three bottles containing different amounts of water
- lab sheet

PROCEDURE

1. Blow down an inside edge of each bottle. What do you hear? Which bottle makes the lowest sound? Which makes the highest sound?

2. Grip each bottle tightly as you blow into it again. Does that change the sound?

CONCLUSIONS

When you blow into a bottle, the air inside vibrates and produces a tone. The more water there is in the bottle, the shorter the column of air above it, and the higher the note when the air vibrates. Gripping the bottle does not affect the air inside or the sound it produces.

Note:

This activity presents an intriguing puzzle. You might demonstrate first and then ask others to experiment with the bottles themselves, and try to figure out why tapping and blowing produce different results.

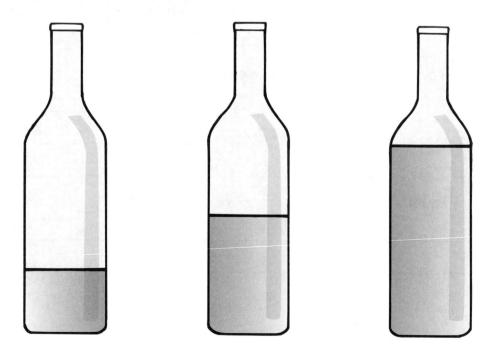

Blow

Blow

Blow

Which bottle flute makes the highest note? _____

_____

Which makes the lowest? _____

_____

What vibrates to produce the notes you hear? _____

_____

What happens when you grip each bottle as you blow into it? _____

_____

Newton's Laws

A scientist named Isaac Newton experimented and developed three laws of motion that hold true for matter on earth. The laws are as follows:

Law 1—An object in motion will remain in motion, and an object at rest will stay at rest unless a force acts on it.

Law 2—Acceleration of an object increases as the amount of force causing acceleration increases. The larger the mass of the item, the larger the force needed to result in acceleration.

Law 3—For every action there is an equal and opposite reaction.

These laws are at work everyday as you play on the playground. When you swing on the swing or kick the soccer ball to the net, you are experiencing Newton's laws.

Directions: Below are examples of motion on the playground. On the line next to the number, write the number of the law that is at work.

_____ **1.** You swing the baseball bat and hit the ball. It doesn't go as far as when the older boys hit the ball.

_____ **2.** You are standing on the merry-go-round waiting for someone to push it. When it does get pushed, you fall backward.

_____ **3.** You are playing marbles. You shoot one into another. The one you hit stops, but the one it hits moves out of the circle.

_____ **4.** You are in the school swimming pool gripping the edge. You push off the wall with your feet and shoot forward in the water.

_____ **5.** You are helping your teacher build a rock garden during recess. You are pushing a wheelbarrow full of rocks and then dump them. Pushing the wheelbarrow back to school is much easier.

Inertia

Inertia is the tendency of an object in motion to stay in motion. That is part of Newton's first law of motion. You can experience this in many ways on the playground. Imagine running across the schoolyard as fast as you can for ten steps. Imagine trying to stop your feet and not moving forward another inch. What would happen to the rest of your body? Your body would continue to move forward!

Directions: Look around the playground. Watch people playing. Choose an activity that is showing inertia. Below, draw a picture of the action. Then, on the lines write about the action describing how it shows inertia.

_____

_____

_____

_____

Simple and Compound Machines

Laws of Motion Experiments

MOMENTUM

Newton's second law of motion states that acceleration of an object increases as the amount of force causing acceleration increases.

Momentum makes you go fast when you are sledding down a hill. It is the force the sled has when it's moving. Do this activity to show momentum. Make a hill by placing a grooved ruler on a thick book. Place the fan-folded paper a thumb's width away from the base of the "hill." (Look at the picture.) Roll the marble down the "hill." What happens when the marble "sled" hits the paper? Mark the position of the paper with a piece of tape labeled **G** for "gentle."

Materials
- grooved ruler
- 2 thick books
- half sheet of paper (fan-folded)
- marble
- tape
- pen

Stack another book to make the hill steeper. Replace the paper to its position and roll the marble again. Label where the paper ends up with tape labeled **S** for "steep." Now compare the results of the two slidings. Do you have more momentum sledding down a steep or gentle hill?

FORCEFUL FORCES

Whenever you push an object, the object pushes back at you with the same force. Try this activity to better understand the idea.

Materials
- skateboard or roller skates
- proper protective equipment
- school wall

1. Stand next to the school wall on a skateboard or roller skates. Give the wall a gentle push. What happens?

2. Repeat step 1 but this time give a harder push. What happens now? What pushed you?

"MAGIC" TRICK

Stack seven of the pennies on a smooth table. Place another penny a few inches to the right or left of the stack. Use your finger to flick the single penny hard, so that it hits the bottom of the stack. If you hit the stack just right, you'll find that the pennies won't fall over. What happens instead? Why?

Materials
- 8 pennies

Action and Reaction

Newton's third law of motion states that for every action there is an equal and opposite reaction. For example, if you let go of an inflated balloon, the balloon will move forward while the air will be pushed backward.

Directions: Try as many of these activities as you can. Then, think of two activities of your own. Describe the reactions in the chart.

ACTION	REACTION
Kick a ball.	
Pull a rubber band and let go.	
Push a partner on a swing.	
Hit a ball with a bat.	
Push against a wall.	

Simple and Compound Machines

Measuring Friction

Friction is the force that slows down and stops moving objects. In this activity, you will observe the effects of different surface materials on friction.

MATERIALS

- plastic tray
- felt
- plastic food wrap
- plastic cup
- sandpaper
- pennies
- string
- wax paper
- tape
- rocks

PROCEDURE

1. Punch holes in the plastic tray and cup. Connect the cup to the tray as shown in the illustration.

2. Tape a piece of felt material to the table beneath the tray.

3. Place a few small rocks in the tray.

4. Begin placing pennies in the cup until the tray begins to move on the felt.

5. Count the pennies needed to begin the motion. Record the number in the chart below.

6. Repeat the activity with sandpaper, wax paper, and plastic food wrap. Record the number of pennies in each trial.

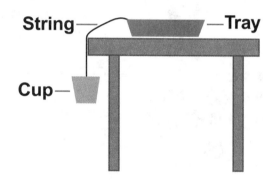

Type of Material	Number of Pennies Needed
Felt	
Sandpaper	
Wax paper	
Plastic food wrap	

Magnetic Attraction

QUESTIONS   Open a can with an electric can opener. Why does the can stay suspended while the can opener works? A magnet holds the can in place. Think about other familiar things that might contain a magnet.

INFORMATION   A magnet is an object that attracts metals such as iron and steel. The ends of a magnet are called **poles**. A magnet has a north pole and a south pole. Opposite poles **attract**; the north pole of one magnet attracts the south pole of another magnet. Like poles **repel**; the north pole of one magnet pushes away the north pole of another magnet.

MATERIALS

- magnets
- objects to explore:
    wood block, thread, steel pin, aluminum foil, copper wire, paper clip, penny, shoelace, plastic straw, steel wool, nail, metal can, metal spoon

PROCEDURE   Fill in the prediction column of the data table to indicate whether items will be attracted to magnets. Then, explore and find out which items are attracted to magnets. Sort the objects into two groups: items that are attracted to magnets, and those that are not.

CONCLUSIONS   What do conductors have in common? Discuss what the insulators have in common. Can you make up a rule that would help identify which items are conductors and which are insulators? Discuss what this list has in common with the items that are magnetic.

What items are attracted to magnets? Not all metals are magnetic.

PREDICTION   Think about how magnets are used to make our lives easier. Write about some magnets we use in everyday life.

Real-World Applications
- Discuss how inventors use magnets.
- Discuss when you wouldn't want a metal to be magnetic.

Simple and Compound Machines

Magnetic Attraction, cont.

Directions: First, make a prediction, then test each item. Hold each item next to the magnet to determine whether it is magnetic. Write your observations below on the chart.

ITEM	YOUR PREDICTION	IS IT MAGNETIC?	WHAT IS IT MADE OF?
Wood block			
Thread			
Steel pin			
Aluminum foil			
Copper wire			
Paper clip			
Penny			
Shoelace			
Steel wool			
Nail			
Metal can			
Metal spoon			
Plastic straw			

Were there any items that surprised you? _____

What did you observe about the magnetic items? _____

Sort the items into two groups. Draw a picture of each item in its proper category.

Magnetic	Non-Magnetic

Are All Metals Magnetic?

QUESTIONS   Have you ever wondered if all metals are equally magnetic? Try this simple test to see. Try to pick up a quarter with a magnet. Now, try a steel pin. Was there a difference?

INFORMATION   Most materials, even wood, copper, and water do not seem to respond to magnets. Actually, all materials can respond to magnetic force, but some so weakly that the force is not observable in everyday life. Items that respond well to magnets are iron, nickel, and cobalt.

MATERIALS

- magnet
- sharpened pencil (graphite)
- straight pin (steel)
- aluminum foil
- copper wire
- paper clip (steel)
- penny (copper-plated zinc)
- steel wool
- nail (iron)
- aluminum can
- dime (copper and nickel)

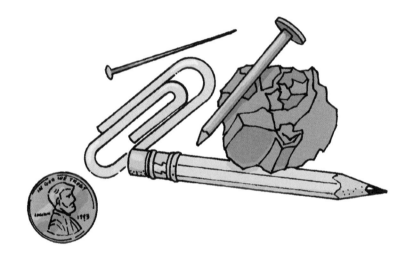

PROCEDURE   Test each of the items for its reaction to the magnet. Complete the table. Research the composition of the different metal items (content is in parentheses in the materials list).

CONCLUSIONS   Study and discuss the completed table. Have students determine what types of metals are always magnetic. What types of metals are not attracted to the magnet?

PREDICTION   Collect as many different metals as you can find. From what you know about different types of metals, predict which ones will be attracted to a magnet and which ones will not.

> **Real-World Applications**
> Discuss how mechanics may magnetize their screwdrivers to retrieve lost screws.

Name _____

Directions: List the items being tested in the table. Predict and then test each item against a magnet. Record whether each item is magnetic or nonmagnetic.

ITEM	YOUR PREDICTION	IS IT MAGNETIC?	WHAT IS IT MADE OF?

Research the items to determine their composition. Study the table.

What types of metals are always magnetic? _____

_____

_____

What types of metals are never magnetic? _____

_____

_____

_____

Forms of Energy

Energy is what makes motion and change possible. It is the ability to do work. Energy is needed to make items move, from a car that takes you to school to your hair blowing in the breeze as you walk there. Energy is also needed to make matter change, such as when fire burns wood to ashes.

There are two types of energy. There is **kinetic energy**, which is energy that exists because something is moving, like a bus driving away from the bus stop. And there is **potential energy**, which is energy that exists because of its position. It gives the ability to do work in the future. This is like the car parked in the parking lot waiting to be turned on to take you to school.

Look at the pictures below. The one on the left shows potential energy. The rock can do work if it rolls down the hill. The one on the right shows kinetic energy. It is actually moving.

Potential   **Kinetic**

Directions: Decide if the statement is an example of potential or kinetic energy. Write **Potential** or **Kinetic** on the line. Then, draw an example of kinetic energy in the box.

_____ 1. A bicycle locked in a bike rack

_____ 2. The gym teacher jogging to school

_____ 3. A wrecking ball breaking up the old school building

_____ 4. The river you pass on the way to school

_____ 5. Your dog watching you leave for school

_____ 6. Your mother waving goodbye at the door

Simple and Compound Machines

Name _____

DIFFERENT ENERGY

Tie the rope to the bucket handle. Across from you have a partner stand on a chair and hold the bucket so it hangs in front. Have him or her hold the bucket, then let it go. Would you have to get out of the way to avoid being hit when it swings back in your direction? Why or why not? Suppose your partner pushed the bucket away instead of just letting it go. Would that change your answer?

Materials
• bucket
• rope
• partner

_____

_____

NO GRAVITY?

Imagine what the earth would be like without gravity. Write five things that would be different. On a separate sheet of paper, use these five ideas in a story about you and others experiencing the lack of gravity.

Materials
• writing paper
• pen

1. _____

2. _____

3. _____

4. _____

5. _____

BOUNCING BALLS

Do you think bigger balls bounce higher than smaller ones? Get four or five balls of different sizes. Design your own experiment that will help you find the answer. Will you drop the balls from the same height or from different heights? Think about how you will measure the bounces.

Materials
• several different-sized balls
• writing paper
• pencil
• measuring tool

List the balls on a chart. For each ball, record the height of the first bounce. Write several sentences detailing what you have learned.

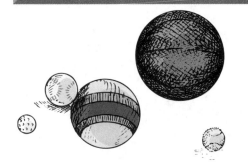

_____

_____

_____

Egg Drop

Gravity is the force which pulls all objects toward the earth. Some materials can insulate and cushion an object from the impact of gravity. Paper, foam cups, cloth, and similar materials are good insulators.

MATERIALS

Collect as many of these materials as possible before beginning the project:

- newspaper
- foam pieces or "peanuts,"
- pantyhose
- pieces of cloth
- string
- one or more raw eggs
- a shoe box or cardboard carton

PROCEDURE

The goal of this experiment is to have an egg survive from the highest possible height. Use the collected packaging materials to protect the egg inside the cardboard carton or shoe box. Be as creative as you can when wrapping the egg. Let an adult hold the package as high as possible or use a ladder to stand on. He or she will drop the package.

Check your egg. Did it break?

_____

If your egg didn't break the first time, have an adult drop it from a higher point. Did it break this time?

_____

From how high do you think the egg can be dropped before it breaks? _____

_____

Simple and Compound Machines

Which Objects Will Slide the Fastest?

QUESTION

What kinds of objects slide the fastest down a ramp?

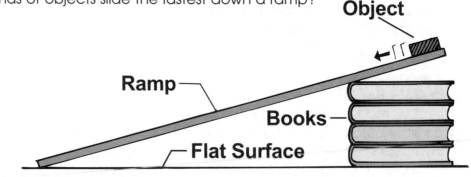

MATERIALS

- ice cube
- penny
- magnet
- ramp
- four books

INFORMATION

A **force** is a push or pull on an object. Forces give energy to an object. For example, a person pushing a bicycle exerts a force upon it. The bicycle also exerts a force on the person. The person must push with more force than the bicycle pushes back in order to move it. This causes an unbalanced force, and unbalanced forces result in motion. **Friction** is a force that opposes motion. Friction is one reason why a book pushed across a table stops moving very quickly, or that some objects slide down a ramp faster than others. The more friction, the slower the object will move. The less friction, the faster the object will move.

PREDICTION

On your record sheet, predict the order in which these items will slide down a ramp: an ice cube, a penny, and a magnet.

PROCEDURE

1. Stack four books and use them to raise one end of the ramp up.
2. One at a time, slide the objects down the ramp. Do not push them. Let them move on their own.

RESULTS

Record the order in which the objects slid down the ramp, from fastest to slowest, on your record sheet.

CONCLUSIONS

Answer the following questions on your record sheet:
Was your prediction correct about which objects would slide the fastest? Why or why not?
If the ramp had been steeper, would the results of your experiment have been any different? Explain your answer.

Name _____

QUESTION   What kinds of objects slide the fastest down a ramp?

PREDICTION   Predict the order in which these items will slide down a ramp, from fastest to slowest: an ice cube, a penny, and a magnet.

_____

_____

_____

RESULTS   Record the order in which the objects slid down the ramp, from fastest to slowest.

_____

_____

_____

CONCLUSIONS

Was your prediction correct about which objects would slide the fastest? _____

Why or why not? _____

_____

If the ramp had been steeper, would the results of your experiment have been any different? Explain your answer.

_____

_____

_____

_____

_____

Name _____

There are three classes of levers—first-class, second-class, and third-class. All levers have a resistance arm, an effort arm, and a fulcrum. Examine the sketches of the three classes of levers below for the positions of the fulcrum, the effort arm, and the resistance arm.

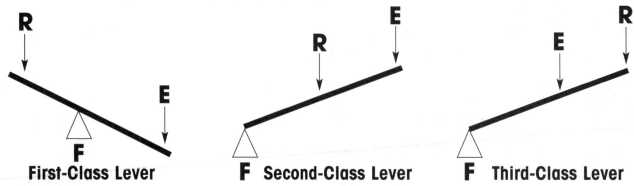

First-Class Lever   **F** **Second-Class Lever**   **F** **Third-Class Lever**

Directions: Make a simple sketch of the events below. Label the fulcrum, the effort arm, and the resistance arm. Identify the class of lever.

1. Two students on a seesaw	**2.** Using a nutcracker
3. Sweeping with a broom	**4.** Using a car jack
5. Rolling a wheelbarrow	**6.** Batting a baseball
7. Hammering a nail in a board	**8.** Swinging a golf club

QUESTION How does weight affect the way a seesaw works?

MATERIALS
- a wooden ruler
- a pencil with flat sides in the shape of a hexagon
- 10 pennies

PROCEDURE

1. Put the pencil on a desk or table. Balance the ruler across the pencil so half of the ruler is on each side.

2. Put a penny in the same place on each end of the ruler.

3. Put a second penny on top of the penny on the right side.

4. Move the two pennies closer to the middle until the system balances. Draw an **X** in the diagram below to show where the two pennies need to be for the seesaw to balance.

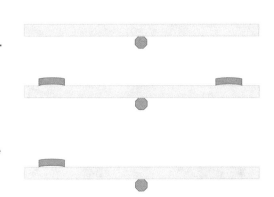

5. Using the numbers of pennies below, predict where the pennies on the right side will need to be for the seesaw to balance. Write your prediction in the chart.

# of Pennies on Left Side	# of Pennies on Right Side	Prediction	Actual
2	3		
1	4		
5	5		
4	6		

6. Check your predictions with your pennies. Write the results in the chart.

Directions: Answer the questions below.

1. What acted as the fulcrum in this experiment? _____

2. Instead of moving the pennies on the right side to make the seesaw balance, do you think you could have moved the fulcrum? Why or why not? _____

_____

3. How could you seesaw with someone who weighs more than you? _____

_____

Less than you? _____

Simple Machines

There are six simple machines that are the basic units of all complex machines: the **lever**, the **wheel and axle**, the **wedge**, the **pulley**, the **inclined plane**, and the **screw**.

RECOGNIZING SIMPLE MACHINES

Which simple machines can you find in each of the tools listed below?

hammer _____   scissors _____

doorstop _____   drill _____

saw _____   screwdriver _____

crowbar _____   monkey wrench _____

BICYCLE PARTS

Study a bicycle carefully. Fill in the blanks with the simple machines you find.

tire _____   kickstand _____

caliper brakes _____   handlebars _____

chain and sprocket _____   gearshift _____

pedal and shaft _____   fork _____

other _____

Six Types of Simple Machines

Machines can increase or decrease a force, or they can change the amount of force needed to do work. There are six machines that are classified as simple machines.

Directions: Use the number pairs to identify the names of the six types of simple machines in the grid below. The horizontal number is first, and the vertical number is second. For example, the number pair 7-8 represents the letter *W*.

	1	2	3	4	5	6	7	8	9
9	E	G	A	D	U	H	C	N	L
8	B	F	Y	C	G	C	W	H	E
7	P	E	J	M	L	K	E	N	L
6	I	L	O	E	N	P	Q	D	R
5	L	R	N	D	S	N	L	T	W
4	A	E	A	Y	L	E	Z	R	E
3	U	X	V	L	A	C	E	E	I
2	S	D	W	F	D	I	P	B	X
1	W	V	G	E	J	A	H	L	K

___ ___ ___ ___ ___
4-3   7-7   2-1   1-9   8-4

___ ___ ___ ___ ___ ___ ___ ___   ___ ___ ___ ___ ___
9-3   3-5   6-8   1-5   6-2   8-9   2-4   5-2   7-2   9-9   3-4   6-5   2-7

___ ___ ___ ___ ___
1-2   4-8   9-6   4-6   3-2

___ ___ ___ ___ ___
7-8   4-1   8-6   2-9   8-3

___ ___ ___ ___ ___ ___
1-7   5-9   7-5   8-1   9-8   3-8

___ ___ ___ ___ ___   ___ ___ ___   ___ ___ ___ ___
1-1   6-9   6-4   9-4   5-7   1-4   5-6   4-5   6-1   9-2   2-6   7-3

Simple and Compound Machines

Special Inclined Planes

Some simple machines are pictures below. Some of these simple machines are special inclined planes, called wedges and screws.

Directions: Put an **X** on the simple machines that are not special inclined planes. Label the special inclined planes either **screw** or **wedge**.

Compound Machines

Often two or more simple machines are combined to make one machine called a **compound machine**.

Directions: Name the simple machines that are combined to make each of the compound machines pictured below.

WORD BANK   wheel and axle   inclined plane (wedge, screw)
                lever   pulley

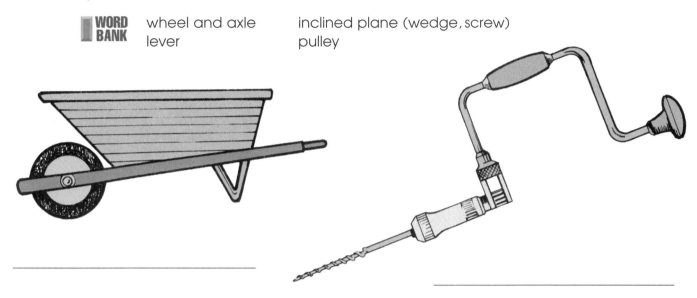

_____   _____

_____

Acids: A group of chemicals containing hydrogen that react in a certain way with other substances; they usually taste sour

Arthropods: Animals with exoskeletons and jointed appendages; the largest percentage of animals in the world

Atom: A tiny particle made of protons, neutrons, and electrons

Bases: Opposite of acids; contain a hydroxide ion and often feel slippery or soapy

Camouflage: Coloring that lets animals blend in with their surroundings so they can escape detection by their predators

Cell: The basic unit of a living thing that performs all of the functions of life

Chemical change: Completely changes the object from one material to another material, resulting in change to its chemical makeup; it usually cannot be reversed

Chromosomes: The thread-like parts of cells that hold genes

Circulatory system: The system made up of the heart, arteries, veins, and capillaries

Climate: The weather in a particular place over a long period of time

Clouds: Water droplets collected on tiny specks of dust or salt particles in the air; basic types are cirrus, cumulus, stratus, nimbus, and alto

Complete metamorphosis: The organism goes through four stages of growth and can look very different from the adult organism

Compound: Matter that is made up of two or more ingredients that are joined together

Compound machine: Two or more simple machines combined to make one machine

Conductor: An item that allows electric current to flow freely

Digestive system: The system that breaks down food, collecting nutrients and getting rid of wastes

Earthquake: A sudden shaking of the ground that occurs when masses of rock change positions below the earth's surface

Ecosystem: A group of plants and animals interacting and living in the same community

Element: Matter that is made up of only one ingredient; examples are oxygen, hydrogen, and carbon

Endocrine system: The system that develops and releases hormones into the blood

Environment: Includes all living and nonliving things with which an organism interacts

Food chain: A group of plants and animals that feed off one another

Food pyramid: A model that shows how many servings of certain foods people should eat each day

Food web: A series of interconnected food chains

Fossil: The remains of plants and animals preserved in rock

Genes: Parts of the cell that determine characteristics living things inherit from their parents; dominant are the strongest traits and recessive are the weakest traits

Genetics: The study of how parents and their offspring have similar and different traits

Germination: The process in which seeds start to change and grow into sprouts, then seedlings, and finally adult plants

Gravity: The force which pulls all objects toward the earth

Hypothesis: An educated guess to a scientific question

Incomplete metamorphosis: The change in the organism is not complete, meaning the young may resemble the adult

Insulator: An item that stops electrons from flowing freely

Glossary

Invertebrates: Animals that do not have a backbone

Kinetic energy: Energy that exists because something is moving, like a bus driving away from the bus stop

Law of Conservation of Mass: Matter cannot be created or destroyed during a chemical change

Matter: Anything that has mass and takes up space

Mixture: Matter that is made up of two or more ingredients that are mixed together

Mohs Hardness Scale: Classifies a mineral's hardness by using a simple scratch test

Mollusks: Animals with soft, boneless bodies; most have shells

Nervous system: The system made up of the brain and spinal cord that send information through the body

Newton's Law of Motion: Objects at rest stay at rest and objects in motion stay in motion; acceleration of an object increases as the amount of force causing acceleration increases; every action has an equal and opposite reaction force

Parallel circuit: Current runs to two or more appliances (bulbs) in separate loops; removing one bulb does not interrupt the circuit so current continues to flow to the other bulb

Periodic Table of Elements: A chart that gives a great deal of information about each of the elements

Photosynthesis: A food-making process that occurs in green plants; it is the main function of the leaves

Physical change: A change that does not involve a change in the basic elements or compounds that make up a substance; it can change in size, shape, or state of matter but does not create something new

Potential energy: Energy that exists because of its position; it has the ability to do work in the future

Procedure: Steps taken in a scientific experiment to test a hypothesis

Reproductive system: The system that allows living things to create new life

Reptiles: An animal that has dry, scaly skin and breathes using lungs

Respiratory system: The system made up of the lungs that takes in oxygen and pushes out carbon dioxide

Scientific method: The way scientists learn and study the world around them by performing experiments to find answers to their questions

Series circuit: Current runs through two or more appliances (bulbs) before returning to the battery; removing a bulb, like a switch being turned off, breaks the circuit

Simple machines: Basic units of all complex machines; the lever, the wheel and axle, the wedge, the pulley, the inclined plane, and the screw

Skeletal system: The system of bones and joints that gives the body its shape

Solar system: System made up of the sun, its nine plants, and their moons

Tornado: A destructive, whirling wind accompanied by a funnel-shaped cloud that takes a narrow path across land

Urinary system: The system made up of the kidneys and bladder that rids the body of waste

Vertebrates: Animals that have a backbone

Volcano: An opening in earth's surface through which gases, lava, and ash erupt

Volt: A measure of the force that pushes current through a conductor

Answer Key

Page 8
Sort 'Em Out

	VERTEBRATES		INVERTEBRATES
1.	dog	1.	octopus
2.	boy	2.	snail
3.	turtle	3.	starfish
4.	frog	4.	lobster
5.	lizard	5.	oyster

Page 11
The Meaning of...
1. A vertebrate is an organism with a backbone. Dogs, humans, and birds are examples.
2. An invertebrate has no backbone. Examples are sponges, mollusks, and flatworms.
3. fish, amphibians, reptiles, birds, and mammals
4. the left and right sides of the body are the same
5. the spine of an organism; it protects the spinal cord
6. an organism that lives off of another and gives nothing in return
7. Cold-blooded means the blood changes temperature with the air or water surrounding the organism. Warm-blooded means the body temperature stays the same, no matter the outside temperature.
8. a special fold of skin

Page 12
Concept Mapping Invertebrates
Maps will vary.

Page 13
Classifying Vertebrates

	FISH	AMPHIBIANS	BIRDS	REPTILES	MAMMALS
Body covering	scales	smooth	feathers	scales or shell	hair or fur
Warm- or cold-blooded	cold	cold	warm	cold	warm
Lungs or gills	gills	gills/lungs	lungs	lungs	lungs
Born alive or hatched	both	hatched	hatched	both	born
Habitat	water	water/land	air and water	water/land	land, air, and water
Name one example		Answers will vary.			

Page 14
Venn Them
Venn diagrams and paragraphs will vary.

Page 15
A Round of Research
Answers will vary.

Page 16
Animal Characteristics Recall
1. b
2. Neighbor
3. a
4. true
5. Answers will vary.

Page 17
Can You Identify These Arthropods?
1. I
2. A
3. C
4. I
5. I

6. A
7. A
8. C
9. C
10. I
11. I
12. I
13. C
14. C
15. C
16. C
17. I
18. I
19. I
20. I
21. I
22. I
23. I
24. I
25. I
26. A
27. A
28. C
29. C
30. C
31. I
32. I
33. I
34. I
35. A
36. A
37. I
38. I
39. I
40. A
41. A
42. I
43. I
44. I
45. A
46. C

Page 18
The World of Arthropods
INSECTS—beetle, termite,

grasshopper, moth, bee, butterfly, cricket, louse, ant, firefly, hornet, gnat, wasp, fly, cicada, aphid, flea, mayfly

ARACHNIDS—tick, black widow, scorpion, brown recluse, garden spider, tarantula, mite

CRUSTACEANS—lobster, barnacle, shrimp, crayfish, water flea, crab, wood louse

Page 19
Earthworms' Soil Conditioning
Answers will vary.

Page 20
Snail Observations
Answers will vary.

Page 21
Have You Seen It?
A. wings—thorax
B. antennae—head
C. eyes—head
D. spiracles—abdomen
E. legs—thorax
F. mouth—head

Page 22
How Does a Frog Catch Its Lunch?
1–4. Answers will vary.
5. Answers will vary. For example, the frog moves its long, sticky tongue quickly to catch insects.
6. Answers will vary.

Page 23
All Kinds of Reptiles

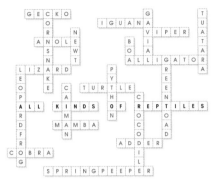

Page 24
Marine Life

Page 25
Mollusks
Answers will vary.

Page 26
Fabulous Seashells

Page 27
Echinoderms
Answers will vary.

Page 28
Some Sharks to Study
Answers will vary.

Page 29
What Can You See?
1. two tubes
2. eyes forward
3. side vision
4. The predators are northern pike, trout, and bass. The prey are carp, sunfish, and catfish.

Page 30
Animal Adaptations and Behavior
1. C
2. K
3. D
4. J
5. I
6. M
7. N
8. A
9. B
10. G
11. O
12. F
13. H
14. E
15. L

Page 31
Animal Adaptations
Animals and answers will vary.

Answer Key

Page 32
Beak Pick-Up
1. Answers will vary.
2. Answers will vary.

Page 33
Hide-and-Seek
1. Animal choices will vary.
2. Camouflage can hide animals from predators and help them sneak up on their prey.
3. Answers may include color and texture.

Page 34
My Animal
Animals and answers will vary.

Page 35
Animal Adaptations
Charts and drawings will vary.

Page 36
Animals and the Environment Recall
1. true
2. b
3. e
4. Food, shelter, and protection are three ways animals use their environment to live and survive.
5. Venn diagrams will vary.

Page 37
Endangered Animals
KOALA
JAGUAR
PUMA
MANATEE
GIANT PANDA
VICUÑA
CHEETAH
COATI
PRONGHORN
ORANGUTAN
Answers will vary.

Page 38
Metamorphosis
A. complete
1. egg
2. larva
3. pupa
4. adult
B. Incomplete
1. egg
2. nymph
3. adult

Page 39
Fascinating Fruit Flies
Observations will vary.
6. The stages are egg, larva, pupa, and adult.

Page 40
Brine Shrimp Exploration
Drawings will vary. Answers will vary.

Page 41
Compare and Contrast
1. Answers will vary.

2. Answers will vary.
3. Answers should include the fact that the human life cycle is more complex.

Page 42
Your Body Systems
skeletal, muscular
nervous, sensory, endocrine
digestive, respiratory,
circulatory, urinary

Page 43
Your Body Parts

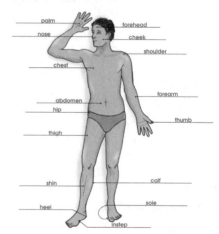

Page 45
Meeting Places
knees, elbows
hips, shoulders
fingers, toes
vertebrae
neck, wrist
skull, pelvis
the head

Page 46
Your Hands and Feet

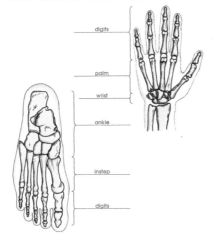

Page 47
Bones of Your Arm

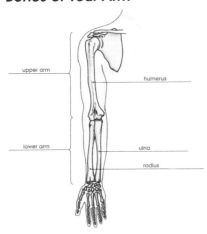

Page 48
Inside Your Teeth

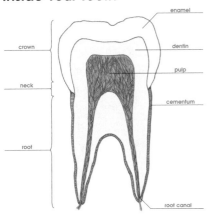

Page 49
Four Kinds of Teeth

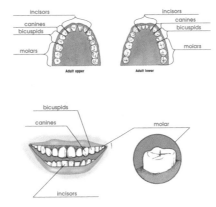

Page 50
Skeletal System Review

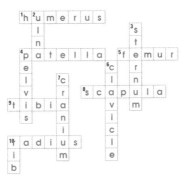

Page 51
The Supportive System

1. Answers may include: The skeleton supports the body. The skeleton protects internal organs. Bone marrow produces new blood cells. Bones store important minerals.

2. the femur

3. the stapes, or stirrup

4. cartilage

5. produces blood cells

6. no

7. compact bone

8. joint

Page 52
Muscle Man

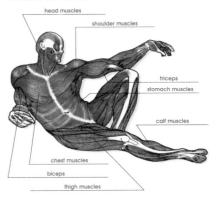

Page 53
Skeletal Muscles

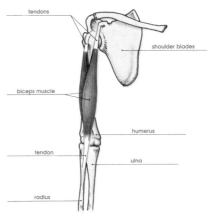

Page 54
Your Muscles

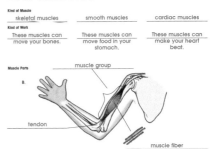

Page 55
The Circulatory System I

1. transporting materials throughout the body and

regulating body temperature
2. cells
3. waste products; liver, lungs, kidneys
4. center, surface
5. Blood vessels contract, allowing little blood to flow through.
A "Hearty" Experiment:
Answers will vary.

Page 56
The Circulatory System II

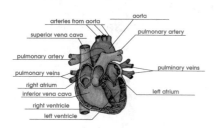

Page 57
Veins and Arteries

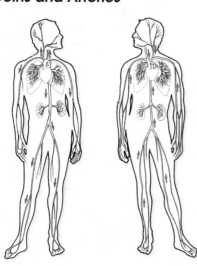

Page 58
Your Heart

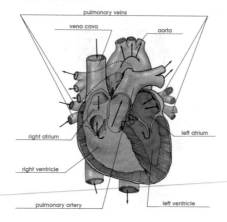

Page 59
Circulatory System Review

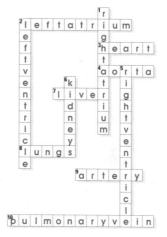

Page 60
The Respiratory System

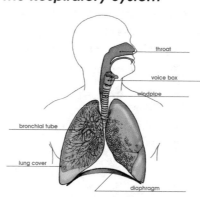

Page 61
Your Lungs

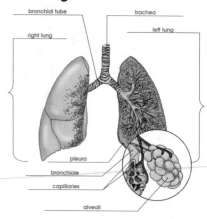

Page 62
Respiratory System Review

Page 64
Breathing and Heart Rates

A person's rate of breathing and the rate at which his or her heart beats both increase after exercise. This is because our bodies need more oxygen when we do strenuous work. Exercise helps a person stay healthy and fit because it helps our hearts and lungs work more efficiently. Exercise helps a person stay in shape and also increases his or her resistance to colds and diseases.

Page 66
Your Digestive System

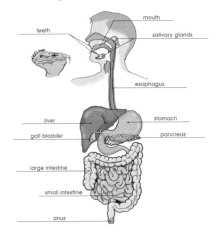

Labels: mouth, teeth, salivary glands, esophagus, liver, stomach, gall bladder, pancreas, large intestine, small intestine, anus

Page 67
The Alimentary Canal

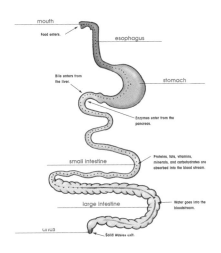

Labels: mouth, Food enters., esophagus, Bile enters from the liver., stomach, Enzymes enter from the pancreas., small intestine, Proteins, fats, vitamins, minerals, and carbohydrates are absorbed into the blood stream., large intestine, Water goes into the bloodstream., anus, Solid wastes exit.

Page 68
The Stomach

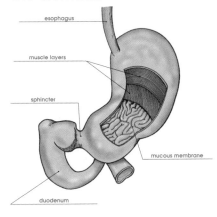

Labels: esophagus, muscle layers, sphincter, mucous membrane, duodenum

Page 69
Digestion in the Mouth

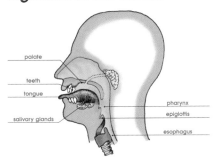

Labels: palate, teeth, tongue, salivary glands, pharynx, epiglottis, esophagus

Page 70
Pancreas, Liver, and Gall Bladder

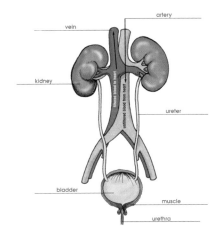

Labels: liver, bile duct, gall bladder, pancreas, duodenum

Page 71
Digestive System Review

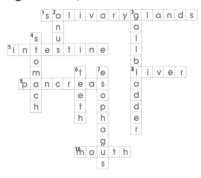

Crossword:
1. salivary glands
2. snu (down)
3. gall bladder (down)
4. s (down)
5. intestine
6. teeth (down)
7. esophagus (down)
8. liver
9. pancreas
10. mouth

Page 72
Blood Scrubbers

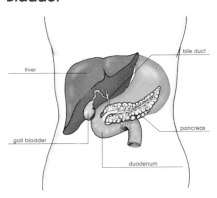

Labels: artery, vein, kidney, filtered blood to heart, unfiltered blood from heart, ureter, bladder, muscle, urethra

Page 73
Waste Removal

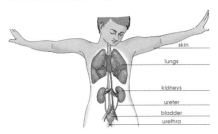

Labels: skin, lungs, kidneys, ureter, bladder, urethra

FUNCTION	EXCRETORY ORGANS			
	Kidneys	Lungs	Skin	Bladder
Removes water	✓	✓	✓	
Brings oxygen to blood		✓		
Removes salt	✓		✓	
Stores urine				✓
Removes carbon dioxide		✓		
Produces urine	✓			
Removes body heat		✓	✓	

Page 74
The Body's Communication System
Answers will vary.

Page 75
The Central Nervous System

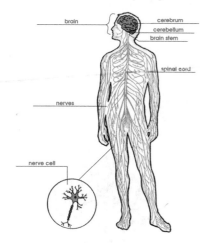

brain
cerebrum
cerebellum
brain stem
spinal cord
nerves
nerve cell

Page 76
Neurons

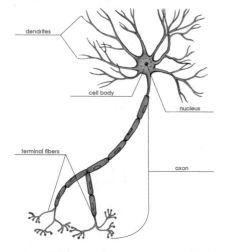

dendrites
cell body
nucleus
terminal fibers
axon

Page 77
Transmitters of Impulses

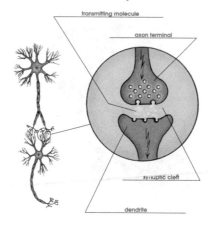

transmitting molecule
axon terminal
synaptic cleft
dendrite

Page 78
The Nervous System

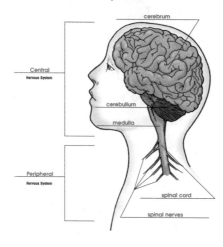

cerebrum
Central Nervous System
cerebellum
medulla
Peripheral Nervous System
spinal cord
spinal nerves

Page 79
Nervous System at Work
1. b
2. a
3. d
4. e
5. c

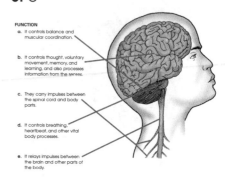

FUNCTION
a. It controls balance and muscular coordination.
b. It controls thought, voluntary movement, memory, and learning, and also processes information from the senses.
c. They carry impulses between the spinal cord and body parts.
d. It controls breathing, heartbeat, and other vital body processes.
e. It relays impulses between the brain and other parts of the body.

Page 80
Autonomic Nervous System

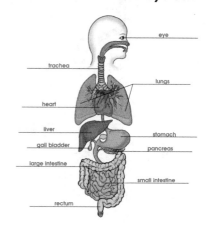

eye
trachea
lungs
heart
liver
stomach
gall bladder
pancreas
large intestine
small intestine
rectum

Page 81
Nervous System Review

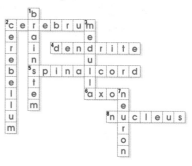

Page 82
The Endocrine System

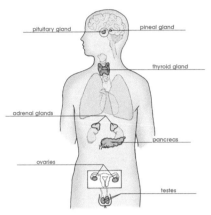

Page 83
Glands at Work

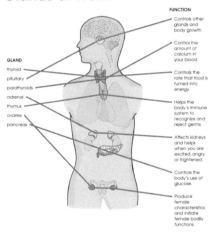

Page 84
The Sensory Systems

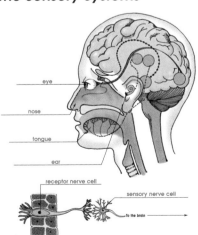

Page 85
The Senses
1. Answers will vary.
2. Answers will vary.

Page 86
Map Your Tongue
1. on the taste buds
2. Answers will vary.
3. Answers will vary.

Page 87
Your Nose

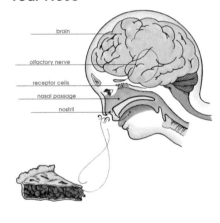

Page 88
Your Ear

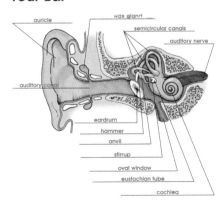

Page 89
Ear, Nose, and Throat Connection

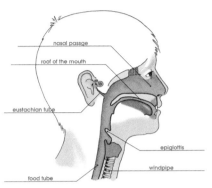

Page 90
Your Eye

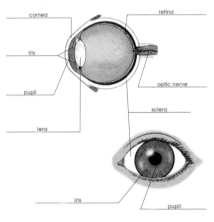

Page 91
Eyes to Brain Connection

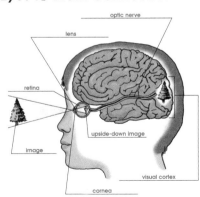

Answer Key

Page 92
Ear and Eye Review

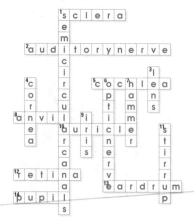

Page 93
Skin Deep

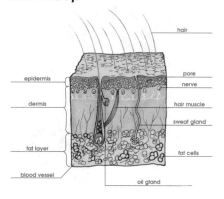

Page 94
Sweaty Palms and Goose Bumps

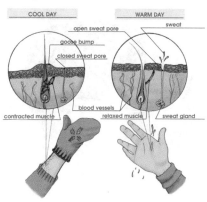

Page 95
Body Tissues

connective tissue

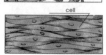

muscle tissue

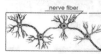

nerve tissue

epithelial tissue

Page 96
Fingerprints

Answers will vary.

Page 97
Your Toenails and Fingernails

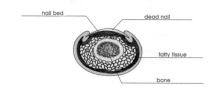

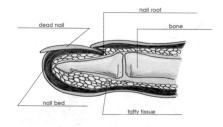

Page 98
Reproductive System

Develops arm and leg buds; heart begins to beat.
Ears, eyes, nose, fingers, and toes are formed.
Has recognizable human features; sex can be determined.
First movements felt; heartbeat can be heard with stethoscope.
Can survive birth with special care.
Fully developed with organs that can function on their own.

Page 99
Birth of a Baby

Page 100
Human Body Recall

1. true
2. c
3. c
4. a
5. c
6. a cold might have an effect on how you breathe (respiratory system). It might also affect the circulatory and digestive systems.

Answer Key

Page 101
Human Body Review

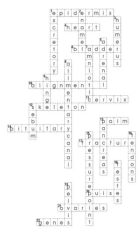

Page 102
Organ Systems

ORGANS	SYSTEMS						
	Digestive	Respiratory	Urinary	Reproductive	Circulatory	Nervous	Endocrine
Bladder			X				
Brain						X	
Heart					X		
Ovaries				X			X
Liver	X						
Pancreas	X						X
Kidney			X				
Spinal Cord						X	
Lungs		X					
Small Intestines	X						
Diaphragm		X					
Mouth	X	X					
Nerves						X	
Testes				X			X
Thyroid Gland							X
Arteries		X			X		
Esophagus	X						
Cerebellum						X	

Page 105
What Do You Remember?
1. the study of how parents and offspring have similar and different traits
2. traits that physically show
3. traits that do not show although they exist in the offspring's genes
4. the passing on of traits from parent to offspring
5. Gregor Mendel. His research showed evidence that traits are passed on through genetic material.
6. He used pea plants. They produce a large number of seeds, they are easily cross-pollinated, and they have obvious contrasting characteristics.

Page 106
Boy or Girl?
1. Answers will vary.
2. All egg cells from the female contain a Y chromosome. The sperm cells have half Y chromosomes and half X chromosomes. Therefore, at fertilization, there is a 50 percent chance that a Y chromosome sperm will fertilize the egg.

Page 107
Inherited Traits
1. C
2. U
3. C
4. U
5. Paragraphs will vary.
6. Answers will vary.

Page 109
Recording Your Data
People look different because there are many possibilities of traits. In order to look identical, every trait must be the same, which occurs when two or more babies form from a single egg that divides and then separates.

Page 110
Designer "Genes"
Answers will vary.

Page 111
Designer "Genes" continued
Answers will vary.

Page 112
Beyond the Looking Glass
1. the basic unit of a living thing that performs all of the functions of life
2. an inherited unit of genetic material that determines a trait
3. Answers will vary.
4. at least 2; one from each parent
5. brown eyes are carried by a dominant gene
6. curly hair, because it is a dominant trait

Page 113
Class Dominance
1. Answers will vary.
2. Answers will vary.

Page 114
Who's Right?
1. that someone prefers to use their right hand to perform different tasks; 90%
2. yes because these people were not naturally right-handed
3. eye
4. 14%; 23%

Page 115
What's Your Dominance?
1. Answers will vary.
2. Answers will vary.

Page 116
A Special Science Tool
a. nosepiece
b. coarse adjustment
c. fine adjustment
d. arm
e. base
f. eyepiece
g. body tube
h. objective
i. stage
j. diaphragm
k. stage clips
l. mirror

Page 118
Animal and Plant Cells
Animal and plant cells share the following structures: nucleus, nuclear membrane, vacuoles, cell membrane, and cytoplasm. A plant cell also has chloroplasts and a cell wall.

Page 121
Definitely Cellular
1. where proteins are made
2. jelly-like substance within the cell; holds other cell parts
3. chromosomes are found here; controls the activity of the rest of the cell parts
4. holds the nucleus together
5. releases energy from the nutrients

6. controls entry into and out of the cell
7. stores and releases chemicals
8. contains water and dissolved minerals

1. cell membrane
2. chloroplast

Page 122
What's the Difference?
1. Answers will vary but may include the fact that no cell membrane and no chloroplast exists in the human cell. Some parts are the same because the cells must function to support the life.
2. Answers will vary.
3. Answers will vary.
4. Answers will vary.

Page 123
What Do You See?
1. Answers will vary.
2. Answers will vary.
3. Answers will vary.

Page 124
Very Cheeky
1. Answers will vary.
2. Answers will vary.
3. The dye makes things clearer and more defined in the lens.
4. Chloroplast gives plants food. Animals don't make their own food.

Page 127
Animal or Plant?

CHARACTERISTIC	PLANT	ANIMAL
Living organisms	✓	✓
Formed from cells	✓	✓
Cells have chlorophyll	✓	
Makes its own food	✓	
Gets food from outside		✓
Moves from place to place		✓
Has limited movement	✓	
Can reproduce its own kind	✓	✓
Depends on sun's energy	✓	✓

Page 128
Photosynthesis

Page 129
Plant or Animal?

CHARACTERISTIC	PLANT	ANIMAL
Made of cells	✓	✓
Able to move from one place to another		✓
Able to produce its own food to supply its energy needs	✓	
Relies on food that it eats to supply its energy needs		✓
Most reproduce through seeds	✓	
Most reproduce through eggs		✓
Continues to grow and develop throughout its entire life	✓	
Stops growing and developing as it gets older		✓
Obtains and uses energy to grow and develop	✓	✓
Adapts to its environment	✓	✓
Contains chlorophyll in its cells	✓	

Charts and answers will vary.

Page 130
Root Systems

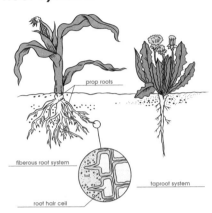

Page 131
Inside a Root

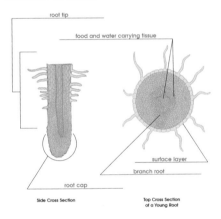

Page 132
Roots and Shoots
Answers will vary.

Page 133
What Color of Light Helps Plants Grow?
1. No
2. The one under the clear dome grew the best.
3. The plant under the red dome grew poorly.
4. Answers will vary. For example, plants need light to grow properly. If no light reaches that area in space, plants cannot produce their own food for continued growth.
5. Answers will vary. For example, some pollution may block out certain frequencies of light which plants need to grow.

Page 135
How Does Your Garden Grow?
1. Answers will vary. For example, the sprout emerged first. This will vary depending on the direction of the seed's orientation when planted.
2. Answers will vary.
3. Answers will vary.

Page 137
What Does Your Garden Need to Grow?
1. Answers will vary. For example, the plant in carton #3 grew the best because it received sunlight and an appropriate amount of water.
2. Answers will vary.

Page 138
Plant Pipelines
monocot; dicot
Answers may include:
1. red in the veins of the leaves

2. red holes across the top of the cut
3. veins
4. No food would get to the top because the food path would be interrupted, and the plant might die.

Page 140
Growing Mold
1. Answers will vary. For example, the moist bread which was placed in the dark produced the most mold.
2. The dry piece of bread which was placed in the light had the most mold growth.
3. Answers will vary but should include darker areas with moist conditions.
4. shadows
5. Answers will vary. For example, the best conditions may include moist areas with darkness.

Page 143
Is Your Soil the Best or Is Mine?
1–3. Answers will vary.

Page 144
A Seedy Start
1. warmth, air, and water
2. through seeds
3. the seed coat, the embryo, the food supply
4. it sprouts
5. the roots

Page 145
Sailing Seeds
1. man plants seeds
2. seeds travel in water
3. seeds stick to leg
4. seeds travel by wind
5. birds carry seeds

Page 146
Sprouting Radishes
Answers will vary.

Page 147
A Tree From a Seed
Answers will vary.

Page 148
Tree Foods
Answers will vary.

Page 151
Parts of a Flower
Most flowers have these four main parts: calyx, corolla, stamens, pistils. The parts and elements of the students' chosen flowers should be labeled.

Page 152
Making Seeds
1. petal—red
2. sepal—green
3. stamen—brown
4. pistil—yellow
5. ovary—blue

Page 153
All About Growing

Page 157
Look Closer
1. Consumers—organisms that eat
2. Producers—all green plants
3. Sun—provides energy for everything on earth
4. Pesticides—chemicals used to eliminate pests such as bugs
5. Food chain—a system, like a chain, by which organisms get their food
6. Food web—food chains interwoven together
7. Domino effect—When one organism in a food chain is affected, other organisms in the chain and in the food web are impacted as well.
8. Energy—element necessary for life

1. domino effect
2. Answers will vary.

Page 158
Chain Reactions Everywhere
Answers will vary.

Page 159
Your Daily Menu
Answers will vary.

Page 160
Shop Around
1. Answers will vary.
2. Answers will vary.
3. Answers will vary.

Page 161
Which Is It?
1. a. producer
   b. herbivore
   c. carnivore
2. a. producer
   b. herbivore
   c. omnivore
3. a. producer
   b. herbivore
   c. carnivore

Page 162
Eating Out in the Habitat
Food webs will vary depending on the habitat chosen.

Page 163
Spin a Food Web
Answers will vary.

Answer Key

Page 164
What We Need
Fruit—1
Milk—2, 8, 12
Fats and Sweets—3, 11
Vegetables—4, 9
Meat—5, 10
Grains—6, 7

Page 165
Name That Vegetable
Answers will vary.

Page 166
Where's the Energy?
1. the amount of energy supplied by carbohydrates, proteins, and fats as they are digested
2. proteins, carbohydrates, and fats
3. carbohydrates and proteins; eating too many fats is unhealthy
4. you gain weight

Page 167
What's Your Output?
Answers will vary.

Page 168
Nutrition Facts About Crackers
Answers will vary.

Page 169
Nutrition Facts About Cereals
Answers will vary.

Page 170
You Are What You Eat

	CORN BALLS	YOUR CEREAL
What kind of grain(s) is used?	corn	Answers will vary.
Is sugar used?	yes	
What position is sugar on the list of ingredients?	2nd	
List other sweeteners	corn syrup molasses	
How many calories per serving without milk?	110	
How many calories per serving when eaten with 1/2 cup of skim milk?	150	
How much protein per serving?	1 g	
How many vitamins and minerals does the cereal contain?	10	
How much cholesterol is in one serving?	0 mg	
How much fat is in one serving?	0 g	
How much carbohydrate is in one serving?	26 g	

Page 171
Burning Calories to Stay Healthy
Answers will vary.

Page 172
Reading the Label
1. 2 teas. every 6 hours
2. 1 teas. every 6 hours
3. drowsiness
4. child under 5; pregnant or nursing mother
5. 4
6. August 1993
7. Consult your physician.
8. coughs due to colds and flu

Page 173
Caution: Poison!

Page 174
Enlightening Information
1. abiotic: sun, sky, water, rock biotic: butterfly, dragonfly, fish, turtle, cattails, snails, frogs, bugs
2. The living things in the picture depend on each other for food.
3. pond
4. Circle all the living things—plants and animals.
5. Frogs eat insects; insects eat plants; plants grow in water; fish live in water; etc.
6. frogs, fish, turtles, dragonflies, butterflies, etc.

Page 175
It's a Small World
1. plants and animals
2. based on their physical structures and behaviors
3. they all contain living things; their size
4. food, water, temperature, and minerals
5. a species must move to another habitat or die out

Page 176
What's in Your Neighborhood?
1. the place that people did not walk through
2. the place where a lot of people walk through

Page 177
Incredible Ecosystems
Answers will vary.

Page 178
Make a Difference
Answers will vary.

Page 179
Home, Sweet Home
Charts and Venn diagrams will vary.

Page 180
Habitat in a Jar
Observations will vary. Changes will vary depending on the care students gave to the terrarium.

Page 181
Habitat Happenings
Paragraphs and sketches will vary.

Page 182
Habitat Visit
Answers will vary.

Page 183
Habitat Recall
1. b
2. a
3. true
4. c
5. a
Answers will vary.

Page 185
Investigating a Pond
Answers will vary.

Page 186
Life on a Rotting Log
1. lichen, moss, mushrooms
2. The roots create open spaces in the log.
3. The log offers plants a source of food, protection, and a place to grow
4. salamander, ants, earthworms, chipmunk
5. They eat and chew on the log. A lichen is made up of an algae and a fungus. The algae makes food by means of photosynthesis. The fungus absorbs the water that the algae needs to live.

Page 187
Mohs Hardness Scale

MOHS HARDNESS SCALE		
HARDNESS	MINERAL	COMMON TESTS
1	Talc	Fingernail will scratch it.
2	Gypsum	
3	Calcite	Fingernail will not scratch it; a copper penny will.
4	Fluorite	Knife blade or window glass will scratch it.
5	Apatite	
6	Feldspar/Orthoclase	
7	Quartz	Will scratch a steel knife or window glass.
8	Topaz	
9	Corundum	
10	Diamond	Will scratch all common materials.

Page 188
Name That Mineral

The Unknown Minerals

HARDNESS	COLOR	LUSTER	MINERAL
Will scratch a steel knife or window glass.	yellow	glassy	Quartz
Will scratch a steel knife or window glass.	gray	glassy	Feldspar
A copper penny will scratch it	black	pearly	Mica
Fingernail will scratch it	white	pearly	Talc
Knife blade or window glass will scratch it.	black	glassy	Hornblende

Page 189
Classy Rocks
igneous
metamorphic
metamorphic
sedimentary
sedimentary
igneous
sedimentary
metamorphic
igneous
sedimentary
cooled magma
layers of loose material, etc.
rock that has been changed, etc.

Page 190
Mineral Identifications

MINERAL	HARDNESS	SPECIFIC GRAVITY	STREAK COLOR	LUSTER
Siderite	3.5-4	3.85	white	pearly
Gypsum	2	2.32	white	vitreous
Kaolinite	2-2.5	2.6	white	dull
Halite	2.5	2.16	white	glassy
Fluorite	4	3-3.3	white	glassy
Calcite	3	2.7	white	waxy
Barite	3-3.5	4.3-4.6	white	vitreous
Pyrite	6-6.5	5.02	green-black	metallic
Galena	2.5-2.7	7.4-7.6	lead-gray	metallic
Magnetite	6	5.2	black	metallic
Topaz	8	3.4-3.6	colorless	glassy

1. gypsum, kaolinite, halite
2. gypsum, kaolinite, halite, calcite, galena
3. pyrite, magnetite, topaz
4. topaz

Page 191
Rocks and Minerals

Answer Key

Page 193
Rock Crystals Record Sheet
Conclusions: Possible answer: Sugar is a crystal that can dissolve in water.
Answers will vary.

Page 194
Erosion by Glaciers
1. Answers will vary. For example, grit has become embedded into the ice.
2. U
3. Answers will vary. For example, grit has carved striations (scratches) on the soap.
4. Yes. Answers will vary. For example, striation would be deeper.
5. striation
6. Answers will vary. Some examples of glacial movement includes: repeated carving of the topography; multiple layers of striations; debris (till) pushed to different locations.

Page 195
Glaciers
1. B
2. G
3. J
4. C
5. L
6. K
7. N
8. I
9. M
10. E
11. F
12. D
13. H
14. A

Page 196
Fossil Models
Answers will vary.

Page 197
The Center of the Earth

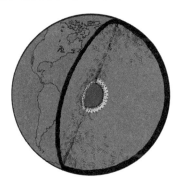

Page 198
The Layered Look
1. inner core
2. outer core
3. mantle
4. crust
5. crust
6. Answers will vary.

Page 199
Molten Rocks
1. obsidian
2. granite
3. olivine
4. feldspar
5. diorite
6. quartz
7. basalt
8. igneous
9. buildings, statues, cutting tools, decorative objects, sand, glass, electronic equipment
10. western U.S., Mexico, Hawaii, Italy, South Africa, Canada, North Carolina, Georgia

Page 200
Five Types of Mountains

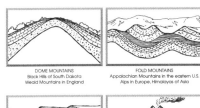

Page 201
Volcanoes

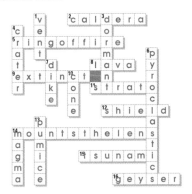

Answer Key

Page 202
Earth's Moving Plates

Page 203
Bending the Earth's Crust

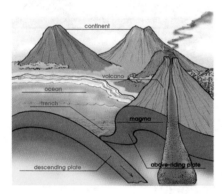

Page 204
The Science of Earthquakes

1. tsunami
2. seismic
3. epicenter
4. San Andreas
5. seismograph
6. focus
7. fault
8. shock waves
9. Ring of Fire
10. primary; seismology

Page 205
All About Earthquakes

fault 1	San Francisco 15	strike-slip fault 14	focus 4
normal fault 12	Richter scale 6	primary waves 7	Buffalo, NY 9
secondary waves 8	surface waves 10	oil and fossils 11	epicenter 5
reverse fault 13	San Andreas Fault 3	seismograph 2	seismologist 16

Page 206
Where Is the New Madrid Fault?

3. **a.** 1950 mi
b. 1170 mi
c. 975 mi
d. 390 mi
e. 390 mi
f. 780 mi
Missouri
Memphis, St. Louis, Little Rock

Page 208
U.S. Climate Zones

Answers will vary.
6-continental
1-alpine
1-alpine, 10-subarctic, 3-tundra
7-subtropical, 2-steppe, 5-desert
7-subtropical, 9-tropical
6-continental

Page 209
Balloon Barometer

Answers will vary.

Page 211
Warm and Cold Front Movement

1. blue. Answers will vary. For example, it sinks to the bottom of the container.
2. red. Answers will vary. For example, it floats on top of the room temperature water.
3. blue water
4. red water
5. blue water
6. cold air
7. cold fronts
8. Answers will vary. For example, in cold fronts, cold air is more dense and moves more quickly thus creating a greater rate of change.

Page 213
What's Your Prediction?

1. rain within 24 hours
2. increasing wind; rain in 12-18 hours
3. (June) rain, with high wind, then clearing within 36 hours (December) rain or snow, with high wind, then clearing and colder within 36 hours
4. clearing within a few hours
5. end of storm—clearing and colder
6. fair weather
7. Rain may be on the way.
8. It's raining.
9. severe storms
10. falling rapidly

Page 214
Water, Water Everywhere

Answers will vary.
EVAPORATION; SATURATED
solid, liquid, gas

Page 215
Rain Maker
Answers will vary.

Page 216
Cloud Words
1. feathery clouds
2. feathery, piled-up clouds
3. feathery clouds in sheets (or stretched out)
4. high, piled-up clouds
5. high clouds in sheets (or stretched out)
6. rain clouds in sheets (or stretched out)
7. clouds in sheets (or layers or stretched out)
8. piled-up clouds in sheets (or stretched out)
9. piled-up clouds
10. piled-up rain clouds

Page 217
Name That Cloud
1. Cirrus
2. Cirrocumulus
3. Cirrostratus
4. Altocumulus
5. Altostratus
6. Nimbostratus
7. Stratus
8. Stratocumulus
9. Cumulus
10. Cumulonimbus

Page 218
Clouds and Fog Review
1. Nimbus: rain. Cirrus: fair, with rain possible within two days. Cumulus: fair weather.

Cumulonimbus: thundershowers.
2.

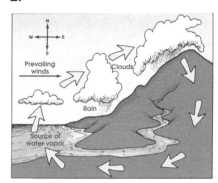

3. Stratus: low. Cirrus: high. Cirrocumulus: high. Cumulus: low to middle. Altostratus: middle.

Page 219
Temperature High and Lows Around the World
1. Libya
2. 100°, -80°, 180°
3. 100°, 14°, 86°
4. Alaska; Hawaii is closer to the equator than Alaska and therefore has less seasonal temperature variation; Hawaii is surrounded by water, which helps to keep its overall temperature warmer than Alaska's.

Page 221
Precipitation Highs and Lows Around the World
1. They are surrounded by the ocean; they are in latitudes of fairly high humidity.
2. In the western mountains— the Cascades, the Sierras, and the Rockies. (*Any one of the following*) The prevailing westerly winds carry moisture from the Pacific Ocean; the humidity from the ocean is pushed up these high western mountain ranges, where it condenses as precipitation.
3. (*Any two of the following*) There are no mountains to cause humid air to rise and condense as precipitation; the prevailing winds are southwest, blowing from land to ocean, so they do not carry much humidity; the prevailing winds are the trade winds, which are gentle and do not bring storms.
4. Cherrapunji is in monsoon country. In the summer the land becomes much warmer than the ocean, creating lower air pressure inland and causing the wind to shift direction and blow inland from the sea. This suddenly brings heavy rains and high humidity. Monsoons move into India from the southwest and "retreat" at the end of the season in the same direction, so the southwest, where Cherrapunji is located, gets more monsoon rain than any other part of India. In addition, Cherrapunji is in the foothills on the windward side of the Himalaya Mountains.

Answer Key

Page 222
A Magic Square of Weather

mass of air that surrounds Earth	air that rushes in from the north and south to warm the air along the equator	calm areas of Earth where there is little wind	a gas in the upper part of Earth's atmosphere
1	15	14	4
cold air from the ocean that moves into the warmer land	the zone of the atmosphere above the troposphere	the zone of the atmosphere above the stratosphere	a movement of air close to Earth's surface
12	6	7	9
the outer zone of Earth's atmosphere	air above Earth that is warmed by the reflection of the sun's rays and is prevented from easily passing back into space	transfer of heat by currents of air or water	strong, steady winds high in the atmosphere; used by pilots
8	10	11	5
cold air from land that moves out to warmer air over oceans	zone of the atmosphere which affects the transmission of radio waves	the zone of the atmosphere which is closest to the surface of Earth	the line along which air masses meet
13	3	12	16

34; 4 squares in each corner
4 squares in center

Page 223
Symbol Sense
A. 6
B. 10
C. 1
D. 16
E. 14
F. 2
G. 13
H. 4 (Symbols 5, 7, 12, and 15 are the "fakes")
I. 9
J. wrong label
K. 11
L. 8
M. 3
N. wrong label

Page 224
Weather Instruments
1. radiosonde
2. doppler
3. ceilometer
4. rain gauge
5. radar
6. anemometer
7. vane
8. barometer
9. thermometer
10. thermograph

11. hygrometer
Answer: solar energy

Page 225
Atmospheric Circulation
doldrums, trade winds, prevailing easterlies, prevailing westerlies, horse latitudes

Page 226
Stormy Weather

Page 227
Weather Trivia
1. T
2. F
3. F
4. T
5. F
6. F
7. T
8. F
9. T
10. T
11. T
12. T
13. T
14. F
15. F
16. F
17. F
18. F
19. T
20. F
21. T
22. T
23. F
24. T

Page 228
Weather Trivia
25. T
26. F
27. F
28. T
29. F
30. F
31. T
32. F
33. T
34. F
35. T
36. T
37. T
38. F
39. T
40. T
41. T
42. F
43. T
44. F

Page 229
What Do You Know About Tornadoes?
1. F
2. T
3. T
4. T
5. F
6. T
7. F
8. T
9. F
10. T

11. T
12. T
13. T
14. T
15. T
16. T
17. T
18. T
19. T
20. T
21. T
22. F
23. F
24. F

Page 231
Tornado Fury
1. The vortex is the pattern of movement of molecules as the air or water passes through a small opening.
2. Actual tornadoes move upward. The tornado in this bottle moved downward.
3. A vortex is the path of the water moving down the drain.
4. As the temperature patterns change drastically, the air pressure can change.
5. A vortex resembles a funnel.

Page 232
What's in a Name?
Before 1950
1860—Hurricane 1
The Great Hurricane of 1780
The Late Gale at St. Joseph
1950-1952
Hurricane King
Hurricane Easy
Hurricane Able

1952-1978
Hurricane Audrey
Hurricane Eloise
Hurricane Hazel
1978-Present
Hurricane Hugo
Hurricane George
Hurricane Mitch

Page 233
Aftershocks and Body Waves

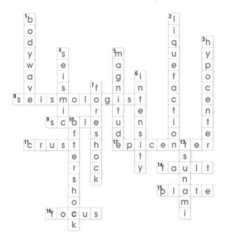

Page 234
Defining Droughts
1. Definitions 5 and 6
2. Definition 1
3. Definition 4
4. Definition 3
5. Definition 2
6. Definition 1
7. Definitions 2, 4, and 6
8. Definition 5

Page 235
The Effects of El Niño
1. T
2. T
3. F—El Niños slow easterly winds across the tropical Pacific to an almost standstill.
4. F—The El Niño effect increases hurricane activity in the North Pacific, but it decreases it in the North Atlantic.
5. T
6. F—Alaska experienced warmer and drier weather than normal that season.
7. T—Incidentally, the region is accustomed to only one typhoon every three years.
8. T
9. F—Stronger than normal trade winds predict El Niños.
10. T
11. T
12. F—El Niños can affect the entire globe.
13. T
14. F—Fish and birds die or leave the region during El Niños.
15. T
16. F—The most severe El Niño of the twentieth century occurred in 1982-1983.

Page 236
Weather Wisdom
1. True; a sudden change in air pressure may affect arthritic joints, bunions, even old wounds.
2. True; most animals feel changes in air pressure and feel uncomfortable and restless before a storm.
3. False
4. True; frogs are popular weather forecasters in almost

every country.

5. True

6. True; skies are even a better predictor than animals. A red sky indicates a passing front.

7. False; but it may show the effects of a previous bad winter.

8. True; hot, humid nights mean rain.

Page 237
Natural Weather Forecasters

1. B
2. H
3. A
4. I
5. E
6. C
7. L
8. G
9. K
10. F
11. J
12. D

Page 238
The Wind-Chill Factor

1. -2°
2. 26°
3. 37°
4. Temperature = - 40°, wind speed = 40 mph.
5. Answers will vary.

Page 239
What Are You Wearing?

1. air temperature, air pressure, wind, humidity
2. shorts, T-shirt

3. barometer—air pressure anemometer—wind
4. Answers will vary.

Page 240
Earth and Moon

1. earth's diameter = 7,926 miles, moon's diameter = 2,160 miles
2. Answers will vary.
3. seasons

Page 241
Changing Faces

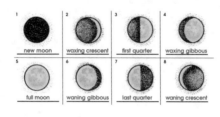

Page 242
High Tide

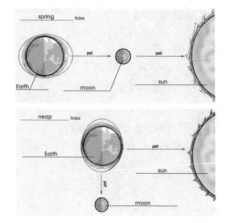

Page 243
A Sunny Star

1. ball of hot, glowing gases with no ground
2. 863,710 miles in diameter. It is average in size.
3. four seasons
4. Life as we know it would stop.

Page 244
Our Closest Star—the Sun

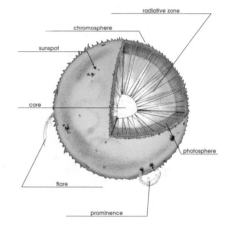

Page 245
The Seasons

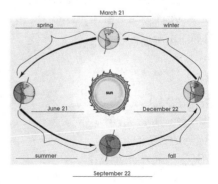

Answer Key

Page 246
Planets of the Solar System

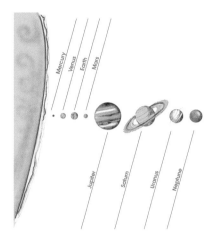

Page 247
Puzzling Planets

Page 248
Physical Characteristics of the Planets
Answers will vary.
1. The inner plants' distances are shorter.
2. It took longer.
3. because Neptune is further away than Mercury
4. The year is longer the further away the planet is from the sun.

Page 249
The North Star

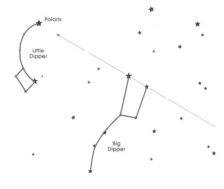

Page 250
Constellations of the Zodiac
1. Sagittarius
2. Aquarius
3. Gemini
4. Capricornus
5. Scorpio
6. Pisces
7. Taurus
8. Cancer
9. Virgo
10. Libra
11. Aries
12. Leo

Page 251
Hello Out There!
1. Hey from Earth
2. Messages will vary.

Page 252
Galaxies
elliptical
barred spiral
spiral
irregular

Page 253
Astronomical Alterations
2. quasar, D
3. pulsar, F
4. orbit, H
5. Mars, L
6. planet, A
7. moon, B
8. star, J
9. sun, E
10. comet, G
11. axis, I
12. meteor, C

Page 254
Our Solar System

Page 255
July 20, 1969
1. luna
2. satellite
3. eclipse
4. *Apollo*
5. NASA
6. astronauts
7. miles
8. craters
9. orbit
10. solar
11. Saturn
12. gravity
Neil Armstrong

Page 256
In Your Own Words
Paragraphs will vary.

Page 257
Periodic Table of Elements

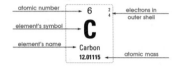

atomic number — 6   2
                      4 — electrons in outer shell

element's symbol — **C**

element's name — Carbon
              12.01115 — atomic mass

Page 258
Atoms

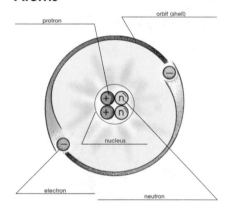

orbit (shell)
protron
nucleus
electron
neutron

Page 259
Name That Molecule!

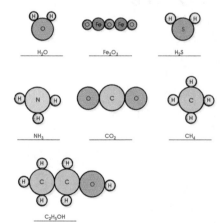

H_2O Fe_2O_3 H_2S

NH_3 CO_2 CH_4

C_2H_5OH

Page 260
Chemical Magic Square

What is your answer? _____34_____

This element is located directly above lithium.	This element is located to the left of sulfur.	This element is located directly below carbon.	This element is located directly above magnesium.	
1	15	14	4	34
This element is located to the right of sodium.	This element is located to the left of nitrogen.	This element is located directly above phosphorus.	This element is located directly above chlorine.	
12	6	7	9	34
This element is located to the left of fluorine.	This element is located below helium.	This element is located directly above potassium.	This element is located directly above aluminum.	
8	10	11	5	34
This element is located to the left of silicon.	This element is located directly below hydrogen.	This element is located directly above neon.	This element is located to the left of chlorine.	
13	3	2	16	34
34	34	34	34	

Page 263
Acids and Bases

SUBSTANCE	BLUE LITMUS	RED LITMUS	ACID, BASE OR NEITHER
Lemon juice	red	red	acid
Vinegar	red	red	acid
Ammonia	blue	blue	base
Orange juice	red	red	acid
Tea	red	red	acid
Milk	blue	red	neither
Baking soda and water	blue	red	base
Cleanser and water	blue	blue	base
Water	blue	red	neither (b)
Vinegar and salt	red	red	acid
Grapefruit juice	red	red	acid
Antacid pills and water	blue	blue	base
Cola	blue	red	neither (a)

Page 264
What's the Matter?
1. anything that has mass and takes up space
2. elements, compounds, and mixtures
3. Answers will vary.
4. Answers will vary.
5. an observable characteristic that can be used to identify something
6. Answers will vary.

Page 265
Its Own Space
Both the water and the marbles are matter. They each occupy their own space. When you add the marbles to the water, the water is moved out of the way, raising the water level.

Page 266
Milk Shake Mixture
Yes.

Page 267
Milk Shake Mixture Record Sheet
ice cream, fruit, milk
Answers will vary.

Page 269
Make It Mix Record Sheet
It mixes for a minute and then separates.
The oil and water stayed mixed.
Then, they float (are suspended) throughout the water.
An emulsifier causes the oil droplets to suspend in the water.

Page 270
Salt and Ice
Answers will vary.
Data will vary.

Page 272
Crystal Picture Tests
Answers will vary.

Page 273
Changes in the States of Matter
1. solidification
2. condensation
3. vaporization
4. melting
5. boiling
6. evaporation
7. freezing
8. sublimation
9. liquefaction

scientist

Page 274
Physical and Chemical Changes
1. C
2. P
3. P
4. C
5. C
6. P
7. P
8. P
9. P
10. C
11. C
12. P
13. C
14. C
15. C
16. P
17. P
18. C
19. C
20. C

21. C
22. C
23. P

Page 275
Physical Properties of Matter

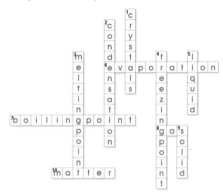

Page 277
Melt Down
D, C, A, B

Page 279
A Chemical Change
1. chemical
2. chemical
3. physical
4. physical
5. chemical
6. chemical

Page 280–281
Chemical Changes
Activity 1—Observations should include that the writing done with the lemon juice is not obvious on the paper until dried and held to the light. This is a chemical change because it cannot be changed back.

Activity 2—Observations should include that when the vinegar is on the steel wool heat is generated and rust is created. These are evidence that a chemical change took place.

Page 282
Facts About Light Energy
1. F
2. T
3. F
4. T
5. T
6. T
7. T
8. T
9. F
10. F
11. T
12. T
13. T
14. T
15. T
16. T
17. F
18. T
19. F
20. T
21. T
22. T

Page 283
Light Waves
Answers will vary.

Page 284
The Behavior of Light
1. bent
2. reflected

3. light
4. real image
5. virtual
6. mirror
7. concave
8. retina
9. convex
10. focal
11. lens
12. index
13. image
14. photon
15. flat

Page 286
Making Rainbows
Pictures will vary.

Page 287
Let the Sun Shine In
Answers will vary.
Blue light has shorter wave lengths than red light.
orange, yellow, green, blue, indigo

Page 288
What Is Electricity?
1. battery
2. bulb
3. resistor
4. charge
5. electrode
6. circuit
7. insulator
8. conductor
9. switch
10. positive
11. negative
12. watt

13. ohm
14. fuse
15. ampere
16. generator
17. volt
18. turbine

Page 289
Charge It
1. within an atom
2. move toward or attract
3. move away from or repel
4. a type of electrical energy found freely in nature
5. an imbalance of positive and negative charges

Page 290
Do I Detect a Charge?
1. It became charged.
2. The foam peanuts moved away or toward the object with the charge.
3. the objects that caused the foam peanuts to move toward each other
4. the objects that caused the foam peanuts to move away from each other

Page 292
Series Circuit
In a series circuit, current runs through two or more appliances (the bulbs) before returning to the battery. Removing a bulb, like a switch being turned off, breaks the circuit.

Page 294
Parallel Circuit
In a parallel circuit like this, current runs to two or more appliances (bulbs) in separate loops. Removing one bulb does not interrupt the circuit, so current continues to flow to the other bulb.

Page 295
Dry Cells

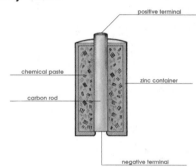

Page 296
How Many Volts?

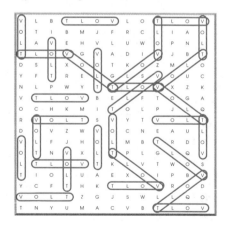

30

Answer Key

Page 298
Conductors and Insulators
Answers will vary.

Page 300
Understanding Insulation
Answers will vary.

Page 301
What's That Sound?
Answers will vary.

Page 303
Bottle Flutes
the one with the most water
the one with the least water
The air vibrates.
It has no effect.

Page 304
Newton's Laws
Answers will vary.
1. 2
2. 1, 3
3. 1, 2, 3
4. 1, 3
5. 2

Page 305
Inertia
Answers will vary.

Page 307
Action and Reaction
Answers will vary.

Page 308
Measuring Friction
Answers will vary.

Page 310
Magnetic Friction
Answers will vary.
Not all metals are magnetic.

Page 312
Are All Metals Magnetic?
Answers will vary.

Page 313
Forms of Energy
1. potential
2. kinetic
3. kinetic
4. kinetic
5. potential
6. kinetic

Page 314
Energy Experiments
Answers will vary.

Page 315
Egg Drop
Answers will vary.

Page 317
Which Objects Will Slide the Fastest?
Answers will vary.

Page 318
Three Classes of Levers
1. first
2. second
3. third
4. first
5. second
6. third
7. third
8. third

Page 319
Lever Experiments
1. the pencil
2. Yes; you could move the fulcrum to balance the seesaw.
3. You could have the person move closer to the fulcrum; you could move closer to the fulcrum.

Page 320
Simple Machines

hammer	lever	scissors	levers
doorstop	wedge	drill	screw
saw	wedge	screwdriver	wheel and axle
crowbar	lever	monkey wrench	wheel and axle

BICYCLE PARTS
Study a bicycle carefully. Fill in the blanks with the simple machines you find.

tire	wheel and axle	kickstand	inclined plane
caliper brakes	lever	handlebars	lever
chain and sprocket	pulley	gearshift	wheel and axle
pedal and shaft	wheel and axle	fork	lever
other			

Page 321
Six Types of Simple Machines
lever
inclined plane
screw
wedge
pulley
wheel and axle

Page 322
Special Inclined Planes

Page 323
Compound Machines

lever, wheel and axle

screw, wheel and axle

pulley, wheel and axle, lever